Savoring France

WILLIAMS-SONOMA

Savoring France

Recipes and Reflections on French Cooking

Recipes and Text
GEORGEANNE BRENNAN

General Editor
CHUCK WILLIAMS

Recipe Photography
NOEL BARNHURST

Travel Photography
STEVEN ROTHFELD

Illustrations
MARLENE McLOUGHLIN

BORDERS.

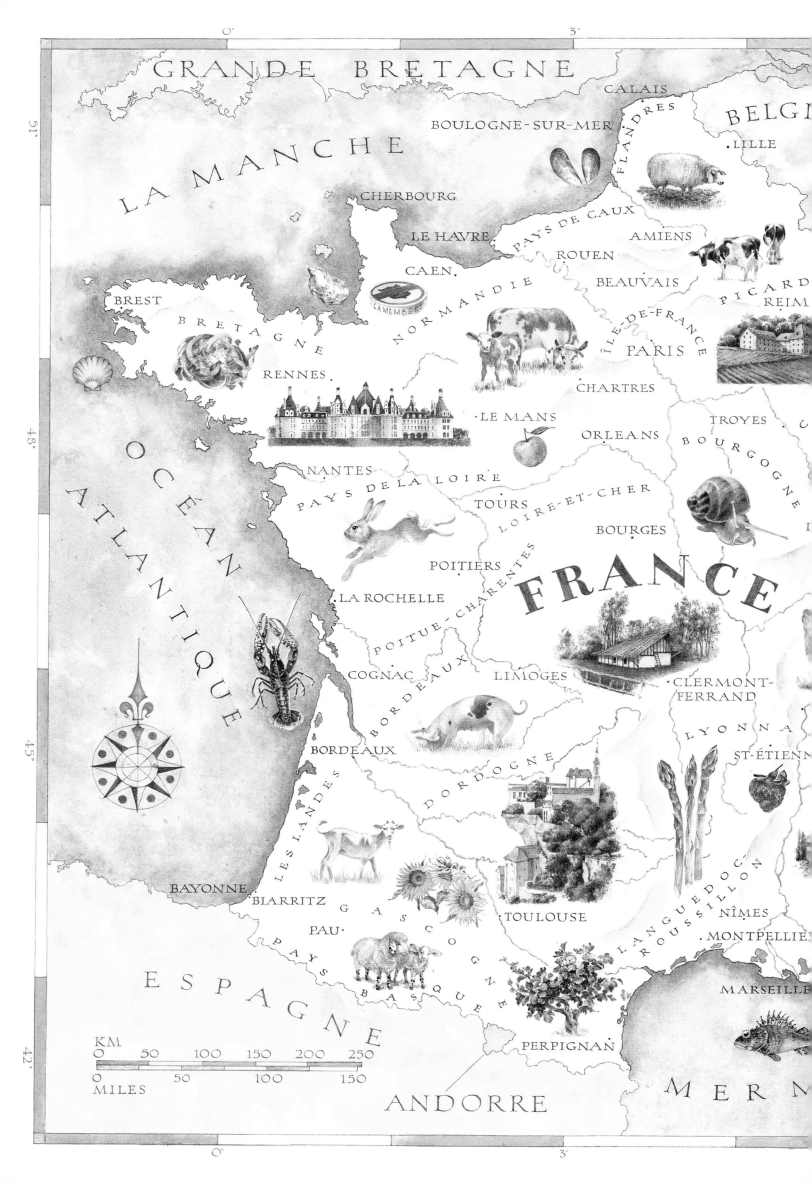

GRANDE BRETAGNE

CALAIS

BOULOGNE-SUR-MER

FLANDRES

BELGI

LILLE

LA MANCHE

CHERBOURG

PAYS DE CAUX

AMIENS

LE HAVRE

ROUEN

BEAUVAIS

PICARD

REIM

CAEN

CAMEMBERT

NORMANDIE

BREST

BRETAGNE

ÎLE-DE-FRANCE

PARIS

RENNES

CHARTRES

LE MANS

ORLEANS

TROYES

BOURGOGNE

NANTES

PAYS DE LA LOIRE

TOURS

LOIRE-ET-CHER

BOURGES

OCÉAN

ATLANTIQUE

POITIERS

FRANCE

LA ROCHELLE

POITUE-CHARENTES

COGNAC

LIMOGES

CLERMONT-
FERRAND

BORDEAUX

LYONNA

ST-ÉTIENN

DORDOGNE

LES LANDES

BAYONNE

BIARRITZ

GASCOGNE

PAU

PAYS BASQUE

TOULOUSE

LANGUEDOC

ROUSSILLON

NÎMES

MONTPELLIE

ESPAGNE

MARSEILLE

KM
0   50   100   150   200   250

0   50   100   150
MILES

PERPIGNAN

ANDORRE

MER M

Contents

L'INTRODUCTION

The French Table

Eating in France is a national pastime, one that regulates the pace of life and expands life's pleasurable moments to an everyday affair. I discovered this when I first went to France as a student, and later participated in it when I lived there raising goats, making cheese, and sharing the rhythm of daily life. For nearly thirty years now, I have owned a home deep in the Provençal countryside. I have spent many, many happy times in that house, so I confess that I am prone to see France from a romantic rural perspective that I sometimes think distorts the reality, much like looking through a pane of old glass. Thus, it always astonishes me, year after year, to see the things I love about French food—the pattern of eating, the fine quality of and respect for ingredients, the passion for seasonality and for local products—still in evidence from one end of the country to the other, in hamlets, villages, cities, and even in Paris.

The eating rituals are the same. Breakfast typically begins with fresh bread and croissants from the bakery and a steaming cup or bowl of coffee with hot milk, or maybe a cup of hot chocolate. The bread is carefully spread from edge to edge with butter and jam or sometimes honey. About one-third of a baguette, slit in

Above: Fashionable cafés and *pâtisseries* are nestled among the high-rent apartments in the Marais, the Right Bank Parisian *quartier* that was deserted by its royal occupants during the 1789 Revolution.

half, is common, so it takes a while to eat it all. The croissant is not rushed either, but instead torn leisurely into bite-sized pieces. The coffee, which is very hot, is sipped slowly. Packaged cereals and assorted fruit juices are making inroads into the French breakfast, but at village cafés, hotels, autoroute stops, and many homes, people still ease into the day with bread and a hot drink.

Come midday, people all over France sit down at the same time, from twelve or twelve-thirty until one-thirty or two. Shops and businesses close and people eat lunch. Once I was at an amusement park and all the rides stopped from twelve to two-thirty. In the smaller communities, where it is still feasible for people to dine together, the children are picked up at school and brought home for lunch with the family. Elsewhere, the children eat their three-course meal at the school canteen, but it is not a hurried affair. Restaurants, brasseries, bistros, and office cafeterias fill with people in search of *le déjeuner*, although not an ordinary lunch by most contemporary standards. An aperitif

is likely to be enjoyed first. It is not necessarily alcoholic, maybe just a bottle of Perrier or other sparkling water with a twist of lemon, or perhaps a glass of juice. This is followed by a starter, such as soup, a composed salad, a wedge of quiche, or charcuterie. Then comes a main course accompanied with vegetables, and finally cheese and a dessert. Usually, the meal is enjoyed with wine. It is a calming ritual, one that gives a break during the day to even the most humble laborer, as evidenced by the rural restaurants where masons, electricians, truckers, and all the others who make the country work sit down and relax over a good, long three-course meal, finishing with a *café express*.

At four or five o'clock, it's time for *un goûter*, a late-afternoon snack. Children have biscuits or, best of all, bread spread with butter and squares of chocolate along with something to drink. Adults are more likely to halt their work for a cup of coffee or tea and a sweet. In the countryside, neighbors go visiting at this time and take coffee together.

By the end of the workday, when people leave their offices, fields, factories, and shops, they often head for a local café to have an aperitif with friends, putting the final note to the workday and beginning a time of relaxation with friends and family. Dinner follows

Left: Tender, white-tipped radishes, fresh from the field, are invariably eaten simply with sweet butter and salt. **Above:** While its name translates to "New Bridge," Pont Neuf is in fact the oldest bridge in Paris. Its first stones were laid in 1578, although it was not inaugurated until 1607.

shortly thereafter and is similar to the midday meal, but lighter if lunch was substantial. I find these traditions peaceful and civilized, allowing, as they do, for hours each day to share with friends and family.

A large part of the French passion for food and for eating is predicated on a love for and an understanding of the land and what it produces each season. There is tremendous local pride in regional products, *les produits du terroir,* that seems not only undimin- ished today, but increasingly celebrated. Many a time when I have gone to visit friends for lunch, the main event before or after the meal is foraging for wild greens or hunting for mushrooms, snail gathering or cherry picking. In an urban environment, the event might be stopping at a special cheese shop where the owner does his or her own aging, or perhaps a trip to an especially fine *pâtisserie* or charcuterie.

Restaurants proudly tout *menus du terroir,* both simple and grand. In Forcalquier, the Hostellerie des Deux Lions sits at the edge of the town square, a classic traveler's hotel of the last century or so. The aperitif list includes a *vin de noix,* a walnut wine made from the harvest of the famous orchards in the nearby Valley of Jabron. Among the first courses offered will always be a seasonal vegetable or a soup made from one. The main courses feature local herb- grazed lamb and a daube made with a regional wine in the local style, using orange peel.

The owner also ages in house the cheeses that make up the next course. When I first sampled his lavender-seasoned goat cheese, I was swept away. It was perfection. I asked how its extraordinary taste was accomplished, and the owner brought out a shallow cardboard box of loose lavender stems and flowers. He showed me how he used the lavender seeds, which

Left: The French seem to possess an innate aesthetic, evident in the composition of this quintessential country garden of neat rows of greens bordered by pink poppies. **Right top:** Row of tables and chairs await customers at Café de Flore, a legendary literary hangout that once hosted such famous Parisian residents as Jean-Paul Sartre, Albert Camus, and Simone de Beauvoir. **Right bottom:** A tempting array of desserts are displayed in this *pâtisserie* window in Auxerre, a Burgundy town on the Yonne River.

Above top: A shallow stream meanders though the vine-yard-covered hills around Banyuls, where the sunny climate nourishes grapes that produce well-regarded sweet wines.
Above bottom: Melons, among the most appealing of fruits with their trickle of sweet juice, are cultivated in the fields around Aix-en-Provence, Avignon, and Cavaillon. **Right:** In Paris, the city of lovers, a young couple share a kiss on the sun-dappled Place Saint-Sulpice.

looked like tiny black specks in his hand, and then revealed a little jar, which he explained was a mixture of the seeds and the dried lavender stems, but not the blossoms, which he said were too strong. The cheese was made "just over there," in the hills near Banon, and the lavender was from his own planting.

All over France, this same scene is repeated. People care about their food and its source. Even today, when France, like other industrial-ized countries, has a highly developed delivery system of fresh fruits, vegetables, fish, cheeses, and meats, there remains a deep understanding of and value attached to high-quality *produits du terroir*.

The importance of seasonality can best be observed in the local markets, where in spring you'll find heaps of berries, the tiny cherries called *girottes,* asparagus, and artichokes. Come summer, these will have been replaced by tomatoes, sweet peppers (capsicums), eggplants (aubergines), peaches, plums, and melons. A few months later the scene will have changed again, with a preponderance of cabbages, wild mushrooms, greens, squashes, apples, and quinces. Winter finds sturdy kales, nuts, pota-toes, escarole (Batavian endive), and frisée. Of

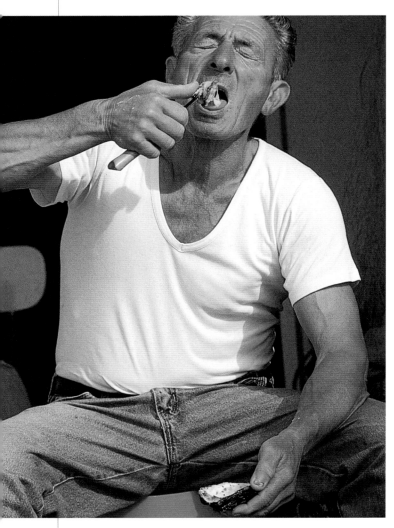

course, the seasons vary from region to region and climate to climate, so that residents in the Alps will find themselves without strawberries when their counterparts in the southwest are already enjoying them.

When traveling in France you can learn much about that region's food and its people by simply looking in the windows of the charcuteries, *pâtisseries,* cheese stores, and wine shops and by reading the posted restaurant menus. You'll discover products that are specific to that region, like the *poumonier* sausages of Savoy, the *gâteau Basque,* or the plum puddings of Brittany. Everywhere you will see a distinctive *vin du pays,* the local wine.

The role of the French artisans and the people's appreciation and respect for them can't be underestimated. Cheese makers, *charcutiers, pâstissiers, fermiers,* fishermen, and wine makers who work on their own or with just a few employees, often in very traditional ways, are instrumental in carrying out the French desire for fine-quality foodstuffs. Cheese, for example, is an integral part of the French meal, both as a separate course and in cooking, and the French have hundreds of different varieties from which to choose, many of them made by local artisanal cheese makers. In the alpine summer pastures, some shepherds still make cheese from the milk of their charges, and later bring the wheels down from the hills to age and then to sell. Goat cheeses wrapped in brown chestnut leaves speak of the cheese tradition of Banon, where the *fromagers* know that the green leaves carry too much tannin and impart a slightly bitter taste to the cheese, rather than the faint nuttiness the brown leaves bring.

It is because of such artisans that any Frenchman can purchase virtually an entire meal and be assured of quality as fine as, if not better than, homemade. From the *boulanger* comes the fresh bread, several baguettes, or maybe a special loaf made with olives or walnuts. The *charcutier* provides the first course and the main one. To begin, perhaps, *jambon*

cru, a nice slice of rabbit pâté, or sliced *saucisson* is accompanied with tiny cornichon pickles. A whole roasted chicken, its skin golden, crispy, and well scented with herbs, forms the center-piece of the menu, or perhaps a fine stew, rich with wine. The *épicerie* is the source of very ripe tomatoes, which are sliced onto a platter and offered after the chicken. Then the cheese course, selected, of course, by the *fromager.* And from the wonderful selection at the *pâtisserie,* a dessert is chosen. Carefully selected wines are poured throughout the meal. The *charcutier* and *pâtissier,* in particular, make it easy to prepare a fine meal, for they free the cook to concen-trate on preparing only one or two dishes. It is a custom I find eminently practical.

I hope that in this book I convey not only my affection for France, its food, and its way of life, but also the notions of simplicity that lie behind much of the passion for food that exists there. More often than not it is that simplicity that typifies the French table, a table of uncomplicated fare, prepared in season, and enjoyed in a leisurely atmosphere in the com-pany of friends and family.

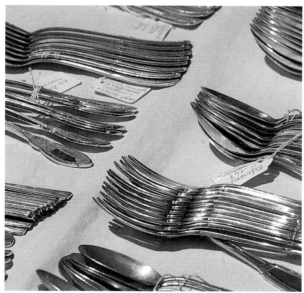

Left top: The magnificent snowcapped French Alps are home to some of the world's finest resorts, from the chal-lenging ski slopes of Chamonix and Megève to the luxuri-ous spas surrounding Lake Geneva. **Left middle:** Brittany's jagged coastline attracts both sightseers and fishermen.
Left bottom: In the port town of Bastia, a Corsican savors an oyster fresh from the sea. **Above top:** Birthplace of Paul Cézanne, Aix-en-Provence was once the capital of Provence and is still considered an epicenter of culture and cuisine.
Above bottom: For the tenacious shopper, flea markets offer a trove of household treasures.

LES ENTREES

*The first course
always sets the tone,
preparing the palate
for what is to follow.*

IN FRANCE, the first course of a meal is given as much attention, if not more, than the main course. It is, after all, the beginning that sets the tone for what is to follow, that prepares the palate and starts the digestive juices flowing.

When ordering in a French restaurant from a prix fixe menu, I seem to spend more time choosing my first course than on anything else. The possibilities are always intriguing, because they are so wide ranging. I might have a plate of charcuterie, a composed salad, shellfish, a warm cheese, an egg dish, a vegetable composition, a tart, crepes, a quiche, or a soup. When preparing a meal at home, the variations become even more significant, because the first course that you choose determines where you will focus your efforts in the kitchen. Should a composed salad, a warm cheese, or charcuterie be your choice, then little time is required to produce it. Purchased charcuterie requires only arranging on a plate. A salad might necessitate some chopping and slicing, as well as arranging, and the cheese will need to be heated. A soup, tart, quiche, homemade charcuterie, or a vegetable dish is more time-consuming and demands at least a modicum of culinary skill.

A restaurant charcuterie selection leads quickly to a taste of the local products, frequently *à la maison*, that is, made by the chef. In small family-run restaurants these might be prepared from recipes handed down through the generations, so not only do you have a chance to sample the *terroir*, but also a bit of history. In Rouen, I've been seduced by duck pâté with Armagnac, in the south by *pâté maison* with juniper berries and marc, in the Basque country by *jambon du pays* rubbed with the hot pepper of Espellete, and in Savoy by *poumoniers,* pork sausages made with lungs and spinach or chard.

The variety of French charcuterie served as a first course is astonishing. Terrines, pâtés, *rillettes,* sausages, and ham—all prepared in dozens of different ways, sometimes in a flaky crust or in aspic—are constructed using duck, pork, wild game, rabbit, fish, vegetables, and shellfish. Slices of headcheese, pickled tongue,

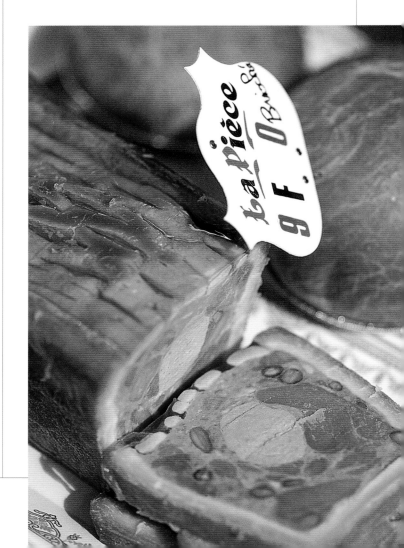

and salads of tongues and cheeks are among some of the other traditional preparations that use variety meats.

Shellfish are a wonderful way to start a meal, especially if you are near the sea. Many restaurants are known for their fresh *coquillage,* displayed near the entrance on banks of crushed ice decorated with fresh lemons and seaweed to tempt the customer. Oysters, shrimp, crab, tiny clams, sea urchins, and whelks all figure in the choices, depending upon the season.

But then, it's difficult to pass up such specialties as oyster soup on the Brittany coast, a wild mushroom omelet in the Périgord, grilled anchovies along the Mediterranean, or lentil and duck breast salad in the Auvergne.

Seasonality determines which vegetables or fruits appear as a first course, either *au naturel* or as part of a salad, quiche, tart, or omelet. Thus in spring, look for asparagus, artichokes, and cherries; in summer, tomatoes, eggplants (aubergines), zucchini (courgettes), peppers, and melons; in fall, mushrooms, figs, and apples; in winter, leeks, pumpkins, and truffles. Sometimes, with seasonal vegetables, the best way to sample or serve them is as simply as

Above top: In the Basque village of Espelette, peppers are hung outside to dry. They are then typically mixed with garlic, bread crumbs, olive oil, tomatoes, and fish stock to make *rouille,* a spicy red-orange sauce usually served with fish soup. **Above middle:** *Gavage,* the practice of forcibly feeding a goose or duck in order to enlarge its liver artificially, results in a rich, flavorful, and succulent foie gras. **Above bottom:** Charcuterie, the generic term used to describe a variety of meat products such as pâtés, terrines, *rillettes,* hams, and sausages, also denotes the shop in which such foods are sold. **Right:** Pâtés come in many different forms, from the common *pâté de campagne* (country style) to the more unusual *pâté de grive* (thrush). Here, a *pâté en croûte* (baked in pastry) conceals a treasure at its heart. **Far right:** An afternoon aperitif caps a visit to the market in Lyons. The city, situated on the banks of the Rhône and Saône Rivers, is considered the gastronomic capital of the country.

possible, allowing the extraordinary flavor of perfect ripeness to have full impact. Asparagus with a tarragon vinaigrette, a warm artichoke with olive oil and a little garlic, and grilled figs are all uncomplicated preparations permissible with wonderfully fresh ingredients.

Composed and mixed salads are frequently assertive expressions of *cuisine du terroir,* both in traditional and innovative dishes. A *salade niçoise* speaks of Mediterranean Provence with its tuna and anchovies, potatoes, tomatoes, and beans, all perfumed with olive oil and herbs, while a Norman salad is made with apples and walnuts and dressed with cream and cider vinegar. A *salade savoyarde* will have chunks of cheese—Beaufort or Emmentaler—walnuts, and lardons, tossed with a local walnut oil and a wine vinegar. Near the borders of Spain, around Perpignan and Biarritz, look for salads made with fish, seasoned with saffron and peppers, while fish salads of the northern coasts are likely to be full of *coquillage,* local shellfish.

Tarts, crepes, and quiches are served hot or at room temperature and are among the most

tempting of offerings. In the south, *pissaladière,* its crust thickly spread with a golden confit of onions and topped with anchovy fillets and locally produced olives, is mouth-watering. In the north, one finds instead a comparable tart made with leeks and dotted with a local cheese. 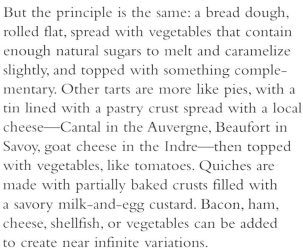 But the principle is the same: a bread dough, rolled flat, spread with vegetables that contain enough natural sugars to melt and caramelize slightly, and topped with something complementary. Other tarts are more like pies, with a tin lined with a pastry crust spread with a local cheese—Cantal in the Auvergne, Beaufort in Savoy, goat cheese in the Indre—then topped with vegetables, like tomatoes. Quiches are made with partially baked crusts filled with a savory milk-and-egg custard. Bacon, ham, cheese, shellfish, or vegetables can be added to create near infinite variations.

Of all the possibilities for first courses, though, I think it is soups that offer the greatest range. The soup can be as rustic and humble as onion soup, but ladle it into individual bowls, add a thick slice of chewy bread, some dollops of butter, dashes of olive oil, and lots of grated Gruyère to each one, and then bake until a golden crust forms and you have a sublime transformation. Vegetable soup with beans, potatoes, and a little pasta is equally transformed by the addition of *pistou,* the thick basil-garlic sauce that is stirred in at the last moment. Or consider Provençal *bourride,* the origins of which lie with local fishermen. It starts in the most modest manner, with a potful of heads and bones, a few vegetables, and a little wine. Then you add chunks of fish, the leftovers from the catch, and poach them in the liquid. Next you beat aioli, the garlic-rich mayonnaise of the region, and a few egg yolks into the broth to produce a delicate garlic cream that you ladle over bread slices placed in soup plates. Finally, set a bowl of aioli on the table to spoon into the soup at your pleasure and you have entered paradise.

Regardless of choice, hot or cold, simple or elaborate, purchased or homemade, the first course is as careful a consideration in the home as it is in restaurants. Rarely have I eaten a meal in anyone's home in France, lunch or dinner, when a first course wasn't offered. One of my best friends in France is a mason named Pascal, who is also an employee of his village. Two days a week he performs the duties of the *garde champêtre,* an appointed office that includes, among other disparate duties, directing traffic in case of an accident, making sure the fire engine is always running, winding the church clock once a week, and officiating at elections and ceremonies. On the days he works for the village, he always comes home at lunch. He is the cook of the family, saying that cooking is

relaxing, therapeutic, and calming for him. On Mondays and Tuesdays, his battered masonry truck pulls up the road at noon, and Pascal, after a pastis, tends to preparing lunch for whomever is there. I always feel fortunate when I'm present.

Most recently, and of fond memory, we were served a first course of *jambon cru* with olives, followed by panfried salmon steaks finished with saffron, white wine, and raisins; a little escarole salad; and finally, a cheese. The meal concluded with *café express* before he went back to work. Lunch was leisurely, full of lively conversation and good, simple food.

Left: The Musée du Louvre, first constructed as a fortress in 1190 and now home to one of the world's most significant art collections, is partially concealed here by trees growing on the bank of the Seine. **Right top:** Horses graze in a field outside the Cévennes city of Nîmes, an important crossroads in ancient times and now famous for its Roman ruins, festivals, and bullfights. **Right bottom:** There are over four hundred different kinds of French cheeses, which, like wines and sausages, are often named after their place of origin, such as Camembert, Brie, and Roquefort.

Above top: The spire of Bonnieux's twelfth-century church rises against Lubéron's limestone mountain range. **Above bottom:** An aperitif is always a time for conversation and conviviality. **Right:** In Burgundy, the Côte d'Or is home to some of the world's most famous red wines.

French meals are an indefinable experience that seems difficult to capture away from French soil. The aperitif—that half hour or so of making a transition from the work world to the private, pleasurable world of the table— begins it, and the first course establishes it. The preludes to the main course allow and even force the participants to a slower pace. Food is eaten leisurely, with time and emphasis given to conversation and conviviality. Business and work are put aside, and politics, theater, or other subjects take their place. It is not only good for the digestion, but as the French will tell you, it is also part of the good life of the French table.

To re-create that ambience at home, in a different country based on a different lifestyle, takes effort, but keep in mind that each course need not be elaborate, only good, and that the beginning of a meal can be as simple as steamed vegetables dressed with an herb and a vinaigrette, a platter of tomatoes, or a slice or two of ham.

Provence

Pissaladière

onion confit pizza

This is the pizza of Provence, rich with onions that have been cooked down with herbs, butter, and olive oil to make a thick, golden confit.

ONION CONFIT

¼ cup (2 oz/60 g) unsalted butter

3½ lb (1.75 kg) yellow onions, sliced ¼ inch (6 mm) thick

2 fresh bay leaves or 1 dried bay leaf

4 large fresh thyme sprigs

4 fresh winter savory sprigs

1 teaspoon freshly ground pepper

½ teaspoon salt

4 tablespoons (2 fl oz/60 ml) extra-virgin olive oil

DOUGH

5 teaspoons (2 packages) active dry yeast

1 cup (8 fl oz/250 ml) warm water (105°F/41°C)

1 teaspoon sugar

1 teaspoon salt

2 tablespoons extra-virgin olive oil

about 3½ cups (17½ oz/545 g) all-purpose (plain) flour

20 anchovy fillets

20 oil-cured black olives

2 teaspoons olive oil

2 tablespoons minced fresh marjoram

❦ Preheat an oven to 300°F (150°C).

❦ To make the onion confit, cut the butter into several pieces and place in a shallow baking dish large enough to hold the onions in a heaping layer 1–1½ inches (2.5–4 cm) deep. If the onions are spread too thinly, they will fry rather than "melt" into a confit. Put in the oven to melt, about 5 minutes. Remove the dish and place half the sliced onions in it. Tear the bay leaves into 2 or 3 pieces and scatter half of the pieces over the onions. Then add 2 each of the thyme and winter savory sprigs, ½ teaspoon of the pepper, and ¼ teaspoon of the salt. Drizzle with 2 tablespoons of the olive oil. Repeat with the remaining onions, seasonings, and olive oil, piling them on top. Return the dish to the oven and continue to bake, turning the onions every 10–15 minutes, until they are a light golden brown and have reduced in volume by nearly half, 1–1½ hours. Remove from the oven and discard the thyme, winter savory, and bay.

❦ Meanwhile, make the dough: In a small bowl, dissolve the yeast in the warm water. Add the sugar and let stand until foamy, about 5 minutes.

❦ In a food processor, combine the yeast mixture, the salt, 1 tablespoon of the olive oil, and 3 cups (15 oz/470 g) of the flour. Process until the ingredients come together into a ball. If the dough is too wet, add as much of the remaining ½ cup (2½ oz/ 75 g) flour, a little at a time, as needed to form a smooth, firm ball. If the dough is too dry, add dribbles of warm water until the ball forms. Continue to process after the ball has formed until the dough is silky but firm, 3–4 minutes. Turn out the dough onto a well-floured work surface and knead until the dough is smooth and elastic, 4–5 minutes.

❦ Oil a large bowl with the remaining 1 tablespoon olive oil. Place the dough ball in the bowl and turn the ball to coat the surface with oil. Cover with a clean, damp kitchen towel and let stand in a warm place until the dough doubles in size, 1–1½ hours. Punch down the dough, re-cover the bowl with the towel, and let rest for another 30 minutes.

❦ Position a rack in the upper third of an oven and preheat to 500°F (260°C).

❦ Punch down the dough and turn out onto a floured work surface. Roll out the dough into a rectangle about 13 by 19 inches (33 by 48 cm). Sprinkle a little flour on the bottom of a 12-by-18-inch (30-by-45-cm) baking sheet. Lay the dough on it, patting it up the sides to make a crust. Spread the surface with the onion confit, then arrange the anchovies and olives evenly over the surface.

❦ Bake until the bottom of the crust is crisp and the edge is lightly browned, 12–15 minutes. Remove from the oven. While hot, drizzle with the 2 teaspoons olive oil, then sprinkle with the marjoram.

❦ To serve, cut the *pissaladière* into rectangles about 3 by 3½ inches (7.5 by 9 cm) and serve warm or at room temperature.

serves 10

Salade de Melon et Figues avec Crème au Basilic

melon and fig salad with basil cream

Very ripe, intensely sweet figs and melons, both daily summer fare in the warm regions of central and southwestern France, are often lightly dressed with a sauce made of cream and basil.

½ cup (4 fl oz/125 ml) heavy (double) cream

2½ tablespoons fresh lemon juice

¼ cup (⅓ oz/10 g) minced fresh basil, plus sprigs for garnish

1½ teaspoons sugar

3 cups (18 oz/560 g) cubed cantaloupe, honeydew, or other sweet melon (1-inch/2.5-cm cubes)

1–1½ lb (500–750 g) very ripe figs, each quartered lengthwise

♛ In a bowl, stir together the cream, lemon juice, minced basil, and sugar. Cover and refrigerate for at least 1 hour or for up to 6 hours.

♛ When ready to serve, divide the melon and figs among 4 individual plates. Pour a little of the cream mixture over each plate of fruit, then garnish each with a basil sprig.

serves 4

The best way to serve seasonal fruits is as simply as possible, allowing the extraordinary flavor of perfect ripeness to have full impact.

Alsace-Lorraine

Quiche Lorraine

Quiches of all kinds are an indelible part of the French patrimony. One summer my son, who was only about thirteen at the time, made a study of quiches, which he loved. During a trip from Haute Provence to just north of Lyons, he bought one in every village we stopped at and promptly ate it, commenting each time on the texture of the custard, the amount of filling, and the flakiness of the crust. He still remembers the one he deemed to be the best that summer, from Villelaure, in the Lubéron.

Quiche wagons, found in the open markets, offer the savory pies fresh, large and small, and with varying ingredients. They are baked sur place *and delivered warm right into your hands. It's impossible to bypass one of these portable kitchens, and almost impossible not to eat the pies out of hand right away. Quiche Lorraine is the simplest of the family, but its flavors are intense and enormously satisfying.*

PASTRY

2 cups (10 oz/315 g) all-purpose (plain) flour

½ teaspoon salt

½ cup (4 oz/125 g) chilled unsalted butter, cut into ½-inch (12-mm) chunks

6 tablespoons (3 fl oz/90 ml) ice water

FILLING

3 eggs

1 cup (8 fl oz/250 ml) heavy (double) cream

1 cup (8 fl oz/250 ml) half-and-half (half cream)

½ teaspoon salt

½ teaspoon freshly ground pepper

⅛ teaspoon ground nutmeg

8 thin slices bacon, cut into ½-inch (12-mm) pieces

To make the pastry, in a bowl, stir together the flour and salt. Using a pastry blender or 2 knives, cut in the butter until pea-sized balls form. Add the ice water 1 tablespoon at a time while turning the dough lightly with a fork and then with your fingertips. (This will help to keep the pastry light and flaky. Do not overwork the dough, or it will become tough.) Gather the dough into a ball (it should be a little crumbly), wrap in plastic wrap, and refrigerate for 15 minutes.

Preheat an oven to 425°F (220°C).

On a floured work surface, roll out the dough into a round about 10½ inches (26.5 cm) in diameter and about ¼ inch (6 mm) thick. Drape the pastry around the rolling pin and carefully transfer to a 9-inch (23-cm) quiche or other straight-sided pan with 1-inch (2.5-cm) sides. Pat into the bottom and sides, and flute the edge or trim even with the rim, depending on the pan. Line the pastry with aluminum foil or parchment (baking) paper and fill with pie weights or dried beans.

Bake the pastry until set but not browned, 12–15 minutes. Remove from the oven and lift out the weights and liner. Prick any bubbles with the tines of a fork and return to the oven until firm and barely colored, 5 minutes longer. Remove from the oven and set aside.

Reduce the oven temperature to 375°F (190°C).

To make the filling, in a bowl, stir together the eggs, cream, half-and-half, salt, pepper, and nutmeg until blended. Scatter the uncooked bacon evenly over the pastry crust. Pour in the egg mixture.

Carefully transfer the quiche to the oven and bake until the top is puffed and lightly golden and a knife inserted into the center comes out clean, 25–30 minutes. Transfer to a rack and let stand for 15 minutes. Serve warm or at room temperature.

serves 6

Provence

Tellines à l'Arlésienne

sautéed garlic clams

On a stretch of sandy Mediterranean beach near Arles, tellines, tiny clams not much larger than the nail on one's little finger, are found. Sautéed in olive oil with garlic and parsley and served in their shells, they are an aperitif tradition at cafés and homes throughout the area, and they may also appear in larger quantities as a first course. On market day in nearby Isle-sur-la-Sorgue, shoppers can be seen picking tellines from the small plastic containers in which the vendors pack them, then licking their fingers as they explore the market. The small clams or mussels that abound in other areas of coastal France and elsewhere may be prepared in the same way. Any of the classic aperitifs are suitable partners, although I am partial to pairing them with a glass of chilled Provençal rosé.

1 lb (500 g) small clams or 2 lb (1 kg) mussels

¼ cup (2 fl oz/60 ml) extra-virgin olive oil

4 cloves garlic, minced

¼ cup (⅓ oz/10 g) minced fresh flat-leaf (Italian) parsley

❦ Rinse the clams or mussels thoroughly under running water to remove any grit, sand, or dirt, scrubbing with a brush if necessary. If using mussels, clip any beards that are evident with scissors. Discard any clams or mussels that do not close to the touch. Roughly dry the shellfish with a towel.

❦ Select a frying pan large enough to hold all the clams or mussels in no more than 2 scant layers. Place over medium heat and add the olive oil. When hot, add the garlic and sauté for a minute or two, but do not let it brown. Add the clams or mussels and the parsley to the pan, turning the shellfish with a spoon to coat them with the oil. Cook just until the shells open, 2–3 minutes.

❦ Transfer the clams or mussels and their juices to a platter or individual plates, discarding any shellfish that failed to open. Serve immediately.

serves 3 or 4 as an appetizer, 2 as a first course

Bourgogne et Le Lyonnais

Escargots à la Bourguignonne

snails with garlic, butter, and parsley

Large snails abound in Burgundy, but I have made this dish with the smaller petit gris of Provence, which work equally well. The biggest difference is that you might need more than four dozen—not a bad idea. To my thinking, the snails are really an excuse to eat lots of melted garlic and parsley butter, scooped up with bread.

Canned snails and packages of large shells are readily available. Stuffed snail shells are classically served in dishes with indentations for each snail, where the butter pools as it melts. Special tongs for holding the shells and a small two-pronged fork for digging out the snails are provided for each diner.

1 cup (8 oz/250 g) salted butter, at room temperature

6 cloves garlic, minced

½ cup (¾ oz/20 g) minced fresh flat-leaf (Italian) parsley

1 teaspoon freshly ground pepper

4 dozen canned snails, drained

4 dozen snail shells

❦ Preheat an oven to 450°F (230°C).

❦ In a bowl, combine the butter, garlic, parsley, and pepper and mix well with a wooden spoon.

❦ Slip a snail into each shell, pushing it toward the back with a small spoon. Then tuck in a plug of the seasoned butter, about 2 teaspoons, pushing it deep into the shell and smoothing it at the opening.

❦ Arrange the snails, the butter facing up, on snail plates with individual indentations, and place the plates on a baking sheet. Alternatively, pack them snugly together in a shallow baking dish.

❦ Bake until the snails are hot and the butter is beginning to melt, 10–12 minutes. If using snail plates, put them on individual serving plates. If the snails have been cooked in a baking dish, transfer them to small plates or shallow bowls, being careful not to lose any of the garlicky butter. Serve at once.

serves 4

SAVORING FRANCE

Le Sud-Ouest

Omelette aux Champignons Sauvages

wild mushroom omelet

In the Périgord, as in other areas of France, the fall mushroom season is eagerly awaited. When it arrives, locals can be spotted with baskets on their arms, even in the rain, carrying home their forest finds. At least once, usually early in the season, wild mushrooms, such as the cèpes and chanterelles that are particularly abundant in the region, are made into a simple omelet.

3½ tablespoons unsalted butter

½ shallot, minced

½ lb (250 g) fresh cèpe mushrooms or a mixture of cèpes and chanterelles, brushed clean and thinly sliced

½ teaspoon fresh thyme leaves

¾ teaspoon salt

¾ teaspoon freshly ground pepper

6 eggs

1 tablespoon minced fresh flat-leaf (Italian) parsley

☙ In a small frying pan over medium heat, melt 2 tablespoons of the butter. Add the shallot and sauté until translucent, 1–2 minutes. Add the mushrooms and thyme and sauté until soft, 2–3 minutes. Sprinkle with ¼ teaspoon each of the salt and pepper. Set aside. In a bowl, whisk the eggs with the remaining ½ teaspoon each salt and pepper until frothy.

☙ In a 12-inch (30-cm) frying pan over medium heat, melt the remaining 1½ tablespoons butter. Add the eggs and stir until they begin to thicken, just a few seconds. Reduce the heat to low. As the eggs set along the sides of the pan, lift the edges with a spatula and tip the pan to let the uncooked egg run underneath. Cook until the omelet is set and the bottom is lightly golden, 30–40 seconds longer.

☙ Using a slotted spoon, transfer the mushrooms to the omelet, covering half of it to within about 1 inch (2.5 cm) of the edge. Sprinkle with half of the parsley. Pulling the pan up and toward you, and using a spatula, flip the uncovered half over the covered half. Cook until the inner edges are slightly firm, another 30–40 seconds. Transfer to a warmed platter and sprinkle with the remaining parsley. Cut into wedges and serve immediately.

serves 3 or 4

Pour Commencer, un Peu de Fromage

We tend to think of cheese coming at the end of a French repast, but it is surprising how often it is used to begin (*pour commencer*) a meal, either with aperitifs or as an element of the first course. When I kept a herd of goats in Provence and made my own cheese from their milk, I sometimes put bits left over from larger rounds into a jar of olive oil. They were then spread on toasts for aperitif time. Now at the market I see little individual cheeses packed in olive oil, labeled *pour l'apéro*—"for the aperitif." *Gougères,* cheese-flavored puff pastries, are another way cheese is presented as a partner to aperitifs, or sometimes cubes of a special local cheese are served.

One of my favorite first courses to make and to eat is a disk of warm goat cheese served atop a well-dressed salad of frisée, a perfect marriage of flavors and textures. Cheese appears in tarts and quiches, too, as elements in composed salads, and in sauces napping elegant first-course crepes or quenelles.

Le Sud-Ouest

Tarte au Roquefort
et Tomates

fresh tomato tart with roquefort

*I discovered this dish when a friend invited me to
a picnic. The same filling can top a pizza crust.*

PASTRY

1 cup (5 oz/155 g) all-purpose (plain) flour

½ teaspoon salt

*⅓ cup (3 oz/90 g) chilled unsalted butter, cut
into ½-inch (12-mm) chunks*

3 tablespoons ice water

FILLING

*6 oz (185 g) Roquefort cheese, at room
temperature*

2 tablespoons half-and-half (half cream) or milk

2 tomatoes, sliced ¼ inch (6 mm) thick

½ teaspoon freshly ground pepper

½ teaspoon minced fresh thyme

1 teaspoon extra-virgin olive oil

❧ To make the pastry, in a bowl, stir together the
flour and salt. Using a pastry blender or 2 knives, cut
in the butter until pea-sized balls form. Add the ice
water 1 tablespoon at a time while turning the
dough lightly with a fork and then with your fingertips. (Do not overwork, or it will become tough.)
Gather the crumbly dough into a ball, wrap in plastic wrap, and refrigerate for 15 minutes.

❧ Preheat an oven to 400°F (200°C). On a floured
work surface, roll out the dough into a round about
10½ inches (26.5 cm) in diameter and about ¼ inch
(6 mm) thick. Carefully transfer to a 9-inch (23-cm)
tart pan with a removable bottom and ½-inch (12-
mm) sides. Pat into the bottom and sides and trim
the edge even with the rim.

❧ In a small bowl, using a fork, mash the cheese
together with the half-and-half or milk. Spread evenly over the bottom of the pastry. Cover with the
tomato slices in a tightly packed single layer. Sprinkle
with the pepper, thyme, and olive oil.

❧ Bake until the crust is lightly golden and the
tomatoes have collapsed, 20–25 minutes. Transfer to
a rack and let stand for 30 minutes. Serve warm or at
room temperature.

serves 6–8

Ile-de-France

Les Crudités

trio of crudités

At home, I either serve crudités on small oval dishes called raviers, *with a different crudité on each, or combine the three on an individual* ravier *for each person.*

3 beets

5 carrots, peeled and finely grated

3 tomatoes, sliced

6 tablespoons (3 fl oz/90 ml) extra-virgin olive oil

1 teaspoon Dijon mustard

4 tablespoons (2 fl oz/60 ml) red wine vinegar

¾ teaspoon salt

¾ teaspoon freshly ground pepper

8 butter (Boston) lettuce leaves

2 tablespoons minced fresh flat-leaf (Italian) parsley

❀ Trim off the beet greens, leaving 1 inch (2.5 cm) of the stem. Place the beets in a saucepan, add water to cover, and bring to a boil over medium–high heat. Reduce the heat to medium–low, cover, and cook until tender when pierced with a fork, about 1 hour. Drain and, when cool enough to handle, peel the beets. Cut into ½-inch (12-mm) cubes. Place in a bowl and set aside.

❀ Place the carrots and tomatoes in separate bowls. In another bowl, using a fork, stir together 4 tablespoons (2 fl oz/60 ml) of the olive oil and the mustard until thickened. Mix in 3 tablespoons of the vinegar and ½ teaspoon each of the salt and pepper to form a vinaigrette.

❀ Pour half of the vinaigrette over the beets and turn to coat. Pour the other half over the carrots and turn. Sprinkle the remaining 2 tablespoons oil, 1 tablespoon vinegar, and ¼ teaspoon each salt and pepper over the tomatoes and turn them.

❀ Arrange the lettuces leaves on a platter or individual plates. Spoon separate piles of the seasoned vegetables on top of the lettuce. Sprinkle everything with the parsley and serve.

serves 4

Provence

Sardines Marinées aux Tomates et Huile d'Olive

sardines marinated with olive oil and tomatoes

Sardines are considered a delicacy along the Mediterranean, where they are often fried, then dressed in a sauce and served at room temperature, as with this dish. Sardines have long been plentiful in these waters, and many local dishes, including a bouillabaisse, are made with them. One of my favorite preparations is the simplest: grilling them over an open fire where the skin crisps and the meat takes on a smoky flavor. My neighbor and I sometimes grill sardines in the fireplace in her dining room, delivering them straight from the grill to the table.

When choosing sardines, look for those with bright, clear eyes and slippery skin. A dull-eyed, dry-skinned fish is not a fresh one. Allow at least four sardines per person if they are served fried or grilled without a sauce.

¼ cup (2 fl oz/60 ml) olive oil

½ cup (2½ oz/75 g) all-purpose (plain) flour

12 fresh sardines, about 3 lb (1.5 kg) total weight, cleaned

½ teaspoon salt

1 teaspoon freshly ground pepper

¼ cup (2 fl oz/60 ml) red wine vinegar

MARINADE

2 tablespoons olive oil

1 yellow or white onion, minced

1 fennel stalk, about 6 inches (15 cm) long

1 clove garlic

1 fresh bay leaf or ½ dried bay leaf

2 ripe tomatoes, peeled, seeded, and chopped

❧ In a frying pan over medium heat, warm the olive oil. While the oil is heating, spread the flour on a plate and roll the sardines in it to coat lightly.

❧ When the oil is hot, place the sardines, a few at a time, into the pan and fry on the first side until the skin is crispy and golden, 2–3 minutes. Turn and fry on the second side until crispy and golden and the meat pulls easily away from the bone, another minute or so. Using a slotted spatula, transfer to paper towels to drain. Repeat until all the sardines are cooked. Sprinkle them with the salt and pepper and arrange on a platter.

❧ Pour off all but 2 tablespoons of the oil from the pan and return to medium heat. Add the vinegar and deglaze the pan, stirring with a wooden spoon to dislodge any browned bits from the pan bottom. Remove from the heat and pour the vinegar mixture over the sardines.

❧ To make the marinade, in another frying pan over medium heat, warm the olive oil. When it is hot, add the onion, fennel, garlic, and bay leaf. Sauté until the onion is translucent, 1–2 minutes. Add the tomatoes, raise the heat to high, and cook for 2–3 minutes to reduce some of the liquid.

❧ Pour the hot marinade over the sardines. Let cool to room temperature, 10–15 minutes, then cover and refrigerate for 12–24 hours before serving.

❧ Serve slightly chilled or at room temperature.

serves 4

Le Centre

Crème de Potiron
au Cerfeuil

cream of winter squash soup with chervil

Chervil, one of the classic herbs of French cooking, adds a delicate and slightly surprising licorice flavor to this smooth, light soup. Traditionally a cooking pumpkin would be used, but dense, meaty butternut and acorn squashes are now popular as well.

1 butternut squash, about 2 lb (1 kg)

1 teaspoon plus 1 tablespoon unsalted butter

1 yellow or white onion, chopped

1 cup (8 fl oz/250 ml) chicken stock

⅔ cup (5 fl oz/160 ml) water

3 tablespoons minced fresh chervil

½ teaspoon salt

½ teaspoon freshly ground pepper

1⅓ cups (11 fl oz/340 ml) milk

❦ Preheat an oven to 350°F (180°C). Cut the squash in half lengthwise. Scoop out and discard the seeds and fibers. Using the 1 teaspoon butter, rub the cavities and cut edges of the squash. Place cut sides down on a baking sheet.

❦ Bake until the flesh is very soft when pierced with a fork, 45–50 minutes. Remove from the oven and, when cool enough to handle, scrape the pulp into a bowl; discard the skin. In a saucepan over medium heat, melt the 1 tablespoon butter. When it foams, add the onion and sauté until soft, 4–5 minutes. Add the chicken stock, water, 2 tablespoons of the chervil, and ¼ teaspoon each of the salt and pepper. Simmer, uncovered, for 15 minutes to blend the flavors. Add the squash, stir well, and simmer for another 5 minutes to heat through.

❦ Remove from the heat and let cool slightly. Working in batches, place in a blender or food processor. With the machine running, add the milk in a steady stream and process until smooth. Return the purée to the saucepan over medium heat and add the remaining ¼ teaspoon each salt and pepper. Cook, stirring continuously, until hot but not boiling.

❦ To serve, ladle into warmed bowls. Garnish each bowl with an equal amount of the remaining chervil.

serves 4

Champagne et Le Nord

Salade de Champignons,
Celeris, et Fromage
de Chèvre Sec

mushroom, celery, and goat cheese salad

A refreshing, easy-to-prepare salad frequently made in French households combines thinly sliced mushrooms with celery, more common in the north, or with fennel, the custom in the south. The important thing is that the mushroom caps must still be tightly closed, without the slightest evidence of gills other than the faint pink line where they will eventually appear. If the gills are showing, the mushrooms are not fresh and firm enough to use raw in this salad. Hard, aged goat cheese has a strong, peppery flavor. If you prefer a milder taste, grate it instead of shaving, or substitute another dry cheese such as Parmesan.

¼ cup (2 fl oz/60 ml) extra-virgin olive oil

3 tablespoons fresh lemon juice

scant ½ teaspoon salt

scant ½ teaspoon freshly ground pepper

4 tablespoons (⅓ oz/10 g) chopped fresh flat-leaf (Italian) parsley

¾ lb (375 g) firm fresh white button mushrooms, brushed clean

4 celery stalks, trimmed

1–2-oz (30–60-g) piece hard, aged goat cheese

❦ In a large bowl, stir together the olive oil, lemon juice, salt, pepper, and 2 tablespoons of the parsley to form a vinaigrette. Set aside.

❦ Using a mandoline or a very sharp knife, slice the mushrooms paper-thin. Repeat with the celery. Using a vegetable peeler, shave the cheese into paper-thin slices or curls.

❦ Add the mushrooms, celery, and half of the cheese to the bowl holding the vinaigrette and toss well to coat the vegetables.

❦ Divide the salad evenly among individual plates. Garnish with the remaining cheese and 2 tablespoons parsley. Serve at once.

serves 4

Provence

Ratatouille

Perfumed with the region's olive oil, wild thyme, and garlic, ratatouille is the summer vegetable stew of Provence, cooked up when potagers *and market gardens are full of peppers, eggplants, and zucchini.*

Traditionally, the different vegetables are cooked separately, then combined at the end with the tomatoes. I have rarely eaten a ratatouille prepared this way at the home of French friends, however, although I have occasionally made it that way myself. Instead, my friends invariably go into their gardens, harvest the abundance of zucchini, peppers, eggplants, tomatoes, and basil, return to the kitchen, and cook the vegetables together to make a scrumptious plate. The proportions regularly vary according to what is ready to pick and personal taste. What doesn't vary is that the dish is always well spiced with the local herbs, including wild thyme, rosemary, sage, and winter savory. The specific herbs and their combination depend upon the hand and taste of the cook, although thyme is typically present and seems to me to give ratatouille its distinctive perfume.

Ratatouille, although a popular first course, is sometimes served as a side dish or a main course, and is also used as a topping for egg dishes.

2 generous tablespoons extra-virgin olive oil

2 small yellow or white onions, chopped

2 eggplants (aubergines), cut into 1-inch (2.5-cm) cubes

4 cloves garlic, minced

2 zucchini (courgettes), cut into 1-inch (2.5-cm) cubes

2 large green, red, or yellow bell peppers (capsicums), seeded and cut into 1-inch (2.5-cm) pieces

8–10 ripe tomatoes, peeled, seeded, and coarsely chopped

3 fresh thyme sprigs

1 fresh rosemary sprig

1 dried bay leaf

½ teaspoon salt

½ teaspoon freshly ground pepper

¼ cup (⅓ oz/10 g) minced fresh basil

In a large, heavy saucepan or soup pot over medium heat, warm the olive oil. When it is hot, reduce the heat to medium-low, add the onions, and sauté until translucent, about 2 minutes. Add the eggplants and garlic and sauté, stirring often, until the eggplant cubes are slightly softened, 3–4 minutes.

Add the zucchini and bell peppers and continue to sauté, stirring and turning, until softened, another 4–5 minutes. Add the tomatoes, thyme, rosemary, bay leaf, salt, and pepper and stir and turn for another 2–3 minutes.

Cover, reduce the heat to low, and cook, stirring occasionally, until the vegetables are soft and have somewhat blended together, about 40 minutes.

Stir in the basil and remove from the heat. Transfer to a serving bowl and serve hot, at room temperature, or cold.

serves 10

Les Pyrénées et Gascogne

Brochettes de Pruneaux au Romarin

bacon-wrapped prunes on
rosemary skewers

*In southern France, rosemary grows wild, and the stiff
branches, stripped of all but their uppermost leaves,
are often used as skewers. Here, skewered prunes (such
as those from Agen in Touraine) and bacon become
lightly infused with the flavor of rosemary and
the delightful smokiness of the fire. Dried figs might
be substituted for the prunes.*

16 pitted prunes

8 slices bacon, cut in half crosswise

4 sturdy rosemary branches, leaves removed and
tips whittled to a point

♛ Prepare a fire in a charcoal grill with a cover.

♛ Wrap each prune with a half slice of bacon and
fasten it with a toothpick. Thread 4 wrapped prunes
onto each of 4 rosemary skewers, being careful not to
pack them together too tightly.

♛ When the coals are hot, push them to the sides
of the fire pan and place a drip pan in the bottom of
the grill. Place the skewers on the grill rack over it
and grill, uncovered, until the bacon is golden on the
first side, 2–3 minutes. Turn the skewers and grill 2–3
minutes longer to brown the second side lightly.

♛ Cover the grill and close the vents. Cook for
2–3 minutes longer. Lift the cover and turn the
skewers to check the bacon. It should be very crisp.

♛ Divide the skewers among individual plates and
serve hot or warm.

serves 4

Bretagne

Moules à la Marinière

mussels in white wine

Mussels are an important part of local French fare along both the Mediterranean and Atlantic coastlines. There are myriad preparations and variations, but I have remained especially fond of the moules à la marinière *that I first had at a tiny restaurant partially built into the rock on Mont-Saint-Michel. After visiting the thousand-year-old monastery built on the summit of what was once an island, my companion and I succumbed to the posted menu and stepped inside. Once we were seated, a huge bowl of mussels in steaming hot broth was brought to each of us. It was hard to decide which was better, the tender mussels we pried from the blue-black shells or the broth of Muscadet, butter, and garlic that we soaked up to the last drop with our bread.*

1 tablespoon unsalted butter

1 tablespoon extra-virgin olive oil

½ yellow or white onion, chopped

1 clove garlic, minced

½ teaspoon freshly ground pepper

4–5 lb (2–2.5 kg) mussels, well scrubbed and debearded

2 cups (16 fl oz / 500 ml) Muscadet or other dry white wine

1½ tablespoons minced fresh flat-leaf (Italian) parsley

❀ In the bottom of a pot large enough to accommodate all the mussels, melt the butter with the olive oil over medium-high heat. When the butter foams, add the onion and sauté just until translucent, 2–3 minutes. Add the garlic, pepper, and mussels (discard any that do not close to the touch), pour over the wine, and sprinkle with the parsley.

❀ Cover, reduce the heat to low, and cook just until the mussels open, 10–12 minutes. Uncover and turn the mussels in the broth.

❀ Using a large slotted spoon, scoop the mussels into individual bowls, discarding any that failed to open. Ladle an equal amount of the broth into each bowl. Serve at once.

serves 4

La Crêperie

All towns of any size in France have at least one *crêperie*. It might be a full-fledged restaurant or only a storefront just big enough to house a large hot plate for cooking the paper-thin pancakes and to display an assortment of toppings. Prepared crepes can also be purchased by the dozen in supermarkets, making it easy to serve them at home, either savory or sweet.

Chartres, dominated by its magnificent cathedral, stands out in my mind for its life-saving *crêperies* as well. My husband and I arrived there one December evening after a long flight from California and a drive from Orly airport. We were starving, but too tired to contemplate a serious restaurant meal. We decided on a *crêperie* near the beautifully lit cathedral, and we each consumed a trio of crepes. The first was rather like a salad, filled with tomato, frisée, and bacon. The second was ham for me, sausage for my husband, and the third a simple *crêpe sucrée* with butter and sugar. We washed them all down with a pitcher of white wine and went to bed well satisfied with our first night in France.

Bourgogne et Le Lyonnais

Salade de Foies de Volailles

warm escarole and chicken liver salad

I'm not sure that this is a dish typical of Burgundy, but my memory of eating it there is associated with such pleasure that I always think of it as special to Mâcon. My husband and I were driving south from Paris, planning to stop over in Mâcon and meet friends there. We arrived far behind schedule, tired and very hungry. Our friends took us to a beautiful bistro, where we ordered a bottle of Mâcon blanc and only the chicken liver salad. When our salads appeared, a bed of lovely pale escarole, each topped with three perfectly cooked chicken livers and a warm vinaigrette, we quickly forgot the trials of the drive.

6 cups (6 oz/185 g) escarole (Batavian endive), pale inner leaves only, torn into bite-sized pieces

¼ cup fresh flat-leaf (Italian) parsley sprigs, coarsely chopped

1 cup (1 oz/30 g) very young, small arugula (rocket) leaves, whole or torn in half

12 chicken livers, trimmed and halved

½ teaspoon salt

½ teaspoon freshly ground pepper

2 tablespoons unsalted butter

2½ tablespoons red wine vinegar

½ teaspoon Dijon mustard

½ cup (4 fl oz/125 ml) extra-virgin olive oil

In a bowl, mix together the escarole, parsley, and arugula. Divide evenly among individual plates.

Sprinkle the livers with the salt and pepper. In a sauté pan over medium–high heat, melt the butter. When it foams, add the chicken livers and sauté, turning once, until browned on the outside but pink and creamy inside, 2–3 minutes total. Pour in the vinegar and deglaze the pan, stirring with a wooden spoon to dislodge any browned bits from the pan bottom. Stir in the mustard and olive oil.

Using a slotted spoon, divide the chicken livers evenly among the individual plates. Pour a little dressing from the pan over each salad and serve.

serves 4

Île-de-France

Soupe à l'Oignon Gratinée

gratinéed onion soup

I was fortunate to have eaten at Les Halles, the old central market in Paris, before it was closed down and moved to the outskirts of the city. In those days, little restaurants abounded in the quarter, which was alive and vibrant in the early hours of the morning when trucks rumbled in from all over France to supply le ventre de Paris— *"the belly of Paris"—as Zola so aptly called it. One of the renowned dishes was onion soup covered with slices of bread, topped with cheese and butter, and then browned to form a crust. After a night on the town, people from all walks of life joined the market workers to eat the rich, hot soup, served with extra slices of the garlicky toasted bread.*

The only tricky part of this soup is to slice the onions very, very thinly. Thick slices or chopped bits simply don't create the same effect.

6 tablespoons (3 oz/90 g) unsalted butter

1 tablespoon extra-virgin olive oil

2 lb (1 kg) yellow onions, very thinly sliced

½ teaspoon sugar

½ teaspoon salt

1½ tablespoons all-purpose (plain) flour

8 cups (64 fl oz/2 l) beef stock

2 cups (16 fl oz/500 ml) water

1 cup (8 fl oz/250 ml) dry white wine

1 teaspoon freshly ground pepper

TOPPING

12–16 slices coarse country bread, each ½ inch (12 mm) thick

2 cloves garlic, halved

3 tablespoons extra-virgin olive oil

2 cups (8 oz/250 g) shredded Gruyère or Emmentaler cheese

2 tablespoons unsalted butter, cut into small bits

In a heavy saucepan over medium heat, melt the butter with the olive oil. When the butter foams, add the onions and stir and cook until translucent, 4–5 minutes. Reduce the heat to low, cover, and cook, stirring occasionally, until the onions turn lightly golden, about 15 minutes. Uncover, sprinkle with the sugar and salt, and raise the heat to medium. Cook uncovered, stirring often, until the onions are golden brown, 30–40 minutes.

Sprinkle the flour over the onions and continue to stir until the flour is browned, 2–3 minutes. Pour in the stock and the water, a little at a time, while continuing to stir. Raise the heat to high and bring to a boil. Add the wine and stir in the pepper. Reduce the heat to low, cover, and cook until the onions begin to dissolve, about 45 minutes.

While the soup is cooking, make the topping: Preheat a broiler (griller). Place the bread on a baking sheet and slip under the broiler 4–5 inches (10–13 cm) from the heat source. Broil (grill), turning once, just long enough to dry out, but not brown, 3–4 minutes on each side. Remove from the broiler and rub both sides with the garlic cloves. Then brush both sides with the olive oil. Return to the broiler and toast, turning once, until lightly golden, 2–3 minutes on each side. Set aside.

Preheat an oven to 450°F (230°C).

Place 6–8 individual ovenproof bowls on a baking sheet. Ladle the hot soup into them. Top each with 2 pieces of the toast, then sprinkle the cheese evenly over the tops. Dot evenly with the butter. Place in the oven and cook until a golden crust forms on the top and the soup bubbles around the edges, about 15 minutes.

Serve immediately.

serves 6–8

Bourgogne et Le Lyonnais

Jambon Persillé

parsleyed salt-cured ham

This is a traditional preparation of Burgundy, but now it is found all over France. It makes a beautiful charcuterie first course, with the bright green parsley and deep red ham glistening in the wine-scented jelly. Serve it with mustard and cornichons on the side, accompanied with a chilled white wine.

Jambon cru, or "raw ham," is ham that has been cured in salt. It is a popular charcuterie item throughout France, with each region using different breeds of pigs and customizing their curing technique. Bayonne, in the Pyrenees, is especially famous for its hams.

1 piece boneless jambon cru or prosciutto, about 2 lb (1 kg)

3 whole cloves

5 yellow or white onions

1 veal shank, about ½ lb (250 g)

1 calf's foot, about 1½–2 lb (750 g–1 kg)

2 fresh chervil sprigs

2 fresh tarragon sprigs

2 fresh thyme sprigs

1 clove garlic

2 shallots

4 cups (32 fl oz/1 l) water

1 bottle (24 fl oz/750 ml) dry white wine

¼ cup (2 fl oz/60 ml) plus 5 tablespoons (2½ fl oz/75 ml) Cognac

2 tablespoons powdered pectin

2 tablespoons white wine vinegar

1 teaspoon freshly ground pepper

½–⅔ cup (¾–1 oz/20–30 g) minced fresh flat-leaf (Italian) parsley

☙ Place the ham in a large pot, add water to cover, and let soak overnight to remove some of the salt.

☙ The next day, pour off the water. In the same large pot, combine the ham with water to cover and bring to a boil over medium-high heat. Reduce the heat to low, cover, and cook for 1 hour.

☙ Pour off the cooking water and rinse the ham in cold water. Wash the pot and return the ham to it. Stick the 3 cloves in 1 onion and then add all

5 onions to the pot along with the veal shank, calf's foot, chervil, tarragon, thyme, garlic, shallots, water, wine, and the ¼ cup (2 fl oz/60 ml) Cognac.

☙ Place over medium-high heat, bring to a boil, skim off any foam that collects on the surface, and reduce the heat to low. Cover and simmer, occasionally skimming off any foam, until the ham can be separated with a fork, about 1 hour.

☙ Remove the ham and the other meats from the cooking liquid and set aside. Pour the liquid through a sieve and discard the vegetables and herbs. Then line the sieve with several layers of cheesecloth (muslin), place over a clean saucepan, and pour the liquid through it again. Set aside.

☙ Using a fork, tear the ham, including any fat, into chunky pieces. Strip the veal from the shank bone and tear the meat into small pieces, discarding any fat. Pack half of the ham and the veal into a 2-qt (2-l) glass or ceramic bowl.

☙ Bring the liquid to a simmer over medium heat. Pour one-fourth of the hot liquid into another bowl and add the pectin, stirring until completely dissolved. Stir the liquid-pectin mixture into the liquid remaining in the pan and remove it from the heat.

☙ Sprinkle the ham with 1 tablespoon of the vinegar, 2 tablespoons of the Cognac, and ½ teaspoon of the pepper. Pour half of the liquid over the ham, then sprinkle with about half of the parsley. Add the remaining ham and then sprinkle with the remaining 1 tablespoon vinegar, 3 tablespoons Cognac, ½ teaspoon pepper, and the parsley. Pour the remaining liquid over all. The ham may float to the surface, but it will eventually settle.

☙ Cover and refrigerate overnight to set the jelly and chill thoroughly. It will keep refrigerated for up to 2 weeks. To serve, using a very sharp knife, cut into slices ½ inch (12 mm) thick and carefully remove them from the bowl.

serves 15

The beginning of a meal can be as simple as steamed vegetables dressed with a vinaigrette, a platter of tomatoes, or a slice or two of ham.

Le Sud-Ouest

Salade Verte aux Confit de Gésiers

green salad with confit of gizzards

For this classic confit, gizzards of duck, turkey, or chicken are slowly cooked until they become meltingly tender. Thinly sliced and reheated, they are added to salads, which, in the region along the Dordogne River in the Périgord, seem to appear on nearly every menu. There, the exceptionally large and tender gizzards from the ducks fattened for foie gras are used, but the same process works successfully on other gizzards.

CONFIT

2 lb (1 kg) chicken, duck, or turkey gizzards

¼ cup (2 oz/60 g) unsalted butter

2 shallots, minced

2 juniper berries, crushed

1 teaspoon fresh thyme leaves

1 teaspoon fresh winter savory leaves

1 teaspoon salt

½ teaspoon freshly ground pepper

SALAD

¼ cup (2 fl oz/60 ml) walnut oil

2–3 tablespoons red wine vinegar

½ teaspoon salt

½ teaspoon freshly ground pepper

1 head butter (Boston) lettuce

¼ cup (1 oz/30 g) chopped walnuts, toasted

♛ To make the confit, using a sharp knife, peel away the tough outer skins of the gizzards and discard. In a wide saucepan or sauté pan, melt the butter over medium heat. When it foams, add the shallots and gizzards. Reduce the heat to low and cook, turning occasionally, until completely browned, about 15 minutes. Add the juniper berries, thyme, winter savory, salt, pepper, and enough water to reach about two-thirds up the sides of the gizzards. Cover and cook over the lowest heat possible until the gizzards are very, very tender and can be easily sliced with a knife, 2½–3 hours.

✿ Remove from the heat, let cool, then transfer the gizzards and all their fat and juices to a jar with a lid. Cover tightly and refrigerate. If they are completely covered by their fat, they will keep for several weeks; if not, they will keep 3–4 days.

✿ To make the salad, remove the gizzards from the jar and slice them thinly. In a small saucepan over medium-low heat, warm the gizzards in their own fat until hot. In a salad bowl, combine the walnut oil, vinegar, salt, and pepper and stir with a fork to mix well. Tear the lettuce into pieces and add to the bowl. Toss to coat.

✿ Divide the lettuce evenly among individual plates. Spoon the hot gizzards on top, dividing them evenly. Garnish each plate with one-fourth of the walnuts and serve immediately.

serves 4

Provence

Bourride

fish soup with garlic cream

One of the marvels of the Provence coast, this simple fisherman's stew is transformed by the addition of aioli, homemade garlic mayonnaise. It is classically made with meaty monkfish, but other firm white fish can be used. Although the soup is easy to make, there is one important precaution: under no circumstances should the soup boil once the eggs have been added, as they will separate and nothing will blend them back.

1½ lb (750 g) fish trimmings (heads, tails, backbones) from nonoily fish

2 carrots, quartered

1 yellow onion, quartered

3 fennel stalks or 1 fennel bulb, quartered

3 cloves garlic

1 celery stalk, quartered

4 fresh flat-leaf (Italian) parsley sprigs

3 fresh thyme sprigs

1 teaspoon salt

1 bay leaf

1 piece dried orange peel

8 cups (64 fl oz/2 l) water

2 cups (16 fl oz/500 ml) dry white wine

2 lb (1 kg) monkfish or other firm white fish fillets, cut into 1-inch (2.5-cm) cubes

6 slices day-old coarse country bread, each about 1 inch (2.5 cm) thick

1 cup (8 fl oz/250 ml) aioli (see Le Grand Aïoli, page 111)

4 egg yolks

✿ In a large pot, combine the fish trimmings, carrots, onion, fennel, garlic, celery, parsley, thyme, salt, bay leaf, dried orange peel, and water. Place over medium-high heat and bring to a boil, skimming off any foam that collects on the surface. Reduce the heat to low and simmer, uncovered, for 15 minutes. Skim off any additional foam that forms on the surface. Add the wine, raise the heat to high, and return to a boil. Then reduce the heat to low and simmer, uncovered, for another 15 minutes to infuse the stock with flavor. Using a slotted spoon, scoop out and discard the vegetables and fish trimmings. Line a colander with several layers of cheesecloth (muslin), place over a clean saucepan, and pour the stock through it. You should have about 6 cups (48 fl oz/1.5 l) stock.

✿ Bring the stock to a simmer over medium heat. Add the fish and cook, uncovered, just until the fish is opaque, about 5 minutes. Using the slotted spoon, transfer the fish to a platter and cover loosely with aluminum foil to keep warm.

✿ Place a bread slice in each of 6 bowls. Ladle a little stock into each bowl, just enough for the bread to absorb.

✿ Put half of the aioli into a large bowl and whisk in the egg yolks until blended. In a slow, steady stream, whisk in the broth. Return the mixture to a clean saucepan over very low heat. Cook, stirring gently, until the mixture thickens to the consistency of light cream, 6–7 minutes. Be very careful not to let the mixture boil.

✿ Divide the fish evenly among the bowls and ladle the creamy stock over them. Place the remaining aioli in a bowl and pass at the table, to be added to the soup as desired.

serves 6

Franche-Comté et Les Alpes

Escargots au Bleu
de Bresse

snails with bleu de bresse cheese

*Snails have long been popular in France. People
still gather them from the wild, feeding them herbs,
grasses, and cornmeal for two weeks to purge them
before cooking. At some markets in France, snails are
sold live, purged and ready to cook. Canned
snails are also readily available.*

*In this preparation, which can be made with soft,
creamy blue cheeses such as bleu de Bresse,
bleu d'Auvergne, or others, the snails play the role
of succulent tidbits in the midst of a warm, rich
sauce. Serve with a light red Rhône wine and
crusty bread for scooping up bitefuls.*

2 tablespoons unsalted butter

48 canned snails, drained

¼ cup (2 fl oz/60 ml) crème fraîche

6 oz (180 g) bleu de Bresse cheese or other soft
blue cheese, crumbled

1½ teaspoons freshly ground pepper

2 tablespoons fine fresh bread crumbs

❧ Preheat a broiler (griller). In a frying pan over
medium heat, melt the butter. When it foams, add the
snails and sauté until glistening and warmed through,
about 2 minutes. Add the crème fraîche, half of the
cheese, and the pepper. Cook, stirring, just long
enough to melt the cheese, about 1 minute.

❧ Divide the snails evenly among small flameproof
ramekins. Sprinkle each portion with 1½ teaspoons
of the bread crumbs and one-fourth of the remaining cheese.

❧ Arrange the ramekins on a baking sheet and slip
under the broiler just long enough to melt the
cheese and brown the bread crumbs slightly, 2–3
minutes. Serve at once.

serves 4

Languedoc

Salade de Pissenlit aux
Oeufs Pochès

dandelion salad with poached eggs

*Throughout France, from the Alps to the Pyrenees,
from Normandy to Alsace, the wild greens that have
traditionally been part of the regional rural cuisine are
the harbingers of spring. Dandelion is among the most
pervasive of them and is used in both soups and
salads. To be at their most tender and flavorful, the
leaves must be picked before the flower shoots have
formed, when the plant is still only a rosette. They
are always bitter, which to the French palate is part of
their charm, but leaves that have become mature
are undesirably sharp flavored and tough. The egg
yolk, once broken, mixes with the vinaigrette, here
made with vinaigre de Banyuls in the style
of Languedoc, to make a warm sauce for the leaves.
The dandelion leaves are sometimes mixed
with other greens, as they are here.*

¼ cup (2 fl oz/60 ml) extra-virgin olive oil

3 tablespoons Banyuls or other red wine vinegar

½ shallot, minced

scant ½ teaspoon salt

scant ½ teaspoon freshly ground pepper

2 cups (2 oz/60 g) young, tender dandelion
leaves, each 3–4 inches (7.5–10 cm) long, larger
ones torn in half

3 cups (3 oz/90 g) curly endive (chicory), pale
inner leaves only, torn into bite-sized pieces

4 eggs

❧ In a large bowl, stir together the olive oil, vinegar,
shallot, salt, and pepper to form a vinaigrette. Add the
dandelion and curly endive and toss to coat. Divide
evenly among individual salad bowls.

❧ Pour water to a depth of 1 inch (2.5 cm) in a frying pan and bring just below a simmer over medium
heat. One at a time, carefully break the eggs into the
frying pan and poach them, spooning some of the
hot water over them as they cook, until the whites
are set and the yolks are glazed, 2–3 minutes. Using
a spatula, remove each egg, letting it drain a moment
and blotting briefly on a kitchen towel. Place an egg
atop each salad and serve immediately.

serves 4

Apéritifs

In France, *l'apéritif* is both a beverage and a social activity that encompasses the entire breadth of the society. Twice a day throughout the year, in cafés, restaurants, and homes, people share the ritual of having a drink together and nibbling on a few nuts, olives, or perhaps a square or two of cheese, before sitting down to lunch or dinner. The drink is usually not strong spirits, which would dull the appetite, but a fortified wine such as a sweet vermouth or a spirit-based drink like Campari and water.

Different regions have their specialties, too. In the south, it is pastis, a rather bitter anise-flavored drink served with ice and water, but for which one develops a taste. Suze, Aveze, and Salers, flavored with the bitter gentian root, are specialties of the Auvergne. *Kir,* a

mixture of white wine and crème de cassis that originated in Dijon and takes its name from a former mayor, is quite popular all over the country, but there are variations. In Brittany one is offered *kir Bretagne* made with cider, while in the Cevennes crème de cassis is added to red wine to make a *camisard.*

Fortified *vins maison,* based on local fruits and nuts, are homemade and proudly produced at aperitif time. I love the crisp, refreshing *vin d'orange* made with white wine and bitter oranges, and the dark, spicy *vin de noix,* whose flavor and color come from green walnuts. Champagne, of course, is the aperitif of choice everywhere for celebratory occasions, and *vins doux,* sweet fortified wines, find a local following in the southwest where Banyuls and Rivesaltes are made.

Languedoc

Moules Farcies

gratinéed mussels on the half shell

In the coastal regions of France that border Spain, both on the Mediterranean and Atlantic, mussels are commonly prepared by packing a savory stuffing on top of the already-cooked mollusks.

48 mussels, scrubbed and debearded

1¼–1½ cups (5–6 oz / 155–185 g) fine dried bread crumbs

3 tablespoons minced fresh flat-leaf (Italian) parsley

2 tablespoons minced fresh thyme

½ teaspoon salt

½ teaspoon freshly ground pepper

4 cloves garlic, minced

2 small tomatoes, peeled, seeded, minced, and drained

1½–2 tablespoons extra-virgin olive oil

❦ Preheat an oven to 500°F (260°C). Arrange the mussels in a baking dish in a single layer, discarding any that do not close to the touch. Bake just until the shells open, 8–10 minutes.

❦ Remove from the oven and let cool for about 15 minutes. Discard any mussels that failed to open. Reserve the collected juice in the bottom of the dish. Pull apart the shells of each mussel, holding it over the dish to capture the juices. Using a knife, cut through the muscles that attach the meat to the shell, discarding one shell and leaving the meat resting in the other. Reduce the oven to 450°F (230°C).

❦ In a bowl, combine the bread crumbs, captured mussel juices, parsley, thyme, salt, pepper, and garlic. Mix in the tomatoes. Add enough oil to hold the stuffing together. Cover the mussels in their half shells with about 1 tablespoon of the filling, mounding it to the rim of the shell and packing it tightly. Place the filled shells on a baking sheet.

❦ Bake until the filling is golden brown, 12–14 minutes. If still pale, slip the mussels under a broiler (griller) for 1–2 minutes. Transfer to a platter and serve hot or at room temperature.

serves 8 as an appetizer, 4 as a first course

Salade de Tomme de Savoie aux Noisettes

salad of panfried tomme de savoie with hazelnuts

Hazelnuts, which grow wild on the mountainsides in the valleys of Savoy, are gathered by the inhabitants in the fall and stored as part of the winter larder. The taste for local products remains strong in the area, especially for cheeses such as the mild, round, firm tommes made with cow's milk. If you can't find one, use another supple cheese.

½ cup (2½ oz/75 g) hazelnuts (filberts)

¼ cup (2 fl oz/60 ml) hazelnut oil or extra-virgin olive oil

1 teaspoon Dijon mustard

3 tablespoons red wine vinegar

¼ teaspoon salt

¼ teaspoon freshly ground pepper

6 cups (6 oz/185 g) red or green leaf lettuce leaves, or a mixture, torn into bite-sized pieces

½ cup (2½ oz/75 g) all-purpose (plain) flour

1 tomme de Savoie, ⅓ lb (5 oz/155 g), rind trimmed and cut into 4 slices, each ¼ inch (6 mm) thick

sunflower oil or other light vegetable oil for frying

☙ Preheat an oven to 350°F (180°C). Spread the nuts in a pan and bake for 15 minutes. Stir and continue to bake until lightly golden throughout, about 10 minutes longer. Set aside.

☙ In a large bowl, stir together the hazelnut or olive oil and the mustard until blended. Stir in the vinegar, salt, and pepper to form a vinaigrette. Set aside.

☙ Put the lettuce in the bowl with the vinaigrette and toss to coat. Add half of the nuts and toss again. Divide evenly among individual plates.

☙ Spread the flour on a plate and coat the cheese slices on both sides. In a frying pan over medium-high heat, pour in just enough vegetable oil to form a thin layer. When hot, add the cheese slices, spacing them 1 inch (2.5 cm) apart. Cook, turning once, until golden on both sides, 2–4 minutes total.

☙ Place a piece of cheese atop each salad, sprinkle evenly with the remaining nuts, and serve at once.

serves 4

Normandie

Pâté de Campagne à l'Armagnac

country-style pâté with armagnac

This is my version of a pâté I sampled in Rouen one market day. It was toward noon and the stalls were beginning to close when I spotted a pâté of immense proportions, at least two feet long and nearly a foot wide. It was called grandmother's pâté, essentially a pâté maison, and it was flavored with Armagnac. I had to have a slice, which later, when spread on a fresh baguette, became the first course of a simple lunch. Cornichons are classic accompaniments for this pâté and for others of all kinds.

Hand chopping the ingredients gives an interesting and varied texture, while a machine makes a more uniform pâté. You may need to special order the caul fat or fatback from your butcher. Order a fresh pork liver at the same time. The final texture and flavor of your pâté will be better than if a frozen one is used.

2 lb (1 kg) pork liver

2 lb (1 kg) pork butt

¼ lb (250 g) fatback

¼ cup (2 fl oz/60 ml) Armagnac

1 small head garlic, minced

¼ cup (2 oz/60 g) salt

2 tablespoons coarsely ground pepper

2 tablespoons juniper berries, ground in a spice mill

1 piece caul fat, about 10 by 12 inches (25 by 30 cm), or an equivalent amount of fatback, sliced ¼ inch (6 mm) thick

2 tablespoons all-purpose (plain) flour

½–1 tablespoon water

☙ Preheat an oven to 325°F (165°C).

☙ For a more varied texture, finely chop the liver, pork butt, and fatback separately and set them aside. For a finer, more even texture, cut the meats and fat into chunks, then pass through a meat grinder fitted with a ⅜-inch (1-cm) disk; set aside.

☙ In a small saucepan over medium heat, bring the Armagnac just to a simmer. Immediately light it with a match to burn off the alcohol, let the flames subside, then cool.

☙ In a large bowl, using your hands, mix together the chopped meats and fat, garlic, salt, pepper, ground juniper berries, and Armagnac until thoroughly blended. Fry a tiny nugget of the mixture in a small frying pan, taste, and adjust the seasonings of the mixture, remembering that over time the seasonings will become more pronounced.

☙ Line a 10-by-3-by-3-inch (25-by-7.5-by-7.5-cm) terrine or loaf pan (with a cover) with the caul fat, allowing the edges to overhang the sides. If you are using fatback, line the inside of the container with overlapping pieces, reserving enough to cover the top. Pack the pâté mixture into the pan and cover with the overhang of caul fat or the reserved pieces of fatback. In a small cup, stir together the flour and water to make a paste, then spread it along the edge of the pan where the cover sits. Set the cover on the pan and press it into the paste to create a seal during cooking. Place the terrine in a larger baking pan and pour hot water into the larger pan to reach halfway up the sides of the terrine.

☙ Bake until the juices run clear when the pâté is pierced with a fork, about 2½ hours. Remove from the oven and lift the terrine from the water bath. Uncover the terrine. Cut a piece of aluminum foil slightly larger than the surface of the terrine and place it on top of the cooked meat, pressing it down and into the corners to make a snug fit. Wrap a brick or similar weight with foil and place it on top. The weight should rest directly on the pâté to compact it; this is an important step. Let cool to room temperature.

☙ Pour off any accumulated juices. Refrigerate the pâté, with the weight still in place, for at least 12 hours but preferably 24 hours. Remove the weight and cover the pâté with the lid or plastic wrap and store for up to 10 days.

☙ To serve, cut the pâté into slices ¼–½ inch (6–12 mm) thick.

makes one 3–4-lb (1.5–2-kg) pâté

Bretagne

Soupe aux Huîtres Trois Herbes

oyster soup with three herbs

When I serve this simple yet astonishingly elegant soup, I feel as if I'm in a fine restaurant in Brittany. Depending on which wine you choose, the soup will have a slightly different flavor. It's wonderful made with a Meursault from Burgundy. Although I've included it here as a first course, it also makes a fine main course for a brunch or supper.

12 oysters

2 tablespoons unsalted butter

1 shallot, minced

¾ cup (6 fl oz/180 ml) good-quality dry white wine such as Burgundy, Riesling, or Muscadet

1 teaspoon salt dissolved in ½ cup (4 fl oz/ 125 ml) water

¾ cup (6 fl oz/180 ml) crème fraîche

1 teaspoon minced fresh chives

1 teaspoon minced fresh chervil

1 teaspoon minced fresh tarragon

½ teaspoon freshly ground pepper

♛ First, shuck the oysters: Working with 1 oyster at a time and gripping it flat side up, push the tip of an oyster knife into one side of the hinge (opposite the shell's concentric ridges) and pry upward to open the shell. Run the knife blade along the upper shell to free the oyster from it, then lift off and discard the top shell. Run the knife underneath the oyster to free it from the bottom shell, then slip the oyster and its liquor into a bowl.

♛ In a saucepan over medium heat, melt the butter. When it foams, add the shallot and sauté just until translucent, 1–2 minutes. Add the wine and the oysters and their liquor, then pour the salted water over them. When tiny bubbles begin to form around the edges, stir in the crème fraîche, chives, chervil, and tarragon and sprinkle with the pepper. Continue to cook just long enough to heat through, about 1 minute longer.

♛ Ladle the hot soup into warmed bowls and serve immediately.

serves 4

Franche-Comté et Les Alpes

Salade de Savoie

savoy salad

Two of the important produits du terroir in Savoy are its cheeses and walnuts, both of which are often used with salad greens. Beaufort is the pride of Savoy, and one of the most distinguished cheeses in France. It is pressed from raw milk, aged for at least six months or up to two years, and has a firm, dense texture and a faintly nutty flavor. The Beauforts d'été, those made in summer, have a higher fat content. Sturdy lettuces such as romaine (cos) could be used in place of the escarole, as could frisée or Belgian endive (chicory/witloof). For a main-dish salad, add cubed boiled potatoes.

¼ lb (125 g) lardons or thick-cut bacon (¼ inch/6 mm thick), cut into pieces 1 inch (2.5 cm) long and ¼ inch (6 mm) wide

3 tablespoons walnut oil

2 tablespoons raspberry vinegar

½ teaspoon freshly ground pepper

¼ teaspoon salt

5 cups (5 oz/155 g) escarole (Batavian endive), pale yellow inner leaves only (from about 2 heads), torn into bite-sized pieces

¼ lb (125 g) Beaufort or Gruyère cheese, cubed

¼ cup (1 oz/30 g) coarsely chopped walnuts

♛ In a frying pan over medium heat, fry the lardons or bacon pieces until they are golden brown and have released much of their fat, 7–8 minutes. Using a slotted spoon, transfer to a plate lined with paper towels to drain.

♛ Scoop out ½ teaspoon of the fat from the pan and place in the bottom of a salad bowl. Add the walnut oil, vinegar, pepper, and salt to the salad bowl and mix well with a fork. Add the escarole and toss well to coat. Add the cheese, walnuts, and lardons or bacon, reserving a little of each for garnish. Toss again.

♛ Garnish the salad with the reserved cheese, walnuts, and lardons. Serve immediately.

serves 4

Languedoc

Anchois Grillés au Vinaigre de Banyuls

grilled anchovies with banyuls vinegar

Anchovies, packed in salt or oil, are a staple of the French table, but it is the Mediterranean port of Collioure, in the Roussillon near the Spanish border, that has claimed the anchovy as its own. At one time the small village supported twenty-seven anchovy-salting houses. Today, the majority of the fishing and salting business has moved to the more modern neighboring harbor of Port-Vendres, but the Collioure anchovies remain renowned.

During the May to October season, the fishing boats of Collioure arrive early in the morning, delivering some of their catch to the salting houses, including Sainte Roche Anchois, which you can visit, and the rest to the fresh market. The local restaurants offer fresh grilled or fried anchovies, frequently served with vinaigre de Banyuls, made from the sweet fortified wine of the region.

vegetable oil for oiling grilling basket

45–48 whole fresh anchovies, about 3 lb (1.5 kg) total weight, cleaned

1 tablespoon fresh thyme leaves

2 teaspoons freshly ground pepper

1 teaspoon salt

½ cup (4 fl oz / 125 ml) Banyuls vinegar or sherry vinegar, or 4 lemons, quartered

♛ Prepare a fire in a charcoal grill, or preheat a gas grill. Generously oil the inside and outside of a hinged grilling basket with vegetable oil. Fill with as many anchovies as will fit in a single layer, spacing them ½ inch (12 mm) apart. Sprinkle with a little of the thyme, pepper, and salt. Fasten closed.

♛ Grill over a hot fire, turning once, until the flesh flakes easily from the bone, 2–3 minutes on each side. Transfer to a platter. Repeat until all are cooked.

♛ Serve accompanied with the vinegar or lemon quarters for sprinkling or squeezing over the fish.

serves 4

Languedoc

Salade de Calmars
et Riz au Safran

squid and saffron rice salad

I wanted to make this dish after a market day in Perpignan where I saw young squid for sale and paella being prepared in huge pans. The paella was well garnished with clams, mussels, and shrimp as well as the small squid, and these could be incorporated into this salad as well. It was a hot day and a salad sounded refreshing. I didn't make it that afternoon, but the idea stayed in my mind. The colors, flavors, and textures all blend together to create a festive dish for a starter or a main course for a light meal.

2 lb (1 kg) squid

8 cups (64 fl oz/2 l) water

1 teaspoon salt

RICE

3 cups (24 fl oz/750 ml) water

1 teaspoon salt

¼ teaspoon saffron threads

1½ cups (10½ oz/330 g) long-grain white rice

3 tomatoes, finely chopped

1 green bell pepper (capsicum), seeded and minced

2 serrano chiles, seeded and minced (optional)

½ red (Spanish) onion, finely chopped

¼ cup (⅓ oz/10 g) minced fresh flat-leaf (Italian) parsley

3 tablespoons chopped fresh cilantro (fresh coriander)

3–4 tablespoons fresh lemon juice

2–3 tablespoons olive oil

½ teaspoon salt

½ teaspoon freshly ground pepper

☙ To clean each squid, cut off the tentacles just above the eyes. Grab the tentacles at their base and squeeze to pop out the squid's beak; discard the beak. Cut off the two long strands dangling among the tentacles and discard them. Slit the body lengthwise. Using a knife or the edge of a metal spoon, scrape out the entrails and discard. With your finger, pull out the clear quill (rudimentary shell) and discard. Rinse the squid bodies and tentacles under running water. Cut the tentacles and the bodies in half lengthwise, then cut the bodies into slices ½ inch (12 mm) wide.

☙ In a large pot, bring the water to a boil with the salt. Add the squid and cook just until it becomes opaque and curls, about 45 seconds. Do not over-cook or it will toughen. Drain, rinse with cold running water, and set aside.

☙ To make the rice, combine the water and salt in a saucepan over medium-high heat. Bring to a boil, add the saffron, and stir to dissolve. Add the rice and return the water to a boil. Reduce the heat to low, cover, and cook until the rice is tender and all the water has been absorbed, about 20 minutes. Remove from the heat, spoon into a bowl, and let cool to room temperature, about 30 minutes.

☙ Add the tomatoes, bell pepper, chiles (if using), onion, parsley, and cilantro to the cooled rice and mix well with a fork. Add the squid and mix again. Add the lemon juice, olive oil, salt, and pepper and mix once more. Cover and refrigerate for at least 3 hours or for up to 12 hours before serving.

☙ Transfer to a serving platter and serve chilled.

serves 8

Bretagne

Huîtres Tièdes à la Vinaigrette aux Tomates

warm oysters with tomato-shallot vinaigrette

The majority of French oysters are raised in the numerous oyster parcs *in the coastal waters of Brittany and Normandy. As you pass through the seaside villages, signs point you to the* parcs, *where you can buy freshly harvested oysters of different varieties and sizes. For this dish, you must use the* creuse, *a deep-shelled oyster, or a similar type, rather than the flat* belon *variety, because the well of the shell is needed to hold the sauce. Placing the oysters on a hot bed of rock salt and baking them just long enough to open will warm them slightly, but not cook them through.*

rock salt

4 tomatoes, peeled, seeded, and minced

2 cups (16 fl oz/500 ml) Champagne vinegar

2 shallots, minced

1 tablespoon minced fresh chives

1 teaspoon freshly ground pepper

½ teaspoon salt

4 dozen oysters in their shells

♛ Preheat an oven to 500°F (260°C).

♛ Pour rock salt to a depth of 1 inch (2.5 cm) in 1 large or 2 smaller baking dishes. Place in the oven to heat for 15 minutes.

♛ In a bowl, stir together the tomatoes, vinegar, shallots, chives, pepper, and salt to form a vinaigrette. Set aside.

♛ Remove the baking dish(es) from the oven and place the oysters, rounded side down, on the salt. Return to the oven and bake until the oysters open, 7–8 minutes. Remove from the oven and let cool until the shells can be handled, 3–4 minutes.

♛ Discard any oysters that failed to open. Using a small, sharp knife, cut through the muscle near the hinge that attaches the shells together on each oyster, being careful not to spill any juices. Discard the flat upper shells and place the lower ones on a platter or 4 individual plates.

♛ Spoon a tablespoon of the vinaigrette onto each oyster. Serve immediately.

serves 4

Huîtres

It seems either you like oysters (*huîtres*) or you don't. Initially my children were horrified to see people slurping up the raw, nearly quivering plump morsels and savoring every bit of the salty brine in the shell. But they have been in France with me for those memorable New Year's Eve feasts celebrated with old friends, where platter after platter of oysters with *mignonette* sauce were carried to the table, eventually followed by foie gras. At home every winter, a few weeks before Christmas, I buy a gross of oysters and host an oyster and champagne dinner. The children, now grown, always want to be part of the party. I'm happy to oblige, because not only are they good company, but they have also become experts at opening the delectable bivalves.

Le Sud-Ouest

Terrine de Foie Gras

foie gras terrine

This is the highest expression of French charcuterie, especially if truffles are added. The problem is not so much in the cooking as it is in acquiring a whole fresh duck or goose liver from an animal that has been fattened by gavage, a process in which the animals are force-fed grain so that their livers become enlarged and very fat. Because of its high fat content, the beige to tan liver hardens when chilled and is initially difficult to handle. It is marinated, then placed in a bain-marie over very low heat just long enough to cook it through barely and to release some of its fat. A duck liver that is too large (much over one pound/500 g) or too fat (indicated by a yellow color) is liable to melt too quickly.

The flavor and texture are exquisite and worthy of your best occasion. Serve the foie gras on toasts, accompanied by Sauternes, Montbazillac, or Barsac.

1 fresh foie gras of duck, about 1 lb (500 g), chilled

2 cups (16 fl oz/500 ml) water or milk, at room temperature

½ cup (4 fl oz/125 ml) Cognac

1 teaspoon salt

1 teaspoon freshly ground pepper

½ teaspoon sugar

⚜ Place the chilled liver in a bowl with the water or milk. Let it soften for about 5 minutes. It should be pliable but not melting.

⚜ Remove the liver from the bowl and place on a work surface. Separate the large lobe from the small lobe, pulling them apart with your fingers. You will see small exposed nerves, which must be removed, running two-thirds of the way down the liver. Pull very gently on any exposed nerves. Gentle pulling will often bring out the entire nerve. Then, use a small, sharp knife to slit open both the small and the large lobe. Each slit should run about two-thirds of the way through the center and about two-thirds of the length. Using your fingers or the tip of the knife, remove the remaining network of nerves.

⚜ Put the liver in a bowl and pour the Cognac over it. Sprinkle with the salt, pepper, and sugar, then turn the liver once to coat evenly. Cover the bowl tightly and refrigerate overnight.

⚜ Preheat an oven to 275°F (135°C).

⚜ Uncover the liver; most of the Cognac will have been absorbed. Transfer the liver to a baking dish with a cover that is just large enough to hold it and cover the dish. (Alternatively, use heavy-duty aluminum foil.) Put the dish in a larger baking dish with 3-inch (7.5-cm) sides and pour hot water into the baking dish to reach halfway up the sides of the covered dish.

⚜ Bake until the liver releases a goodly amount of its bright yellow fat and is warmed clear through, about 35 minutes. Put out a small bowl to collect the fat, then position a colander over it. Place the liver in the colander and let drain for 10 minutes.

⚜ Remove the liver from the colander and pack into a terrine just large enough to accommodate it, fitting it back into its original shape as much as possible. Pour the collected fat over to cover. Gently lay a piece of aluminum foil on top of the fat. Cut a piece of cardboard to fit the top of the terrine and place it atop the foil. Then place a 1-lb (500-g) weight on the cardboard. Make sure the weight is evenly distributed. I use a 1-lb (500-g) bag of salt or sugar, slipped into a plastic bag.

⚜ Refrigerate, keeping the weight on the terrine for at least 24 hours. Remove the weight, if desired, but keep the terrine refrigerated for at least 4 days or for up to 2 weeks before serving. The layer of fat seals the foie gras, but once it is broken, the foie gras should be eaten within 2–3 days.

⚜ To serve, scoop away the outer fat. Cut into slices ½ inch (12 mm) thick and serve.

serves 8

The variety of French charcuterie is astonishing, with terrines, pâtés, rillettes, sausages, and ham constructed of duck, pork, wild game, rabbit, fish, vegetables, and shellfish.

Le Centre

Salade de Lentilles et Magret

lentil and parsley salad with duck breast

Thin slices of rare duck breast nearly cover a mound of parsley-flavored lentils in this elegant dish.

1½ cups (10½ oz/330 g) small green lentils

5 cups (40 fl oz/1.25 l) water

2 fresh bay leaves, or 1 dried bay leaf

1½ teaspoons salt

1 duck breast, about ¾ lb (375 g)

½ teaspoon dried thyme

½ teaspoon ground juniper berries

½ teaspoon freshly ground pepper

3 tablespoons extra-virgin olive oil

1 tablespoon fresh lemon juice

¼ cup (⅓ oz/10 g) plus 1 tablespoon chopped fresh flat-leaf (Italian) parsley

3 cups (6 oz/185 g) torn pale inner frisée leaves

♛ Pick over the lentils, discarding any stones or mis-shapen lentils. Place in a saucepan with the water, bay leaves, and 1 teaspoon of the salt. Bring to a boil, reduce the heat to low, and simmer, uncovered, until tender, 20–30 minutes. Drain and let cool.

♛ Preheat an oven to 450°F (230°C). Rub the duck breast with the thyme, juniper, ¼ teaspoon of the salt, and ¼ teaspoon of the pepper. Place on a baking sheet, skin side up. Roast until the skin is crispy and the meat is pink at the center, 20–25 minutes. Let cool slightly, remove the skin, and cut the breast into very thin slices; set aside.

♛ In a bowl, stir together the olive oil, lemon juice, and the remaining ¼ teaspoon each salt and pepper to form a vinaigrette. Mix in the ¼ cup (⅓ oz/10 g) parsley and the lentils; adjust the seasonings.

♛ Divide the frisée among individual plates. Top with the lentils, forming each portion into a cone-shaped mound. Arrange the sliced duck over the lentils and garnish with the remaining 1 tablespoon parsley. Serve at once.

serves 4

Le Sud-Ouest

Brouillade de Truffes

eggs with truffles

This is the quintessential truffle dish made at home and in restaurants throughout the truffle-producing regions of France. If you purchase your truffle in a market, chances are it will be already cleaned. If you find it yourself, or a truffle hunter sells it to you, you will need to rinse it first and gently brush away the dirt with a small, fine-bristled brush.

8 eggs

1 oz (30 g) fresh black truffles, cleaned, if necessary (see note), and finely chopped

½ cup (4 oz/125 g) unsalted butter, cut into 1-inch (2.5-cm) pieces

1 teaspoon salt

2 teaspoons freshly ground white pepper

⚜ Crack the eggs into a heatproof bowl and add the truffles. Whisk together until the eggs are blended. Place the bowl over (not touching) barely simmering water in a saucepan. Add the butter. Whisk the eggs continuously until they have thickened into a creamy mass of tiny curds. This will take about 15 minutes. Whisk in the salt and pepper.

⚜ Serve immediately on warmed plates.

serves 3 or 4

Truffes

The truffle, *le diamant noir* (the black diamond), is an elusive fungus that spends its entire life beneath the surface of the earth. Filaments emerge from the spores of truffles, elongate, then attach themselves to host trees of oak, hazelnut, pine, and linden. From this underground union, mycorrhizae are formed, and eventually the tree's root system is completely invaded. After five to ten years, a crop of truffles has matured at the tree's roots.

During the season, late November through February, the truffles are located by trained dogs or pigs with a keen sense of smell, although of no particular breed. I went truffle hunting once with a friend and two tiny dogs, each weighing no more than three or four pounds. They were so small we lost sight of them whenever they went through the overgrown landscape, their location noted only by the waving of the grass as they plunged along. But they found nearly their weight in truffles.

Provence

Pan Bagnat

tuna, tomato, and olive sandwich

*This sandwich, essentially a salade niçoise on a
roll, is a specialty of Nice. Fillings vary somewhat, as
might be expected, but tuna is nearly always included,
as are tomatoes and olives. It is sold from storefront
sandwich shops, at some traiteurs, and even at modest
cafés located near the center of town—far from the
elegant cafés along the Promenade des Anglais
bordering the Mediterranean. I've often bought one
near the railway station to eat for lunch or dinner on
a long train ride, or for picnic fare on the way to Italy
via the gorges of the Roya River.*

4 large, round, chewy bread rolls

¼ cup (2 fl oz/60 ml) extra-virgin olive oil

2 tablespoons red wine vinegar

4 oz (125 g) water- or oil-packed tuna

1 green bell pepper (capsicum), seeded and
thinly sliced

2 tomatoes, thinly sliced

2 hard-boiled eggs, peeled and sliced

12 anchovy fillets

4–6 lettuce leaves such as butter (Boston), green
leaf, or red leaf

❦ Slit the rolls in half horizontally. Sprinkle the cut
sides evenly with the olive oil and vinegar.

❦ Drain the tuna and place it in a bowl. Using
a fork, flake the tuna into smallish pieces. Divide
evenly among the bottom halves of the rolls. Then
evenly divide the bell pepper, tomatoes, eggs, and
anchovy fillets among them. Cover the filling with
the lettuce leaves. Put the roll tops in place and serve.

serves 4

*A salade niçoise speaks
of Mediterranean Provence,
with its tuna and anchovies,
potatoes, tomatoes and beans,
all perfumed with olive
oil and herbs.*

Provence

Salade Printanière

spring salad

*Maurice, one of my neighbors in Provence, lived
in Nice until he was ten years old. Although it has
been nearly sixty years since he left, he still has
a special affection for his childhood Niçoise food.
He tends a large, ever-evolving potager (kitchen
garden), and in late spring he picks young, tender
fava beans, a purple artichoke or two, and pulls
one of the fresh bulbing white onions. From his
greenhouse comes a tomato. He puts all these in
front of him at the table, plus olive oil, salt, and
vinegar, and proceeds to prepare this salad.*

¼ cup (2 fl oz/60 ml) extra-virgin olive oil

scant ½ teaspoon salt

scant ½ teaspoon freshly ground pepper

2 artichokes

1 lemon, halved

1 lb (500 g) small, tender fava (broad) beans,
shelled

1 small, young white onion or 6 green (spring)
onions, white parts only, finely diced

2 tomatoes, diced

2 tablespoons red wine vinegar

❦ In a salad bowl, using a fork, stir together the olive
oil, salt, and pepper. Set aside.

❦ Working with 1 artichoke at a time, cut off the
stem near the base. Snap off the first layer of leaves.
Cut off the upper third of the artichoke. Rub the cut
surfaces with a lemon half. Continue to pull back
and snap off the leaves until you reach the tender,
inner pale yellow leaves. Cut through the uppermost
part again, removing any remaining leaf tips. Rub
with a lemon half. Using a spoon, scoop out the
furry choke. Cut the artichokes into ¼-inch (6-mm)
cubes and add to the bowl holding the olive oil.

❦ If the fava beans are very young and tender, they
will not need peeling. If their skins are a little tough
and you wish to peel them, drop the shelled favas
into boiling water, boil for 20 seconds, drain, let cool
slightly, and slip off the skins. Let cool completely
and add to the artichokes.

❦ Add the onion and tomatoes to the bowl. Toss to
mix. Add the vinegar and mix again, then serve.

serves 4

Foie Gras

Although most people think of geese when they think of foie gras, ducks are equally fine sources of the fattened liver. Of course, such a bold statement only fuels the continuing argument among gourmands about whether the more intensely flavored duck liver is preferable to the mild, subtly flavored goose liver.

In both cases, the prized oversized organ is achieved by force-feeding the animals an excessive amount of ground corn during the *gavage*, or fattening period. In the region of Périgord Noir, where foie gras is a specialty, the summers are quite hot, and many *éleveurs* raise ducks instead of geese because they can better tolerate the heat. But fattened duck livers are smaller than those of geese, weighing only about a pound (500 g) each, while a goose liver might weigh as much as a pound and a half (750 g), a fact that goose partisans are quick to point out. The debate continues.

Le Sud-Ouest

Foie Gras aux Raisins

sautéed foie gras with grapes

Fresh foie gras cut into slices and then sautéed is a great delicacy. It forms a thin crust on the outside, leaving the inside creamy. Freshly squeezed grape juice and Armagnac or Cognac are combined with the rich pan juices to make a light sauce. Classically, large, sweet Muscat grapes are used in this specialty of Bordeaux.

1 fresh foie gras of duck, about 1 lb (500 g), chilled

1 teaspoon salt

1 teaspoon freshly ground pepper

2–3 tablespoons fresh grape juice, strained

2 tablespoons Armagnac or Cognac

1 cup (6 oz/185 g) Muscat or other sweet grapes, peeled and seeded if desired

☙ Separate the small and large lobes of the liver by slicing between them with a sharp knife. Cut the lobes lengthwise into slices ½ inch (12 mm) thick. Remove the exposed nerves with your fingers or the tip of the knife. Place the slices in a single layer between sheets of waxed paper and refrigerate until thoroughly chilled and hard, about 1 hour.

☙ Place a large frying pan over high heat. Sprinkle the foie gras slices on both sides with the salt and pepper. When the pan is very hot, add the slices and cook just until a crust forms on the first side, 30–40 seconds. Turn and cook for another 30–40 seconds. The pan must be very hot for this step so that a crust quickly forms; overcooking will result in melted foie gras. Transfer the slices to a platter and cover loosely with aluminum foil to keep warm.

☙ Pour off any fat from the pan and return the pan to high heat. Add the grape juice and Armagnac or Cognac and deglaze the pan, stirring with a wooden spoon to dislodge any browned bits from the pan bottom. Continue to stir over high heat until the liquid is reduced by about half. Stir in the grapes and cook, stirring, until just warmed through, about 1 minute.

☙ Arrange the grapes around the foie gras on the platter and pour the hot pan juices over them. Alternatively, arrange the foie gras and grapes on individual plates and top with the pan juices.

serves 3 or 4

Bretagne

Rillettes de Poisson

creamy fish spread

At aperitif time in Brittany, one is more likely to be offered rillettes de poisson than rillettes de porc. True rillettes are made with pork or goose cooked in fat, then shredded and seasoned to make a spread. Because of Brittany's long coastline, it's common to find fish in place of meat in traditional French dishes, such as this one. Here, finely shredded fish is seasoned with mustard and chives and then served atop crackers or grilled toast. It makes an excellent companion to a glass of brut cider or a dry white wine such as Gros Plant or Muscadet.

1 teaspoon salt

4 tablespoons (2 fl oz/60 ml) cider vinegar

1 lb (500 g) mackerel fillet

1 lb (500 g) merlan or cod fillet

2 cups (16 fl oz/500 ml) crème fraîche

½ cup (4 fl oz/125 ml) dry white wine

1 tablespoon Dijon mustard

1 shallot, minced

½ teaspoon freshly ground pepper

juice of 1 lemon

½ cup (¾ oz/20 g) minced fresh chives

24 slices baguette

In a wide, shallow saucepan, pour in water to a depth of 3 inches (7.5 cm). Add ½ teaspoon of the salt and 2 tablespoons of the vinegar. Bring to a simmer over medium heat and add the fish fillets. Poach them gently until just opaque throughout, about 3 minutes. Using a slotted spatula, transfer to a plate and set aside. Discard the cooking water.

In a saucepan over medium–high heat, combine the crème fraîche, wine, the remaining 2 tablespoons vinegar, the mustard, the shallot, the remaining ½ teaspoon salt, and the pepper. Bring to a simmer and cook, stirring, until the mixture is reduced by half, 6–7 minutes. Add the fish fillets, reduce the heat to low, and cook until easily flaked with a fork, about 5 minutes longer. Add the lemon juice and remove from the heat. Using 2 forks, pull the fish into fine bits, then stir to mix until a thick paste forms. Add all but 1 tablespoon of the chives and mix well. Pack snugly into a terrine or bowl. Cover and refrigerate for 24 hours to blend the flavors before serving.

☙ Preheat a broiler (griller). Place the baguette slices on a baking sheet and broil (grill), turning once, until toasted, about 3 minutes total.

☙ Garnish the *rillettes* with the remaining chives and serve cold accompanied with the toasts.

serves 6–8

Provence

Soupe au Pistou

vegetable soup with basil sauce

Pistou is a paste made with olive oil, garlic, basil, and Parmesan cheese to which dried bread, pine nuts, or almonds are added as a thickener. It shows the influence of Italy on the cooking of southeast France, especially Nice. Freshly made pistou *has an intense, sharp flavor that enhances all the other ingredients in the soup, but if left to stand before using, it can become dull and even bitter. The soup itself varies from a humble one of dried beans and pasta to more elaborate ones that may include a favorite ingredient of mine, fresh shelling beans.*

¼ cup (2 fl oz/60 ml) olive oil

2 yellow or white onions, chopped

6 cloves garlic, chopped

8 potatoes such as Red Rose, Belle de Fontenay, or Bintje, about 3 lb (1.5 kg), diced

½ lb (250 g) green beans, trimmed and cut into 1-inch (2.5-cm) lengths

2 cups (1 lb/500 g) fresh shelling beans such as cranberry (borlotti), flageolet, or lima (about 2 lb/ 1 kg unshelled)

3 tomatoes, peeled and chopped, with juice

3 qt (3 l) vegetable stock

2 tablespoons fresh thyme leaves

2 teaspoons salt

2 teaspoons freshly ground pepper

1 teaspoon minced fresh marjoram

1 cup (3 oz/90 g) broken spaghetti or other thin pasta (small pieces)

20 cloves garlic, peeled but left whole

4 cups (4 oz/125 g) fresh basil leaves, coarsely chopped

1½ cups (6 oz/185 g) grated Parmesan cheese

½ cup (2½ oz/75 g) pine nuts

1–1¼ cups (8–10 fl oz/250–310 ml) extra-virgin olive oil

1 teaspoon salt

½ cup (2 oz/60 g) grated Parmesan cheese

☙ In a large soup pot over medium heat, warm the olive oil. Add the onions and garlic and sauté until translucent, about 2 minutes. Add the potatoes, green beans, and shelling beans and cook, stirring almost constantly with a wooden spoon, until the beans are glistening and the potatoes are nearly opaque, 5–6 minutes.

☙ Stir in the tomatoes and their juice. Then add the stock, thyme, salt, pepper, and marjoram. Reduce the heat to low, cover, and simmer, stirring occasionally, until the potatoes and beans are soft, about 40 minutes. Add the pasta and cook until the pasta is done, 10–15 minutes longer.

☙ While the pasta is cooking, make the *pistou:* In a food processor, combine the garlic, basil, cheese, pine nuts, and 3 tablespoons of the olive oil. Purée to form a paste. With the machine running, gradually add enough of the remaining oil to form a thick sauce. Add the salt and process briefly to blend. Alternatively, combine the garlic, basil, cheese, and pine nuts in a mortar and pound them with a pestle until they form a smooth, thick paste. Gradually add the olive oil, stirring with the pestle until a thick sauce forms. Season with the salt.

☙ To serve, ladle the soup into warmed bowls, then stir 1 tablespoon of the *pistou* into each bowl. Garnish each serving with a sprinkling of the cheese. Pass the remaining *pistou* and cheese in separate serving bowls at the table.

serves 12–15

Appellation d'Origine Contrôlée

Appellation d'Origine Contrôlée (AOC) appears on numerous French products. Nîmes black olives, Le Puy lentils, Grenoble walnuts, Bresse poultry, over thirty different cheeses, including Camembert, Roquefort, and Saint-Nectaire, and wines and liqueurs are recipients of the AOC designation. It is a guarantee that the items are of a certain quality and were produced in a particular region under specified conditions.

To win this coveted status, producers present detailed documentation about the uniqueness of their regional product based on its production in a specific *terroir*. This means that not only are the standards for manufacturing, harvesting, handling, and packaging very strict and very specific to the product, but also that the item must come from a precisely defined territory. These criteria are the purchaser's assurance of a certain level of quality. Belon oysters, Banon cheese, and Périgord foie gras are among the products currently under consideration by the French government for an AOC designation.

Le Sud-Ouest

Terrine de Lapin

rabbit terrine

Rabbit terrines are among the most striking in the panoply of French terrines. When sliced, a mosaic of delicate white meat, interlaced with layers of darker sausage meat, is revealed. In this version, created by one of my neighbors in France, pistachios add notes of green, and the livers bring yet another element of pattern to the design.

Have your butcher bone the rabbits, leaving the meat in fillets and the chunks as large as possible. Request the bones and the livers as well.

Serve the terrine as a perfect first course for a summer night along with a chilled Bandol rosé wine.

MARINADE
¼ cup (2 fl oz / 60 ml) Cognac
6 juniper berries, crushed
4 fresh thyme sprigs
1 dried bay leaf
1 teaspoon salt
1 teaspoon freshly ground pepper

2 rabbits, 2 lb (1 kg) each, boned (see note)
⅓ lb (5 oz / 155 g) fatback, sliced into 9 strips each about ¼ inch (6 mm) thick and ½ inch (12 mm) wide
1 lb (500 g) bulk pork sausage
1 egg
6 juniper berries, ground
3 teaspoons Cognac
½ cup (2 oz / 60 g) shelled pistachios

☙ To make the marinade, in a large bowl, combine the Cognac, crushed juniper berries, thyme, bay leaf, salt, and pepper.

☙ Add the rabbit meat and the strips of fatback to the marinade. Turn the meat several times, then cover and refrigerate overnight.

☙ Preheat an oven to 350°F (180°C).

☙ To construct the terrine, remove the rabbit meat and fatback from the marinade. Discard the marinade. In a bowl, mix together the sausage and egg. Pack a 5-cup (40–fl oz/1.25-l) lidded terrine with one-third of the sausage mix. (Alternatively, use a heavy baking dish of the same size and aluminum

foil.) Top with one-fourth of the rabbit meat in an even layer. Lay 3 rows of fatback strips the length of the terrine. Sprinkle with a little ground juniper and 1 teaspoon of the Cognac. Arrange 2 long rows of pistachios on top. Lay the livers in the middle. Repeat the same layering, without the livers, two more times, ending with a layer of rabbit. Fit some of the bones across the top. (I find that the small fore-leg bones fit nicely.) Cooking with the bones on top will help the terrine to jell.

Place the lid on the terrine, making sure it fits snugly. Set in a baking dish with 3-inch (7.5-cm) sides and pour hot water into the baking dish to reach halfway up the sides of the terrine.

Bake until the rabbit meat is opaque, firm, and cooked through, 1½–2 hours.

Remove from the oven and, while still hot, uncover and remove and discard the bones. Cut a piece of aluminum foil slightly larger than the surface of the terrine and place it on top of the cooked meat, pressing it down and into the corners to make

a snug fit. Wrap a brick or similar weight with foil and place it on top. Refrigerate the weighted terrine for 24 hours.

To serve, remove the weight and foil. Heat a knife under hot tap water, wipe dry, and run the hot knife along the edges of the terrine to loosen it. If possible, use a flexible icing spatula to reach beneath and loosen the bottom. (Alternatively, place the base of the mold in very hot water for 5 minutes.) Invert a platter on top of the terrine. Holding both the mold and the platter, invert them together. Lift off the mold. If it does not come free, repeat the loosening process and try again.

To serve, cut into slices 1 inch (2.5 cm) thick.

serves 8–10

LES PLATS

The main dish reflects the French cook's ingenuity and respect for local products.

I AM ALWAYS STRUCK by the richness of French culinary traditions when main dishes are examined. Their fundamental components are, in many ways, the same from region to region. Poultry, fish, lamb, beef, pork, variety meats, cheeses, cream, vegetables, wine, cider, beer, distilled liquor, herbs, and butter, olive oil, or other fat are the sustaining ingredients. They are made into stews, braised, roasted, grilled, or sautéed. But there the similarities end, for each corner of France has its indigenous *produits du terroir*, which, along with seasonal ingredients, personalize basic preparations, making them unique.

I find one of the delights of traveling in France is the tremendous variety of food there. I never tire of looking in the markets and in the windows of shops and seeing what's new or different. The problem, of course, is that if you are staying in a hotel, you can't buy things in the market and then go home and cook them. This was especially difficult for me late one spring when my husband and I were staying in Dijon, in Burgundy. The day was soft and sunny and the market was one of the most beautiful I had ever seen. Every vendor's products were lovingly arranged and the quality was extraordinary. The famous Bresse chickens were neatly stacked, their long necks and heads tucked demurely beneath their breasts. Carefully dressed rabbits, their livers, kidneys, and hearts still attached to the abdominal cavity, were displayed alongside plump guinea hens. Pork and beef roasts, rolled, larded, and artfully tied, and thick slices of veal shank brimming with luscious marrow made my head spin with visions of coq au vin, roast chicken, rabbit a dozen ways, and veal shanks simmering in thick sauce. I could see these dishes served alongside the asparagus two aisles over and with a potato gratin made with the freshly dug potatoes before me and the little glass jars of local cream sold nearby. I longed to make a salad for the imaginary roast chicken. I would use the mâche that an old woman was selling near the upper end of the market mixed with some of the magnificent escarole (Batavian endive) being offered at several stalls, and I would make a raspberry dressing using one of the vinegars. I decided then and there that someday I would rent a house in Burgundy for a week or two and shop and cook to my heart's content. That day, though, I bought what I could that was sensible—or nearly so—including the raspberry vinegar, a bottle of local crème de cassis, a slice of *jambon persillé,* bread, several fresh goat cheeses, and a bouquet of wild narcissus from a little girl selling flowers alongside her mother. We ate the ham and cheese for lunch, along with a bottle of wine. The narcissus smelled heavenly in the warm car, and as we drove south through the vineyards, they reminded me of the wonders of the Dijon market.

When you are not limited to a picnic, you can explore the stews and braises that are central to French cooking. They take many forms. When a young friend was helping me cook one day, he asked, "Do the French always cook with so much wine?" I thought about it for a moment and said yes, because that is one of the ingredients they always have at hand. It is a fermented product that has gone through many stages before being consumed, so it has complex flavors, as wine tasters will tell you. The vocabulary of wine descriptors is rich

Preceding spread: The Dordogne River loops through fertile pastures, where sheep, raised for wool, mutton, or cheese, graze near a field of sunflowers. **Left:** The inhabitants of the small port town of Cancale, in Brittany, are devoted to the cultivation and consumption of some of France's most prized oysters. **Right top:** There are conflicting notions as to what constitutes an authentic bouillabaisse, what seafood, condiments, and seasonings must be included. If shellfish are part of the mix, however, the *langouste* (spiny lobster) is nearly always guaranteed a role. **Right middle:** Since Roman times the Rhône River has provided a link between the north and the south, enabling imported products such as spices to pass through to Lyons and the rest of the Rhône Valley. **Right bottom:** Fish occupies a sizable niche in the French menu, whether simmered in bouillabaisse or *soupe aux poissons,* baked in *cabillaud à la bordelaise* (cod with tomato and onion), or grilled in *loup flambé au fenouil* (sea bass and fennel flamed with Pernod).

indeed, speaking with aromas of peach, of pine, of wild grasses, prune, and berry. This complexity is brought to the stew and helps in the alchemy that creates the final flavors. Thus, a stew made with water or stock is very different from one that includes wine. And depending upon what wine was used, the flavor of the stew varies. In Provence, for example, the menus of some restaurants list which wine was used in making the daube, and every home cook will have a wine that he or she insists is necessary for the ideal result.

Wine is not the only defining component, however. Stews in different regions and during different seasons incorporate countless local specialties, which makes it easy to eat in France without ever becoming bored. In Provence, a stew, whether of rabbit, chicken, beef, or fish, is likely to include olives and garlic. In Normandy, the additions are apples or cream, while in the north and in Alsace, potatoes and cabbage are popular. The stew might marinate in red wine and eau-de-vie in Provence, in cider plus a little Calvados in Normandy, in white wine or beer in Alsace. Locally gathered wild mushrooms might be added to stews in Provence and Languedoc, in

the Périgord, the Berry, and the Alpes, while Belgian endive (chicory/witloof) might be chosen in the Pas-de-Calais and the north. Fish stews are frequently prepared with a fish stock that includes a local white or red wine.

When it comes to braising, cream and cider appear in Normandy and Brittany, but in Savoy and Alsace it is white wine, sometimes the rich, honeyed late-harvest Rieslings that are made there. *Choucroute,* the signature dish of Alsace, is treated to a long braise in white wine, and the sausages of Savoy are often slow cooked in a sauce based on white wine. In Burgundy, local red wines define boeuf bourguignon and coq au vin, but in Corsica a beef stew would be made with a robust island wine. In the south, tomatoes and olive oil set the pattern.

Grilled or poached meats are easy to prepare and remain popular. Grilled fish when

Above: In the area around Charolles, in Burgundy, the prized Charollais beef cattle are raised. They are slaughtered at age six rather than five, the common age for many other breeds, in the belief that the extra year delivers extra flavor.

I'm near the coast or a river, grilled steak anywhere, grilled lamb and pork chops, all seasoned with local ingredients, are always among choices both in restaurants and when cooking at home. When you start with a fine chop, steak, or fish, sometimes the best way to have it is the simplest. Of course, when pan grilling, I always like to deglaze the pan juices with a little wine or vinegar, depending upon what I'm cooking. I started doing this when I was first living in France and my daughter, Ethel, was three. She had spent several nights with our neighbor Françoise when I was in the hospital having her brother. Not surprisingly, Françoise spoiled her, cooking her steak more than once. Later, Ethel always wanted "juice" with her steak, just as Françoise had made it. Watching Françoise cook one day at lunch, I realized that once the meat had been removed from the pan, she was adding a dash or two of wine from the bottle kept near at hand, sizzling and scraping the pan juices, then pouring them over the steak. Ethel was right. It was better that way, and I have done that ever since, using white wine for fish, red for steaks and chops.

Fish, not surprisingly, given France's long coastline and many rivers, play an important main-dish role, and they are treated in a wide variety of ways, as each region adds its unique elements of the *terroir*. In Normandy, you'll find salmon with a bit of cream, in the Loire with a little local white wine. In Savoy, fresh mountain trout are paired with walnuts, in Haute Provence with local almonds. Monkfish, meaty and lobsterlike in both flavor and texture, is a favorite throughout the country and may be served roasted whole or sliced into thick medallions, garnished with local herbs or vegetables. Stews are made of fish as well, and two of the most famous are bouillabaisse from Provence and *cotriade* from Brittany. You'll have a hard time finding either one made the same way twice, though, as every town and village seems to have its own version.

French cooks are creative with roasted main dishes, surrounding them with the seasonal local vegetables that are always at hand. A pork roast cooked in a Provençal kitchen will be well seasoned with the region's herbs before

Below top: A farmer stands near his fields in what the Gauls called the Argoat, the interior of Brittany that was once blanketed by forests and is now a checkerboard of fields, woods, and moors. **Below bottom:** Aix-en-Provence's fashionable cours Mirabeau is lined by seventeenth- and eighteenth-century buildings on one side and elegant cafés on the other.

Above top: Fishing boats at rest along the Brittany coast during low tide. Above bottom: A restaurant charmingly advertises its daily menu on handwritten chalkboards. Right: In the seventeenth century, Saint-Malo was a large, prosperous port, and local mariners became wealthy through trade and piracy. Its ramparts, which once provided protection, now offer a fine spot to view the sea.

being ringed with whole heads of garlic. A roast duck is likely to be slathered with lavender honey, a combination that appears in numerous restaurants throughout Provence. In the Auvergne, though, the duck will be seasoned more simply with salt and pepper, perhaps a clove-studded onion will be inserted into the cavity, and then the bird will be surrounded by turnips that are basted with the duck's juices as it roasts. In Alsace, the pork roast or duck might be seasoned with juniper and surrounded by thick wedges of cabbage. Roasted dishes also frequently include nuts, and walnuts and chestnuts are among the most common. Birds stuffed and then roasted, such as guinea fowl, chicken, pheasant, and turkey, are filled with mixtures created with what is at hand: local bread crumbled and mixed with prunes and walnuts in Gascony, dried apricots in the south, truffles in the Périgord and Haute Provence.

No matter what the main dish is, it is sure to reflect French cooks' ingenuity and respect for local products. The simplest dish, made with prime ingredients, is hard to surpass.

Provence

Canard au Miel de Lavande

duck with lavender honey

Lavender honey speaks distinctly of Haute Provence and the Drôme, where fields of lavender create shimmering waves on the plateaus. The honey doesn't taste like lavender, but it has its faint aroma. Used in sweets and certainly for tartines, it also makes a fragrant glaze for duck or chicken. Added near the end of the cooking, it quickly lacquers a duck to a deep mahogany, or the chicken to a deep gold. Here, the liver of the duck roasts inside the cavity. Spread it on toasts for eating along with the carved bird.

4 teaspoons fresh lavender blossoms or 2 teaspoons dried blossoms

2 teaspoons fresh thyme leaves or ½ teaspoon dried thyme

2 teaspoons fresh winter savory or 1 teaspoon dried savory

12 peppercorns

1½ teaspoons salt

1 duck, about 5½ lb (2.75 kg), with giblets

4 tablespoons (3 oz/90 g) lavender, acacia, or other strong-flavored honey

3 tablespoons red wine

✲ Preheat an oven to 350°F (180°C).

✲ In a mortar or a spice grinder, grind together 2 teaspoons of the fresh lavender blossoms (or 1 teaspoon of the dried), the thyme, winter savory, peppercorns, and salt.

✲ Remove all the inner fat and the giblets from the cavity of the duck. Rinse and pat dry. Using a sharp knife, cut crisscrosses through the fat—but not into the meat—of the breast. Rub the duck inside and out with the herb mixture. Replace the liver, heart, and gizzard in the cavity. Discard the neck. Place the duck, breast side up, on a rack in a roasting pan.

✲ Roast for 2 hours. Remove from the oven and pour off all but 1 tablespoon of the collected fat from the pan. Spread the duck breast with 2 tablespoons of the honey and return to the oven for another 10 minutes. Once again, remove from the oven and, using a large spoon, baste with the pan juices, now mingled with the honey. Return to the oven and roast for another 10 minutes. Remove the duck again, spread with the remaining 2 tablespoons honey and sprinkle with 1 teaspoon of the remaining fresh lavender (or ½ teaspoon of the dried). Roast for 10 minutes longer, then baste again with the pan juices. Cook for 5 minutes longer and remove from the oven. When done, the juices should run pinkish clear when the breast is pierced with the tip of a knife at its thickest part, or an instant-read thermometer inserted into the thickest part registers 165°F (74°C). The duck skin should be crisp and deeply browned.

✲ Transfer the duck to a platter, cover loosely with aluminum foil, and let stand for 10 minutes while you prepare the sauce. Pour off the collected fat, leaving the pan juices, which should measure about 3 tablespoons, in the pan. Put the roasting pan over medium heat and add the remaining 1 teaspoon fresh lavender blossoms (or ½ teaspoon dried) and the red wine. Deglaze the pan, stirring with a wooden spoon to remove any browned bits from the pan bottom. Cook until well blended and slightly reduced, 3–4 minutes. Keep warm.

✲ Remove the giblets from the duck cavity. Carve the duck, separating the wings, legs, and thighs from the body and slicing the breast. Arrange the duck pieces and giblets on a warmed platter. Drizzle with the sauce and serve immediately.

serves 2–4

French cooks are creative with roasted main dishes. A roast duck is slathered with lavender honey in Provence, surrounded with turnips in the Auvergne, seasoned with juniper in Alsace.

Provence

Côtelettes d'Agneau Grillées

grilled lamb chops with fresh thyme

One of the definitive aspects of the food of Provence is the use of wild herbs. Sometimes they are used in combination, as in the case of herbes de Provence, *but they are often used individually as well. In spring, when the wild thyme flowers create veritable carpets of purple and lamb is in season, grilled lamb chops with thyme are cooked for at least one midday Sunday meal, preferably eaten outside. The meal might begin with a platter of asparagus liberally seasoned with tarragon butter, followed by the chops accompanied with new potatoes or sautéed morels.*

The preferred lamb of the region comes from Sisteron in the department of the Alpes-de-Haute-Provence. Sisteron is considered the gateway to Provence, and the lambs raised near there feed on the wild thyme, rosemary, and other herbs and shrubs that cover the hillsides. Sisteron lamb is labeled as such on restaurant menus and in butcher shops, and it is well worth the premium price.

4 lamb sirloin chops, each ½ inch (12 mm) thick

2 teaspoons fresh thyme leaves and blossoms, if possible, finely minced, plus whole blossoms or sprigs for garnish

scant ½ teaspoon salt

½ teaspoon freshly ground pepper

❦ Prepare a fire in a grill.

❦ Rub each chop with ½ teaspoon of the thyme, firmly pressing it into the flesh.

❦ Place the chops on the grill rack. Cook on the first side until browned, 4–5 minutes. Turn and cook until the meat springs back when touched with your finger, 4–5 minutes longer for medium-rare.

❦ Transfer to a warmed platter, season with the salt and pepper, and garnish with whole thyme blossoms or sprigs.

serves 4

Provence

Boeuf aux Carottes

beef with carrots

A traveling cheese-equipment supplier once invited my family and me to dinner at our local bar-tabac (café). I think he was astonished to find Americans making goat cheese in a remote area of Haute Provence and wanted to learn more about us. The owner of the bar-tabac prepared, by request, a plat du jour, *preceded by a simple plate of charcuterie, crudités, or tomatoes, and followed either by ice cream from the deep freeze or a slice of homemade fruit tart. That day Mme Serre's* plat du jour *was boeuf aux carottes. It came to us family style in a large bowl, with boiled potatoes on the side. The woody sprigs of wild thyme were still in the bowl, and I knew the carrots were fresh because earlier in the day I had seen M. Serre pulling them from the kitchen garden. Afterward, I asked Mme Serre for her recipe, which is reproduced here.*

In restaurants, boeuf aux carottes *is served on its own, but at home, it is typically served accompanied with a platter or bowl of fresh egg noodles. The sauce from the stew is ladled over the noodles, and then Gruyère cheese is passed around to sprinkle on top of individual servings. Serve with a red Côtes du Rhône or Côtes de Provence.*

2 tablespoons extra-virgin olive oil

1 large yellow onion, chopped

3 cloves garlic, chopped

3 lb (1.5 kg) boneless beef chuck or a combination of boneless beef chuck and beef shank, cut into 2-inch (5-cm) cubes

2 cups (16 fl oz/500 ml) dry red wine

4 fresh thyme sprigs

1 dried bay leaf

1 teaspoon salt

½ teaspoon freshly ground pepper

2 lb (1 kg) carrots, peeled and cut into 1-inch (2.5-cm) lengths

⚜ In a heavy pot over medium heat, warm the olive oil. Add the onion and garlic and sauté until the onion is nearly translucent, 2–3 minutes. Using a slotted spoon, transfer the onion and garlic to a large plate. Increase the heat to medium-high, add the meat, a few pieces at a time, and turn them to brown on all sides, about 5 minutes. As they are ready, transfer them to the plate holding the onion and garlic.

⚜ When all the meat is browned and removed from the pot, pour in 1 cup (8 fl oz/250 ml) of the wine and deglaze the pan, stirring to scrape up any bits on the bottom. Add the thyme, bay leaf, salt, pepper, and the remaining 1 cup (8 fl oz/250 ml) wine.

⚜ Return the meat, onion, and garlic and any collected juices to the pan. Reduce the heat to low, cover tightly, and cook for 1 hour, stirring from time to time. Add the carrots, cover, and cook, stirring occasionally, until the meat is tender enough to cut with a fork and the sauce has thickened, 1½–2 hours longer. Taste and adjust the seasonings.

⚜ Remove the thyme branches and the bay leaf and discard. Transfer to a warmed serving bowl or serve directly from the pot.

serves 6

Franche-Comté et Les Alpes
Fondue

Some of France's richest, most luscious cheeses are from Savoy, made from the milk of cows that feed on the alpine pastures that define the region. They figure prominently in fondue, a classic Savoyard dish. My friends who live in the Tarentaise, near the huge Courchevel ski resort, swear that they couldn't live without their local Beaufort, reblochon, and tomme de Savoie. They insist that the most important aspect of fondue is using the correct cheeses, which, when they melt, will become smooth and creamy and will delicately coat the dipped cubes of bread. Local traditions vary, but one holds that if you lose your bread to the fondue pot, you have to provide the next bottle of wine. Since fondue is typically a meal for a group, the bottles of wine can become numerous and the night late.

When only a little cheese is left in the pot, a handful or so of bread cubes are added along with two eggs. The mixture cooks to a toasty finish, which is eagerly scooped up with dinner forks, and then a green salad is served. Accompany the fondue with a local wine such as Roussette de Seyssel, Apremont, or a Chardonnay.

4 or 5 cloves garlic

1 bottle (24 fl oz/750 ml) dry white wine such as Apremont or a Sauvignon Blanc

½ teaspoon salt

1½ lb (750 g) Beaufort cheese or a good-quality Swiss Gruyère cheese, shredded or thinly slivered

½ lb (250 g) Comté or Emmentaler cheese, shredded or thinly slivered

⅛ teaspoon ground nutmeg

¼ cup (2 fl oz/60 ml) kirsch

¼ teaspoon freshly ground pepper

1 tablespoon unsalted butter

1½ day-old baguettes, cut into 1-inch (2.5-cm) cubes (about 6 cups/¾ lb/375 g)

2 eggs

♛ Using a garlic press, squeeze the garlic cloves into a fondue pot, discarding the pulp that remains in the press. Pour in the wine, add the salt, and place over medium-high heat. Heat just until bubbles begin to appear along the edge of the pan.

♛ Using a wooden spoon, stir in both cheeses and continue to stir as the cheeses melt. In about 10 minutes the cheeses will be nearly melted and will be a lovely yellow, as if one had melted butter into milk. Add the nutmeg, reduce the heat to medium-low, and add the kirsch, continuing to stir. Add the pepper and stir in the butter. The cheese will now be completely melted.

♛ To serve, light the alcohol, sterno, or electric burner that accompanies the fondue set and place it on the dining table. Bring the hot fondue pot to the table and put it atop the burner. Put the bread cubes in a bowl or basket and set on the table. Guests can help themselves to the bread cubes, spearing them through the crust side so they will stay on better, then swirling the bread in the fondue. When only a little cheese is left, break the eggs into the cheese, stir, and cook until crusty. Everyone then reaches in with a dinner fork and takes a bit.

serves 6

Local traditions vary, but one holds that if you lose your bread to the fondue pot, you have to provide the next bottle of wine.

Languedoc

Lotte de Mer aux Olives et Artichauts

monkfish with olives and artichokes

In spring, one finds artichokes in this simple braise popular along the Mediterranean coast, but in summer and fall it might be sweet red peppers (capsicums), tomatoes, or eggplants (aubergines).

2 lemons, halved

16 small artichokes

3 tablespoons extra-virgin olive oil

1 clove garlic, minced

1¼ lb (625 g) monkfish fillet, cut into slices 1 inch (2.5 cm) thick

1 teaspoon minced fresh thyme

1 teaspoon minced fresh flat-leaf (Italian) parsley

scant ½ teaspoon freshly ground pepper

¼ cup (2 fl oz/60 ml) chicken stock

3 tablespoons dry white wine

¼ cup (1¼ oz/37 g) Niçoise olives or other small Mediterranean-style black olives

❦ Preheat an oven to 400°F (200°C).

❦ Have ready a large bowl of water to which you have added the juice of 1 lemon. Working with 1 artichoke at a time, cut off the stem near the base. Snap off the first layer of leaves. Cut off the upper third of the artichoke. Rub the cut surfaces with a lemon half. Continue to peel back and snap off leaves until you reach the tender, pale inner yellow leaves. Cut off any remaining tough leaf tips. Rub with a lemon. If the choke has developed prickly tips, scoop it out with the edge of a spoon. Cut the artichokes lengthwise into 4 or 6 pieces, and drop into the lemon water. When ready to cook, drain and pat dry.

❦ In a flameproof baking dish over medium heat, warm the olive oil. Add the garlic and artichokes and sauté until the artichokes begin to turn golden and soften, 5–6 minutes. Gently stir in the fish, thyme, parsley, pepper, stock, wine, and olives. Cover and bake until the artichoke bottoms are easily pierced and the fish is opaque throughout, 15–20 minutes.

❦ Using a slotted spoon, transfer the fish to a warmed platter. Spoon the artichokes and olives around the fish, then spoon a little of the broth over all and serve.

serves 4

Huile d'Olive

You know you're in southern France when you see olive trees. The visual border between the north and the south is the silvery gray orchards of olive trees that supply the thick, rich oil, *huile d'olive,* that perfumes the tables of the south. In the early ripening regions around Arles and Avignon, the mills start pressing the fruit in November and the season continues until February, when the last milling ends at Entrevaux, in the nether regions of Haute Provence. But in every case, only the first cold pressing produces a fine-quality oil.

The flavors of these oils vary considerably, depending upon the variety and ripeness of the olives and how well they were handled after harvesting. The justly famous olive oil of Nyons is buttery yellow and very mild. It is used in baking and poured over warm vegetables. From the Moulin Jean-Marie Cornille at Maussane-les-Alpilles, near Les Baux, comes what many consider to be the finest olive oil in all of the south. Sweet, fruity, and a deep golden green, it makes an unctuous vinaigrette for salads of all kinds and a fine, rich aioli.

Normandie

Boudin Noir aux Pommes

blood sausages with pan-grilled apples

*I always thought that the Provençal version of
boudin noir served with mashed potatoes and
applesauce was the ultimate rendition. I was wrong.
Now, I always make them Norman style, with the
apples panfried in butter, topped with the cooked
boudin, and the whole flamed with Calvados. Choose
apples that are sweet and hold their shape during
cooking. I use Golden Delicious, which are always reli-
able and form a nice, crispy brown crust when fried.*

4 tablespoons (2 oz/60 g) unsalted butter

2 lb (1 kg) firm-fleshed apples such as Golden
Delicious, Reinette, or Gala, peeled, cored,
and cut lengthwise into slices a scant 1 inch
(2.5 cm) thick

¼ teaspoon salt

¼ teaspoon freshly ground pepper

¼ teaspoon ground cinnamon

¼ teaspoon ground nutmeg

8 small boudin noir, about 1½ lb (750 g) total
weight

1 tablespoon Calvados

❧ In a large sauté pan over medium heat, melt
3 tablespoons of the butter. When it foams, add the
apples. Reduce the heat to low and cook, turning
often, until the apples are golden brown and begin
to caramelize but still hold their shape, 10–12 minutes. Add the salt, pepper, cinnamon, and nutmeg.
Remove from the heat and cover to keep warm.

❧ Prick the sausages all over with the tines of a fork.
In a frying pan over medium heat, melt the remaining 1 tablespoon butter. When it foams, add the
sausages. Cook, turning often, until crisp and
browned on the outside and firm on the inside,
10–15 minutes.

❧ Spread the hot apples on a platter, top them with
the sausages, and then pour the Calvados over them.
Ignite the Calvados with a match and let the flames
subside. Serve immediately.

serves 4

Franche-Comté et Les Alpes

Crozets au Beurre Noir

crozets with brown butter and gruyère

*Crozets is one of the typical dishes of Savoy. Every
Savoyard, of course, has a different idea of how it
must be prepared. The tiny bits of pasta, not even
½ inch (12 mm) square, are made of either buckwheat
or wheat flour and are usually purchased dried. But
according to the Savoyards that is where the resem-
blance to traditional pasta stops. Crozets needs longer
cooking and, according to my Savoyard friends, is
flavorless if dressed with only butter, salt, and pepper.
One of the favorite preparations is to toss the cooked
pasta in a frying pan with browned butter and
Gruyère cheese. Another version adds lardons as well,
and in yet another crème fraîche replaces the butter.
Crozets can be eaten as a main course, accompanied
with a green salad, or served as a side dish to
accompany meat such as pork or sausages.*

1 lb (500 g) crozets, made from either
buckwheat or wheat flour

1½ teaspoons salt

½ cup (4 oz/125 g) unsalted butter

½–¾ teaspoon freshly ground pepper

½ lb (250 g) Gruyère or Comté cheese,
coarsely grated

❧ Bring a large saucepan three-fourths full of water
to a boil over medium heat. Add the pasta and salt
and cook uncovered, stirring occasionally, until
tender and slightly puffed, about 30 minutes. Drain
well and set aside.

❧ In a frying pan over medium-high heat, melt the
butter and then continue to cook it until it becomes
a dark brown, about 2 minutes. Add the pepper
to taste and the pasta, and turn in the pan to coat
evenly with the butter. Add the cheese and stir just
until it begins to melt, about 2 minutes.

❧ Transfer to a warmed serving bowl or individual
plates and serve immediately.

serves 4

Languedoc

Beignets de Morue

spicy salt cod fritters

The windows of traiteurs *in Perpignan, like those of many other towns in southwestern France, display mounds of freshly fried salt cod fritters, ready to be taken home or on a picnic. Although they can be made with salt cod chunks, if the cod is shredded and folded into the batter, the result is a lighter puff. The squeeze of lime juice at the end heightens the flavor.*

½ lb (250 g) salt cod

1 bay leaf

1 teaspoon extra-virgin olive oil, if needed, plus 1 tablespoon

1 clove garlic

1 small dried red chile or ¼ teaspoon cayenne pepper

1 cup (5 oz / 155 g) all-purpose (plain) flour

1 teaspoon baking powder

¾ cup (6 fl oz / 180 ml) water

1 yellow onion, minced

1 tablespoon minced fresh flat-leaf (Italian) parsley

1 teaspoon fresh lime juice

vegetable oil for deep-frying

2 lemons, quartered

❦ Salt cod must be refreshed in water before cooking. Refreshing will take a minimum of 3 hours and up to 24 hours, depending upon the amount of salt present. Rinse the salt cod under cold running water for 10 minutes, then put it in a large bowl and add water to cover. Let stand for 3–4 hours. Break off a very small piece of the fish, poach it in simmering water for 3–4 minutes, then taste it. If it is still salty, drain the bowl, cover again with cold water, let stand for another 3–4 hours, and test again. The flavor should not be bland, but you should taste a bit of the salt. When refreshed to taste, pour off the water.

❦ To cook the salt cod, fill a saucepan half full with water, add the bay leaf, and place over medium heat. Bring to just below a boil, reduce the heat to low, and add the salt cod. Cook until the fish easily flakes with a fork, about 10 minutes.

❦ Using a slotted spoon, transfer the fish to a plate. Discard the cooking water. When the fish is cool enough to handle, remove any errant bones or pieces of skin. Put the fish in a mortar and crush to a purée with a pestle, or purée the cod in a food processor along with the 1 teaspoon olive oil.

❦ In a mortar or small food processor, crush together the garlic and whole chile or cayenne pepper. Add the garlic mixture to the puréed cod and mix well. Set aside.

❦ In a bowl, stir together the flour, baking powder, water, and the 1 tablespoon olive oil, mixing well to make a thick cream. Add the cod mixture, onion, parsley, and lime juice and mix well.

❦ In a deep-fryer or a deep, heavy saucepan, pour in vegetable oil to a depth of 4 inches (10 cm) and heat to 375°F (190°C), or until a small spoonful of the batter dropped into it puffs and sizzles upon contact. Working in batches, drop the cod mixture by the heaping tablespoonful into the hot oil. Cook until they are puffed and golden, 3–4 minutes. Using a slotted spoon, transfer to paper towels to drain; keep warm. Repeat until all the cod mixture is used.

❦ Arrange the fritters on a warmed platter and serve immediately with the lemon quarters.

makes about 24 fritters; serves 4

Le Centre

Anguille Grillée

grilled eel

France is blessed with thousand of miles of rivers that are populated with aquatic life, including crayfish and eels. In the inland regions of the Loire, the Berry, the Dordogne, and the Garonne, and in the freshwater marshlands where the rivers meet the sea, small eels are part of the table. As usual, they are prepared in a variety of ways—grilled or poached, in sauces or with a vinaigrette—each varying from region to region. In the Berry, where eels are a specialty, walnut oil is used for the vinaigrette.

½ cup (4 oz / 125 g) coarse sea salt

4 small or 1 large eel, about 2 lb (1 kg) total weight, freshly killed and cleaned with skin intact

½ cup (4 fl oz / 125 ml) walnut oil

2 tablespoons red wine vinegar

1 teaspoon minced fresh chives

1 teaspoon minced fresh tarragon

1 teaspoon minced fresh chervil

½ teaspoon salt

½ teaspoon freshly ground pepper

❀ Prepare a fire in a charcoal grill.

❀ Spread the salt on a kitchen towel and lay the eel(s) on it. Wrap the towel around them and briskly rub the skins smooth with the salt. Rinse and dry the eel(s), then cut into 2-inch (5-cm) lengths, discarding the head(s) and tail(s).

❀ Place the eel(s) in a snugly fastened hinged grill basket or directly on the grill rack. Cook, turning once, until the skin is crispy and golden brown and the meat is cooked clear through, 8–10 minutes on each side.

❀ Meanwhile, in a bowl, stir together the walnut oil, vinegar, chives, tarragon, chervil, salt, and pepper to form a vinaigrette.

❀ Transfer the eel pieces to a warmed platter and serve at once. Pass the vinaigrette at the table.

serves 4

Alsace-Lorraine

Choucroute Garnie

sauerkraut with pork, sausages, and potatoes

Alsace, with its strong German influence, has a regional enthusiasm for sauerkraut. Generally, when anyone thinks of sauerkraut, what comes to mind is the traditional Alsatian choucroute garnie, *cooked with fresh bacon and garnished with sausages, various cuts of pork, and potatoes, but there are myriad variations, including some with no meat at all.*

Sauerkraut is fermented cabbage. The cabbage is finely shredded and salted, then packed into a weak brine solution that allows desirable bacteria to form, but inhibits undesirable ones. These welcome bacteria produce the lactic acid that gives the finished dish its flavor. In Alsace, the cabbages grown for sauerkraut are typically large and very, very dense and can weigh up to thirty pounds (15 kg) each.

Once the pickling process is finished, the sauerkraut must be cooked. In this classic version, it is slowly braised in white wine, and assorted meats are buried in it as it simmers. Whether you make your own sauerkraut for this dish or buy it from a charcuterie, you will be in for a treat because it absorbs so many flavors as it cooks. Sauerkraut is sold both cooked and cru, *or "raw." I use the raw here; if you use cooked sauerkraut, the end result will be more souplike.*

Various meats can be used, including duck, salt-cured or fresh ham hocks, smoked pork shoulder, sausage, and goose. Serve with a chilled Sylvaner or Muscadet.

3 lb (1.5 kg) raw or cooked sauerkraut (see note)

1 clove garlic, minced

10 juniper berries

1 dried bay leaf

2 whole cloves

6 peppercorns

¼ cup (2 oz/60 g) pork lard or rendered goose fat

1 large yellow onion, minced

4 smoked ham hocks, about 2 lb (1 kg) total weight

2 cups (16 fl oz/500 ml) dry Riesling, Sylvaner, or other dry white wine

about 1 cup (8 fl oz/250 ml) water

½ teaspoon freshly ground pepper

¼-lb (125-g) piece slab bacon

¼-lb (125-g) piece lean fresh pork belly (optional)

8 firm-fleshed potatoes, peeled

6 pure pork frankfurters

❦ Preheat an oven to 325°F (165°C).

❦ If using raw sauerkraut, in a large bowl, soak the sauerkraut in cold water to cover for 15 minutes to remove some of its saltiness, then taste it. If it is still too salty, soak again. Drain. Put the raw sauerkraut in a clean, dry kitchen towel, gather up the ends, and wring out the excess water. Cooked sauerkraut does not need to be rinsed.

❦ Place the raw or cooked sauerkraut in a bowl, then, using a fork, fluff it to rid it of any clumps.

❦ Place the garlic, juniper berries, bay leaf, cloves, and peppercorns on a square of cheesecloth (muslin), bring the corners together, and tie securely with kitchen string.

❦ In a deep, heavy pan with a lid, warm the lard or goose fat over medium heat. When it melts, add the onion and sauté slowly, reducing the heat if necessary, until the onion is translucent but not browned, about 5 minutes. Add half of the sauerkraut, the cheesecloth bag of seasonings, and the ham hocks, then top with the remaining sauerkraut. Pour over the wine and then add the water nearly to cover. Add the ground pepper and bring to a boil, uncovered.

❦ Cover, place in the oven, and cook for 1 hour. At the end of the hour, stir the sauerkraut, pushing some to the side. Add the bacon and the fresh pork belly, if using, re-cover, and cook for 1 hour longer.

❦ Remove the pan from the oven and stir the sauerkraut. Place the potatoes on the top. Cover and return to the oven to cook until the potatoes soften, about 30 minutes longer.

❦ Just before the sauerkraut is ready, bring a saucepan three-fourths full of water to a boil over high heat. Add the frankfurters, reduce the heat to medium, and cook until hot, 6–8 minutes. Drain and add to the sauerkraut, turning once or twice.

❦ To serve, transfer the sauerkraut to a warmed large, shallow bowl or deep platter. Top with the ham hocks and frankfurters. Cut the bacon and the fresh pork belly, if used, into slices and add them as well. Surround the sauerkraut with the potatoes and serve hot.

serves 6–8

Rôti di Veau à l'Ail

roasted veal with whole garlic

Veal is frequently used in France, and when I am there, I take advantage of the variety of cuts offered.

1 boneless veal loin or rib roast,
about 3½ lb (1.75 kg)

3 tablespoons extra-virgin olive oil

1 teaspoon salt

1 teaspoon freshly ground pepper

2 bay leaves

4 fresh thyme sprigs

¼ lb (125 g) fatback, sliced ¼ inch (6 mm) thick

6 heads garlic

6 cloves garlic

1 cup (8 fl oz/250 ml) dry white wine

½ cup (4 fl oz/125 ml) water

♛ Preheat an oven to 425°F (220°C).

♛ Rub the roast with 1 tablespoon of the olive oil and ¾ teaspoon each of the salt and pepper. Pat the bay leaves and thyme sprigs on top, then lay the sliced fatback along the top. Tie into a neat roll with kitchen string. Cut the upper ¼ inch (6 mm) off the top of each garlic head. Rub the heads with the remaining 2 tablespoons olive oil and sprinkle with the remaining ¼ teaspoon each salt and pepper. Put the roast, fat side up, on a rack in a roasting pan. Place the garlic heads and the garlic cloves in the pan around the rack.

♛ Roast, occasionally basting the garlic heads with the pan juices, until an instant-read thermometer inserted into the thickest part of the roast registers 145°F (63°C), about 1 hour. Transfer the roast and the garlic to a platter, cover loosely, and rest for 10 minutes before carving.

♛ Meanwhile, put the pan on the stove top over medium-low heat. Add the white wine and deglaze, stirring to dislodge any bits on the bottom. Add the water and stir until reduced a bit, 1–2 minutes.

♛ Cut the roast into slices about ½ inch (12 mm) thick, remove the fatback and kitchen string, and arrange on a platter with the garlic heads. Drizzle with a little of the sauce and pass the remaining sauce at the table.

serves 6

Champignons Sauvages

France is a nation possessed by a love for wild mushrooms, or *champignons sauvages,* and I confess I share what can become a near frenzy for both the eating of the beloved fungi and the hunt itself. Fall is the primary season, and from September until the first freeze, when you see cars parked helter-skelter alongside roadsides, you can be virtually certain the owners are hunting mushrooms.

There is a subtle competition among the people in my village to see who gets the first mushrooms. As the season approaches, more and more residents can be seen taking seemingly innocent walks after lunch or in the late afternoon. But close observation will reveal a plastic bag peeking out of a pocket, in discreet preparation for a possible find.

Once found, the women sit in front of their doors, cleaning the mushrooms for everyone to see. Of course, no one asks where they were found—that's a secret.

In local markets, *épiceries,* and even supermarkets, cèpes, *sanguins,* chanterelles or *girolles, pieds de mouton,* and *trompettes de mort* are proudly displayed. Restaurants and home cooks alike present dishes that celebrate the *terroir* and the season, including wild mushroom omelets, gratins, sauces, and grills. It is one of the best times of the year to sit down to a meal in France.

Le Centre

Pintade aux Choux et Marrons

guinea fowl with cabbage and chestnuts

Guinea fowl, or pintade, and pheasant are commonly cooked with cabbage and chestnuts in the chestnut country of the Berry, south of Paris, an area also renowned for its abundance of wild game. The wild boars, which roam the forests, feed on the fallen chestnuts, and in years past, the farmers used to take their pigs out into the chestnut forests to forage for their food, a custom rarely practiced today. If you don't have guinea fowl, you can prepare this dish with chicken or duck with equal success.

2 guinea fowl or pheasants, about 2 lb (1 kg) each

1½ teaspoons salt

1¼ teaspoons freshly ground pepper

4 celery stalks, halved

2 carrots, peeled and halved

4 cloves garlic, minced

6 fresh thyme sprigs

8 slices bacon

3 cups (24 fl oz/750 ml) dry white wine

2 lb (1 kg) fresh chestnuts

6 tablespoons (3 oz/90 g) unsalted butter

1 lb (500 g) fresh chanterelle mushrooms, brushed clean and halved or quartered if large

1 small head cabbage, cored and cut lengthwise into slices ½ inch (12 mm) thick

½ cup (4 fl oz/125 ml) water

❦ Preheat an oven to 350°F (180°C).

❦ Rub the guinea fowl or pheasants with 1 teaspoon each of the salt and pepper. In a roasting pan, combine the celery, carrots, garlic, and thyme. Place the guinea fowl or pheasants on top of the vegetables, then top with the bacon slices. Pour 2 cups (16 fl oz/500 ml) of the wine over all and cover the pan.

❦ Roast until the birds are tender and the juices run clear when the thickest part of the breast is pierced with a knife, 1¼–1½ hours. The timing will depend on the age of the birds and whether they were wild or farm raised. Older or wild birds may be slightly tougher and take longer to cook. Overcooking, however, will result in a dry bird.

While the birds are cooking, prepare the chest-nuts: Using a sharp knife, cut an X on the flat side of each chestnut. Place them on a baking sheet and roast along with the birds until the cut edges begin to lift slightly, about 30 minutes. Remove from the oven, let cool slightly, then peel away the hard shells. With the knife, remove the soft, furry skin surround-ing each nut. Cut the chestnut meats into ½-inch (12-mm) cubes. Set aside.

In a frying pan over medium heat, melt 4 table-spoons (2 oz/60 g) of the butter. When it foams, add the mushrooms and sauté until some juices are released, 6–7 minutes. Add the cubed chestnuts and the remaining 2 tablespoons butter, reduce the heat to low, and cook, stirring often, until the chestnuts soften, 3–4 minutes. Sprinkle with ¼ teaspoon of the salt and the remaining ¼ teaspoon pepper and set aside. Keep warm.

Just before serving, place the cabbage slices on a rack in a steamer over boiling water, cover, and steam just until translucent, about 5 minutes. Remove from the heat, sprinkle with the remaining ¼ teaspoon salt, and set aside. Keep warm.

Remove the birds from the roasting pan. If you prefer to carve them before serving, discard the bacon. Slice off the breast meat and the legs, and keep warm. Remove the carcasses and discard. Otherwise, set the birds aside and keep warm.

Using a slotted spoon, remove the vegetables from the roasting pan and discard. Place the pan on the stove top over high heat and add the remaining 1 cup (8 fl oz/250 ml) wine and the ½ cup (4 fl oz/125 ml) water. Bring to a boil and deglaze the pan, stirring to scrape up any bits clinging to the bottom. Boil until the liquid is reduced to 1 cup (8 fl oz/250 ml).

On a warmed platter, make a bed of the cabbage. Cover it with the mushroom-chestnut mixture, and top with either the breast meat and legs, if carved, or the whole birds. Pour the sauce over all and serve immediately. To carve the whole birds, remove them to another platter.

serves 4

Provence

Le Grand Aïoli

vegetables and salt cod with garlic mayonnaise

In Provence, un grand aïoli might be prepared for a Sunday afternoon summertime gathering of family and friends, with the feast enjoyed outdoors in the shade of a spreading mulberry tree. Or the occasion might be a village celebration, with every local shopkeeper, civil servant, and schoolchild sitting down to a bountiful meal at long tables set up in the main square. In both cases, red wine or a chilled rosé flows freely and lots of fresh bread is served.

12–14 pieces salt cod, about 6 oz (185 g) each

AIOLI

6–10 cloves garlic, minced

½ teaspoon salt

6 egg yolks

2½ cups (20 fl oz/625 ml) extra-virgin olive oil

scant ½ teaspoon freshly ground pepper

24 boiling potatoes such as Yellow Finn, White Rose, or Yukon gold

6 teaspoons salt

36 carrots

5–6 lb (2.5–3 kg) young, tender green beans, trimmed

36 beets

24 eggs

Salt cod must be refreshed in water before cooking. Refreshing will take a minimum of 3 hours and up to 24 hours, depending upon the amount of salt present. Rinse the salt cod under cold running water for 10 minutes, then put it in a large bowl and add water to cover. Let stand for 3–4 hours. Break off a very small piece of the fish, poach it in simmering water for 3–4 minutes, then taste it. If it is still salty, drain the bowl, cover again with cold water, let stand for another 3–4 hours, and test again. The flavor should not be bland, but you should taste a bit of the salt. When refreshed to taste, pour off the water.

Place the fish in a shallow saucepan or frying pan and add water to cover. Bring to a simmer over low heat and poach the fish just until it flakes when poked with a fork, 3–4 minutes. Using a slotted spatula, transfer to a platter and let cool.

To make the aioli, in a mortar or bowl, pound the garlic cloves and salt together with a pestle until a paste forms. Set aside. In a large bowl, whisk together the egg yolks until blended. Very slowly drizzle in about ½ teaspoon of the olive oil, gently whisking it into the egg yolks. Repeat until a thick emulsion forms, usually after about 2 tablespoons have been added. Then whisk in 1 teaspoon olive oil at a time until all the oil is used. Gently stir in the garlic-salt mixture to make a mayonnaise. Season with the pepper. You should have about 2½ cups (20 fl oz/625 ml). Cover and refrigerate until needed.

In a large saucepan, combine the potatoes, 2 teaspoons of the salt, and water to cover. Bring to a boil over medium-high heat, reduce the heat to medium, and cook until easily pierced with the tip of a sharp knife, about 25 minutes. Drain and set aside.

Peel or simply scrub the carrots. Cook them as you cooked the potatoes, using 2 teaspoons salt and cooking for only 20 minutes. Drain and set aside. Cook the beans in the same way, using the remaining 2 teaspoons salt and cooking for only 10–15 minutes. Drain and set aside. Cut off any beet leaves to within ½ inch (12 mm) of the top. Cook them in the same manner but without any salt. The cooking time will be longer, about 1 hour. Drain and set aside. Keep the beets separate from the other vegetables. They may be served peeled or unpeeled.

In a large saucepan, combine the eggs with water to cover. Bring to a boil, reduce the heat to a simmer, and cook for 12 minutes. Pour off the hot water, then fill the pan with cold water to stop the eggs from cooking. Peel and quarter the eggs.

Arrange the vegetables, eggs, and salt cod on serving platters and set them on the table along with several bowls of the aioli. Serve warm or at room temperature.

serves 12–14

Le grand aïoli is one of the great summer feasts of Provence. But its popularity has spread, and the simple peasant meal is now part of the national patrimony.

Bourgogne et Le Lyonnais

Coq au Vin

chicken cooked in wine

This is one of the great triumphs of French farmhouse cooking. Traditionally, a coq, or "rooster," was killed and cooked, and his blood was reserved to enrich the sauce. The rooster, certainly older and tougher than chickens we use today, simmered on the stove for several hours, until the meat virtually fell from the bone. Today, one still finds restaurants and homes that prepare the dish with a rooster or a capon, but more often a young chicken is used. If you should prepare this with a larger, more mature bird, plan on increasing the cooking time considerably.

3 oz (90 g) lean bacon, cut into strips ¼ inch (6 mm) thick and 1 inch (2.5 cm) long

12 pearl onions

4 tablespoons (2 oz / 60 g) unsalted butter

1 chicken, 3½ lb (1.75 g), cut into serving pieces

1 tablespoon all-purpose (plain) flour

2 tablespoons brandy

1 bottle (24 fl oz / 750 ml) red Burgundy or other full-bodied red wine

3 fresh thyme sprigs

3 fresh flat-leaf (Italian) parsley sprigs

1 dried bay leaf

1 teaspoon freshly ground pepper

½ teaspoon salt

½ lb (250 g) fresh white mushrooms, brushed clean

❧ In a saucepan over medium-high heat, combine the bacon strips with cold water to cover. Bring to a boil, reduce the heat to low, and simmer, uncovered, for 10 minutes. Drain, then rinse the bacon under cold water, and pat dry.

❧ Fill a saucepan three-fourths full with water and bring to a boil. Add the pearl onions and boil for 10 minutes. Drain, cut off the root ends, slip off the skins, and trim off the stems if you like.

❧ In a deep, heavy pan with a lid, melt 3 tablespoons of the butter over medium heat. When it foams, reduce the heat to medium-low, add the bacon and onions, and cook, stirring, until lightly browned, about 10 minutes. Using a slotted spoon, transfer the bacon and onions to a plate. Add the chicken and raise the heat to medium. Cook, turning as needed, until the chicken begins to brown, about 10 minutes. Sprinkle with the flour and, turning from time to time, continue to cook until the chicken and the flour are browned, about 5 minutes. Pour the brandy over the chicken, ignite with a long match to burn off the alcohol, and let the flames subside. Return the bacon and onions to the pan. Pour in a little of the wine and deglaze the pan, stirring to dislodge any bits clinging to the bottom. Pour in the remaining wine and add the thyme, parsley, bay leaf, pepper, and salt. Cover and simmer, stirring occasionally, until the chicken is cooked through, 45–60 minutes.

❧ Meanwhile, in a frying pan over medium-high heat, melt the remaining 1 tablespoon butter. When it foams, add the mushrooms and sauté until just lightly golden, 3–4 minutes. Remove from the heat and set aside. About 15 minutes before the chicken is done, add the mushrooms to the chicken.

❧ When the chicken is finished cooking, using a slotted spoon, transfer the chicken, onions, mushrooms, herb sprigs, and bacon to a bowl. Skim off and discard the fat from the pan juices. Increase the heat to high and boil until the liquid is reduced by nearly half, about 5 minutes. Return the chicken, onions, and mushrooms to the pan (and the bacon, if you wish). Reduce the heat to low and cook, stirring, until heated through, 3–4 minutes.

❧ Transfer to a warmed serving dish or serve directly from the pan.

serves 4 or 5

Corsica

Joue de Boeuf

beef cheeks braised in red wine

This dish uses beef cheeks (the thick meat of the face), whose flavor and tenderness are revealed only after long, slow cooking in a regional red wine, such as a hearty red from Corsica or from Languedoc-Roussillon.

1 calf's foot, cut into several pieces

2 lb (1 kg) beef cheeks, cut into 1-inch (2.5-cm) cubes

1 bottle (24 fl oz/750 ml) hearty red wine

3 tablespoons extra-virgin olive oil

2 yellow or white onions, chopped

3 shallots, chopped

2 celery stalks

¼ cup (⅓ oz/10 g) chopped fresh flat-leaf (Italian) parsley

2 teaspoons fresh thyme leaves

1 teaspoon chopped fresh marjoram

1 orange zest strip, 3 inches (7.5 cm) long

½ teaspoon salt

½ teaspoon freshly ground pepper

2 cups (16 fl oz/500 ml) water

☚ Put the foot and beef pieces in a bowl, add the wine, cover, and refrigerate for 24 hours.

☚ In a heavy saucepan over medium heat, warm the olive oil. Add the onions and shallots and sauté just until translucent, 2–3 minutes. Drain the meat, reserving the marinade, and pat dry. Working in batches, add the meat to the saucepan and cook, turning as needed, just until lightly browned, 3–4 minutes. Transfer to a plate.

☚ When all of the meat is browned, return it to the pan. Add the celery, parsley, thyme, marjoram, orange zest, salt, pepper, and the marinade and water. Stir well, cover, reduce the heat to low, and cook until the meat is easily separated with a fork, 3–4 hours.

☚ Discard the celery, then discard the calf's foot, if desired. To serve, spoon into a deep platter.

serves 4

Les Pyrénées et Gascogne

Daube de Sanglier

daube of wild boar

Wild boars—les sangliers—are abundant in the forested areas of France, including Provence, the Alps, and central and southwestern France, where they are hunted with great enthusiasm, either by the single stalker or in a battue. In the latter, hunters station themselves around a given perimeter and slowly advance toward the center, driving any boars before them. In parts of France, especially the Var, wild boars have become so numerous that they are pests, freely coming out of the forest and marauding among the grapes, grain, and other crops.

In the kitchen, the meat of the mature boar is generally turned into a daube, or stew. It is first marinated and then simmered long and slowly in a wine of the region, along with roulade (French-style pancetta). Serve over soft polenta with plenty of good bread to soak up the sauce.

MARINADE

2 tablespoons extra-virgin olive oil

1 yellow or white onion, sliced

6 cloves garlic, crushed and chopped

4 carrots, peeled and cut into slices 1 inch (2.5 cm) thick

4 cups (32 fl oz / 1 l) full-bodied red wine

4 cups (32 fl oz / 1 l) water

½ cup (4 fl oz / 125 ml) red wine vinegar

2 fresh bay leaves or 1 dried bay leaf

1 teaspoon peppercorns

6 juniper berries

1 teaspoon salt

4 whole cloves

1 orange zest strip, about 4 inches (10 cm) long and ½ inch (12 mm) wide

6 fresh thyme branches, each 6 inches (15 cm) long

3 fresh rosemary sprigs, each 6 inches (15 cm) long

6 fresh winter savory sprigs, each 6 inches (15 cm) long

3½ lb (1.75 kg) boneless wild boar meat such as shoulder, cut into 2-inch (5-cm) pieces

2 tablespoons extra-virgin olive oil

5 slices roulade or pancetta, cut into pieces ½ inch (12 mm) wide

1 yellow onion, chopped

4 cloves garlic, minced

2 tablespoons all-purpose (plain) flour

2 fresh bay leaves or 1 dried bay leaf

1 orange zest strip, about 4 inches (10 cm) long and 1 inch (2.5 cm) wide

1 teaspoon salt

1 teaspoon freshly ground pepper

To make the marinade, in a large saucepan over medium heat, warm the olive oil. Add the onion and garlic and sauté until translucent, 2–3 minutes. Add the carrots and sauté until the carrots change color slightly, 1–2 minutes. Add the wine, water, vinegar, bay leaves, peppercorns, juniper berries, salt, cloves, orange zest, and thyme, rosemary, and winter savory sprigs. Bring to a boil, reduce the heat to low, and simmer, uncovered, for 30 minutes to blend the flavors. Let cool to room temperature. Place the meat in a nonaluminum bowl or pot and pour the marinade over it. Cover and refrigerate for 24 hours.

Remove the meat from the marinade and dry thoroughly. Set aside. Strain the marinade, reserving only the liquid. In a heavy saucepan over medium heat, warm the olive oil. Add the roulade or pancetta and sauté until it releases some of its fat but has not colored, about 5–6 minutes. Using a slotted spoon, remove and discard.

Add the onion and garlic to the fat remaining in the pan and sauté over medium heat until translucent, 3–4 minutes. Raise the heat to high, add the meat, and cook, turning often, until it changes color, 8–10 minutes. Sprinkle with the flour and continue to cook, turning, until the flour browns and some of the liquid has been absorbed, another 3–4 minutes. Pour in about ½ cup (4 fl oz / 125 ml) of the marinade and deglaze the pan, stirring to dislodge any browned bits from the pan bottom. Pour in the remaining marinade and add the bay leaves, orange zest, salt, and pepper. Bring to a boil, reduce the heat to very low, cover, and simmer, stirring occasionally, until the meat is very tender, 2–4 hours, depending upon the age of the animal.

Using a slotted spoon, transfer the meat to a dish; keep warm. Boil the liquid until reduced to about 2 cups (16 fl oz / 500 ml), 5–6 minutes. Return the meat to the reduced juices and heat through. Serve the meat with a little of its juices in a deep platter.

serves 6

Provence

Poissons aux Olives et Herbes de Provence

fish with olives and herbes de provence

This is a simple and delicious way to cook these produits du terroir *from southern France. I like to use unpitted olives, but you can pit them if you prefer.*

8 squid, about 1½ lb (750 g) total weight

1⅓ lb (21 oz/655 g) sea bass fillet, about 1 inch (2.5 cm) thick, cut into 4 equal pieces and skin removed

1 tablespoon extra-virgin olive oil

¼ teaspoon dried winter savory

⅛ teaspoon dried rosemary

¼ teaspoon dried thyme

½ teaspoon freshly ground pepper

½ cup (2½ oz/75 g) oil-cured black olives

1 tomato, peeled, seeded, and coarsely chopped

4 fresh thyme sprigs

☙ Preheat an oven to 350°F (180°C).

☙ Working with 1 squid at a time, cut off the tentacles just above the eyes. Squeeze the base of the tentacles to pop out the squid's hard beak. Cut off and discard the 2 long strands dangling among the tentacles. With your finger, pull out the plasticlike quill and entrails from the body. Rinse the bodies and tentacles with cold running water. Cut the tentacles in half lengthwise. Cut the bodies crosswise into rings ½ inch (12 mm) wide.

☙ Cut four 12-inch (30-cm) squares of aluminum foil. Lay a piece of sea bass in the center of each square and brush with the olive oil. Add 2 full sets of tentacles and one-fourth of the squid rings to each. In a cup, stir together the winter savory, rosemary, thyme, and pepper. Sprinkle evenly over the fish. Divide the olives evenly among the packets and top each with one-fourth of the tomato and a thyme sprig. Bring up the edges of the foil, crease together, and then fold to seal tightly. Place on a baking sheet.

☙ Bake until the fish is opaque throughout, 20–25 minutes. To test for doneness, open a packet and pierce with a fork. Transfer to individual plates and let the diners open their own.

serves 4

Herbes de Provence

The herbs that grow wild on the dry, rocky hillsides and plateaus of Provence are one of the defining features of Provençal cooking, whether humble or refined. They perfume the vegetables, meats, eggs, even the fruits and desserts of the region, giving a distinctive character to the food, whether a *grillade*, a stew, or an omelet. The wild herbs tend to be more intense in flavor than cultivated ones because their volatile oils, which give them their aroma and flavor, are not diluted by the irrigation necessary for cultivation.

The main culinary herbs that grow there are thyme, rosemary, lavender, winter savory, sage, sweet bay laurel, marjoram, and marjoram's wild form, called oregano, or *origan* in Provence. Mixtures of these herbs, usually dried, are called *herbes de Provence* and may contain all or only a few of them. Sometimes the dried leaves are reduced to a powder; other times they are left intact or nearly so. The mixtures are used to season pizzas, vegetables, stews, and meats for grilling, and the wise chef keeps a bowl of *herbes de Provence* handy in the kitchen for dipping into whenever a dish needs an aromatic boost.

Champagne et Le Nord

Sole Meunière

sole cooked in butter

Although delicate-fleshed petrale sole is not a true sole (it is actually a Pacific flounder), it is particularly well suited to this classic sole preparation with butter and lemon juice. My favorite accompaniment is boiled potatoes sprinkled with parsley.

½ cup (2½ oz/75 g) all-purpose (plain) flour

4 whole Dover sole or 2 petrale sole, cleaned and skin removed, or sole fillets, 1½–2 lb (750 g–1 kg) total weight, skin removed

5 tablespoons (2½ oz/75 g) unsalted butter

1 teaspoon salt

1 teaspoon freshly ground pepper

juice of 1 lemon

2 tablespoons minced fresh flat-leaf (Italian) parsley

☙ Spread the flour on a plate and dust the fish on both sides, tapping off the excess.

☙ In a large frying pan over medium heat, melt 3 tablespoons of the butter. When it foams, add 2 of the whole sole, sprinkle them with ½ teaspoon each of the salt and pepper, and cook until the underside of the fish is lightly golden and the meat can be lifted from the bone with a fork, about 4 minutes. Turn and cook the other side until golden, about 4 minutes longer. Transfer to a warmed platter and cover loosely with aluminum foil. Cook the remaining 2 sole the same way, adding an additional tablespoon of butter to the pan. If using sole fillets, proceed as directed, but reduce the cooking time to 1½–2 minutes on each side.

☙ Pour off all but 1 tablespoon of the butter in the pan and add the remaining 1 tablespoon butter and the lemon juice. When the butter melts, pour it over the fish and sprinkle with the parsley.

☙ Serve immediately, piping hot.

serves 4

Franche-Comté et Les Alpes

Salade de Poulet Rôti
aux Noix

roast garlic chicken and walnut salad

*One of the main walnut-producing areas of France
is near Grenoble, in the Dauphiné. Consequently,
walnuts and walnut oil are elements in many of the
regional dishes, from first courses to desserts, and often
appear in combination, as they do here, which produces
a complexity of flavors. Garlic, slipped beneath the
skin of the chicken, delicately scents the meat. Together,
the walnuts and garlic form a flavorful companionship,
as the dish shows. This is a substantial warm
main-dish salad to serve for lunch or dinner, preceded
perhaps by a simple charcuterie platter or crudités.*

1 chicken, about 3 lb (1.5 kg)

1½ teaspoons salt

1½ teaspoons freshly ground pepper

4 cloves garlic, thinly sliced lengthwise

½ cup (4 fl oz/125 ml) chicken stock

WALNUT SALAD

¾ cup (3 oz/90 g) coarsely chopped walnuts

3 tablespoons walnut oil

1½ teaspoons Champagne vinegar or white
wine vinegar

1 shallot, minced

¼ teaspoon salt

¼ teaspoon freshly ground pepper

5 cups (5 oz/155 g) green leaf, red leaf, or other
leaf lettuce, or a mixture

☙ Preheat an oven to 350°F (180°C).

☙ Rinse the chicken and pat dry. Rub the chicken
inside and out with the salt and pepper. Using your
fingers and starting at the cavity, gently separate the
skin from the breast meat, reaching as far back
toward the neck and as close to the thighs as possible
to create a pocket. Be careful not to tear the skin. Slip
the garlic slices between the skin and the meat,
spreading them evenly over the breast. Place the
chicken, breast up, on a rack in a roasting pan. Add
the chicken stock to the pan.

☙ Roast, basting occasionally, until the juices run
clear when a knife is inserted into the thigh joint,
about 1¼ hours. Alternatively, insert an instant-read
thermometer into the thickest part of the thigh away
from the bone; it should register 180°F (82°C).
Transfer to a cutting board and let rest for 10 minutes before carving.

☙ While the chicken is roasting, begin to make the
salad: In a small frying pan over low heat, toast the
walnuts, shaking the pan often, until a nut piece is
golden brown when cut in half, about 10 minutes.
Transfer to a plate and set aside.

☙ In a large bowl, stir together the walnut oil, vinegar, shallot, salt, and pepper. Tear the lettuce leaves
into bite-sized pieces, add them to the bowl, and toss
well to coat with the dressing.

☙ Arrange the salad on a platter and sprinkle with
half of the toasted walnuts.

☙ Carve the chicken, slicing the breast meat and
separating the thighs from the legs. Arrange the
thighs, legs, wings, and the sliced breast meat on top
of the salad, including any bits of garlic that slipped
from beneath the skin while carving. Sprinkle with
the remaining walnuts and serve warm.

serves 4

Couscous aux Légumes

vegetable couscous

Couscous is a legacy of France's North African colonial period, and today it is thoroughly integrated into the culture. Couscous restaurants are especially numerous in Paris, but can be found in other urban centers as well. Many traiteurs *sell ready-to-eat couscous, and on market or fair days in cities and villages, it is not unusual to see couscous being cooked and sold from stands. The name refers to both a tiny semolina pasta and the dish. After cooking, either plumped in hot liquid or steamed, the couscous is garnished with vegetables and some of the aromatic broth in which they were cooked. Harissa, a spicy sauce made of chiles, is usually served alongside, and meat can be added as well. In couscous royale the vegetables and broth are crowned with grilled lamb or mutton chops, sautéed chicken, and grilled* merguez, *a spicy North African lamb sausage, but plates with a single meat are common, too.*

HARISSA

6 oz (185 g) small dried red chiles such as árbol or bird's eye

4 cloves garlic

2 tablespoons ground cumin

1 teaspoon salt

1½ cups (12 fl oz/375 ml) extra-virgin olive oil

VEGETABLES

2 tablespoons unsalted butter

2 tablespoons extra-virgin olive oil

2 yellow onions, chopped

2 cloves garlic, chopped

2 small dried red chiles, such as árbol or bird's eye, seeded and crumbled

2 tablespoons ground turmeric

1 teaspoon ground cumin

1 teaspoon fresh thyme leaves

½ teaspoon salt

½ teaspoon freshly ground pepper

⅛ teaspoon saffron threads

8 small new potatoes, unpeeled, halved

1 small head cauliflower, cut into small florets

2 large carrots, peeled and cut into 2-inch (5-cm) lengths

2 cups (16 fl oz/500 ml) vegetable or chicken stock

1 cup (5 oz/155 g) shelled English peas

COUSCOUS

3 cups (24 fl oz/750 ml) boiling water

2 cups (12 oz/375 g) couscous

1 tablespoon unsalted butter

½ teaspoon salt

¼ cup (⅓ oz/10 g) minced fresh mint

¼ cup (⅓ oz/10 g) minced fresh chives

¼ cup (⅓ oz/10 g) minced fresh tarragon

☘ To make the *harissa*, in a mortar, crush the chiles, including their seeds, into fine pieces with a pestle. Add the garlic, cumin, salt, and 2 tablespoons of the olive oil. Continue to crush until a paste forms. Gradually work in the remaining olive oil to form a medium-thick sauce. (This process can also be accomplished in a blender.) Set aside.

☘ To prepare the vegetables, in a deep, heavy frying pan over medium heat, combine the butter and olive oil. When the butter foams, add the onions and garlic and sauté until translucent, 2–3 minutes. Stir in the chiles, turmeric, cumin, thyme, salt, pepper, and saffron. Add the potatoes, cauliflower, and carrots and turn them gently in the butter mixture for a minute or two. Add the stock and stir for 1–2 minutes. Cover tightly, reduce the heat to low, and cook until the potatoes are almost tender when pierced, 15–20 minutes. Add the peas, cover again, and cook until the peas and potatoes are tender, 5–7 minutes longer. Remove from the heat and keep covered.

☘ To prepare the couscous, in a large bowl, combine the boiling water, couscous, butter, and salt. Let stand until the water is absorbed, about 10 minutes. Turn into a fine-mesh sieve and press gently with the back of a wooden spoon to remove excess water. Transfer to a bowl and, using a fork or your fingertips, gently fluff to separate the grains.

☘ Just before serving, spoon a tablespoon or two of the hot stock from the vegetables into the *harissa* and stir to mix. Transfer to a small serving bowl.

☘ To serve, heap the couscous on a platter, spoon a little of the stock and a few vegetables over it, and sprinkle with a little of the mint, chives, and tarragon. Accompany with the remaining vegetables and their stock, the bowl of *harissa,* and the remaining fresh herbs for the diners to add as desired.

serves 4–6

Provence

Bouillabaisse

mediterranean fish soup

Like all traditional dishes, bouillabaisse, a fish soup commonly found in restaurants and homes along France's Mediterranean coast, can take many forms. Its origins are in the fishermen's stews that were typically cooked up on the beaches, after the day's catch was in and sold. In Hyères, near Toulon, I was invited to one such feast by the granddaughter of a fisherman. Although the fish were purchased that morning at the open-air market, the rest of the preparation was the way she had learned from her parents and grand-parents. The cauldron was brought down to the rocks along the sea and set upon a pile of stones, then a driftwood-and-grapevine fire was built beneath it. We cooked the bouillabaisse in the pot and consumed it with plenty of local wine, both red and white.

ROUILLE

2 dried cayenne or other dried red chiles, seeded

4 cloves garlic

1 tablespoon dried bread crumbs

2 egg yolks

½ teaspoon salt

½ cup (4 fl oz / 125 ml) extra-virgin olive oil

SOUP

¼ cup (2 fl oz / 60 ml) extra-virgin olive oil

1 yellow onion, chopped

2 leeks, white part only, chopped

2 tomatoes, peeled and coarsely chopped

2 cloves garlic, crushed

1 fresh bay leaf or ½ dried

2 fresh thyme sprigs

1 fennel stalk, 6 inches (15 cm) long

1 fresh or dried orange zest strip, 2 inches (5 cm) long and 1 inch (2.5 cm) wide

½ teaspoon salt

½ teaspoon freshly ground pepper

2 cups (16 fl oz / 500 ml) dry white wine

1 cup (8 fl oz / 250 ml) water

5 potatoes, about 1½ lb (750 g) total weight, peeled and cut into slices ½ inch (12 mm) thick

¼ teaspoon saffron threads

2 lb (1 kg) firm-fleshed fish steaks or fillets such as monkfish, halibut, or cod, cut into 1½-inch (4-cm) chunks

boiling water, as needed

2 lb (1 kg) tender-fleshed whole fish such as red snapper, ocean perch, or rockfish, cleaned and left whole if small or cut into 1½-inch (4-cm) chunks or filleted if large

1 lb (500 g) mussels, scrubbed and debearded

1 lb (500 g) small crabs

1 tablespoon minced fresh flat-leaf (Italian) parsley

8 slices coarse country bread, each 1 inch (2.5 cm) thick, toasted and rubbed with garlic

❦ To make the *rouille*, in a mortar, combine the chiles and garlic and crush them together with a pestle to make a paste. Add the bread crumbs and mash again. Mix in the egg yolks and the salt to make a smooth paste. Very slowly, drop by drop, whisk in the olive oil until the mixture thickens. Continue adding the oil in a thin stream, whisking constantly, until a mayonnaiselike mixture forms. (Alternatively, make the *rouille* in a blender.) Set aside.

❦ To make the soup, in a heavy-bottomed soup pot over medium-high heat, warm the olive oil. Add the onion and leeks and sauté until translucent, 2–3 minutes. Add the tomatoes, garlic, bay leaf, thyme, fennel, orange zest, salt, and pepper. Stir well and add the wine, water, and potatoes. Bring to a boil, reduce the heat to low, cover, and simmer until the potatoes are nearly tender, about 25 minutes.

❦ Bring the mixture to a rolling boil. Stir in the saffron. Lay the firm-fleshed fish on top of the soup, pour over just enough boiling water to cover, and boil for about 7 minutes to half-cook the fish. Add the tender-fleshed fish, the mussels (discard any that do not close to the touch), and the crabs, adding more boiling water as needed to cover, and boil just until the tender-fleshed fish separates easily with a fork and the mussels open, 3–4 minutes. Using a spatula, transfer the fish and shellfish to a warmed platter, placing the tender-fleshed fish on one part, the firm-fleshed on another. Discard any mussels that failed to open. Using a slotted spoon, transfer the potatoes to the same plate. Ladle a few tablespoons of broth over them and garnish with the parsley. Stir 2–3 tablespoons of broth into the *rouille*. Ladle the remaining broth into a bowl.

❦ Place a slice of bread in the bottom of each soup plate and ladle on some broth. Pass the fish, potatoes, and *rouille* for spooning into the plates.

serves 8

Franche-Comté et Les Alpes

Raclette

melted cheese with boiled potatoes

Raclette is both the name of a Savoyard cheese and a traditional dish. In the old days, before the development of electric raclette grills, chunks of the cheese were put on the hearth near a glowing fire. Diners gathered around, with plates, knives, and forks in hand and a bowl of boiled potatoes and a good vin de Savoie at their sides. As the surface of the cheese melted, it was eagerly scraped off, spread across the potatoes, and consumed, and then all was washed down with the wine. Raclette is now popular all over France, and the electric grills containing eight or more nonstick two-inch (5-cm) squares are common household items. Each diner is given a stack of sliced raclette and puts it into his or her assigned square, where it melts before being spooned over potatoes.

12 boiling potatoes, such as Ratte, Yukon gold, Yellow Finn, or Red or White Rose

1 teaspoon salt, plus salt to taste

1–1½ lb (500–750 g) raclette cheese, cut into 4 equal portions

freshly ground pepper to taste

In a large saucepan, combine the potatoes, the 1 teaspoon salt, and water to cover. Bring to a boil over medium-high heat, reduce the heat to medium, and cook, uncovered, until easily pierced with the tip of a sharp knife, 20–25 minutes. Drain, cover to keep warm, and set aside.

To serve, put a piece of cheese for each person on a separate heatproof plate and set the plates near the fire with a cut side facing the heat. Pass out more plates for the potatoes. While the cheese is melting, each diner lightly mashes some of the potatoes and seasons them to taste with salt and pepper. When the cheese is ready, each diner scrapes the melted portion from his or her piece and spreads it over the potatoes. The rind, left intact, provides a frame for the melting cheese. After the scraping, the cheese is placed near the fire to melt again.

serves 4

Normandie

Rouelle de Veau au Cidre

veal shanks in cider with mushrooms

Veal shanks are a popular and inexpensive cut of meat in France, and because of their marrow and sinew, which melt and dissolve to thicken the sauce, they make excellent braised dishes. The long, slow cooking allows the flavors to blend and the meat to become tender enough to fall from the bone. Veal shanks might be combined with tomatoes, onions, and a turnip or two, or simply cooked in red wine with aromatics. Here, in this Norman preparation, the regional ingredients of cider and cream are used. Serve with pasta and a green salad for a simple country-style meal. Pour a dry cider or a Rosé d'Anjou.

5 tablespoons (2½ oz/75 g) unsalted butter

2½–3 lb (1.25–1.5 kg) veal shanks, cut into slices 1½–2 inches (4–5 cm) thick

¾ teaspoon salt

1 teaspoon freshly ground pepper

2 yellow onions, minced

1½ cups (12 fl oz/375 ml) dry hard cider, or as needed

1 teaspoon fresh thyme leaves

½ lb (250 g) fresh white mushrooms, brushed clean and quartered

⅓ cup (3 fl oz/90 ml) crème fraîche

1 egg yolk, lightly beaten

4 tablespoons (⅓ oz/10 g) minced fresh flat-leaf (Italian) parsley

☙ In a large, heavy pot over medium heat, melt 3 tablespoons of the butter. Meanwhile, rub the veal with the salt and pepper. When the butter foams, add the veal and sauté, turning once, until browned and golden, 4–6 minutes total. Turn to sauté the edges as well, 1–2 minutes longer. Using a slotted spoon, transfer the veal to a platter.

☙ Add the onions to the pot and sauté, stirring, until translucent, 2–3 minutes. Pour the 1½ cups (12 fl oz/375 ml) cider over the onions and, using a spoon, deglaze the pot, stirring to dislodge any browned bits

from the bottom. Reduce the heat to very low and return the veal and any collected juices to the pot. Stir in the thyme, cover, and cook, stirring from time to time, until the veal is tender, 1–1½ hours. Should the meat begin to stick, add a little more cider.

☙ While the veal is cooking, prepare the mushrooms. In a frying pan over medium heat, melt the remaining 2 tablespoons butter. When it foams, add the mushrooms and sauté until lightly golden, 7–8 minutes. Remove from the heat and set aside.

☙ In a small bowl, stir together the crème fraîche, the egg yolk, and 2 tablespoons of the parsley. Set aside.

☙ After the veal has cooked for 1½ hours, add the mushrooms and their juices, stir well, and cook for another 10 minutes to blend the flavors.

☙ Using a slotted spoon, transfer the veal to a warmed serving platter. With the heat still low, whisk the crème fraîche mixture into the sauce in the pot until fully incorporated. Do not allow it to boil.

☙ Pour the sauce over the veal, sprinkle with the remaining 2 tablespoons parsley, and serve.

serves 6

Crème

Some of the finest, richest cream in the world is produced in France, and the French use it generously in their cooking. The dairy regions, where cows feed on lush green pastures, are found in virtually every province except Provence, and the national table reflects the local bounty. Nowhere, though, is the influence of cream as evident as in the dishes of Normandy, where you will find everything from soups and salad dressings to sauces, tarts, and breads made with cream and crème fraîche.

Crème fraîche is especially beguiling to cook with because it is thickened and slightly acidulated, giving it ready-made texture and flavor. It is particularly good for making sauces that are reduced, because it doesn't separate when it is boiled. To make crème fraîche at home, add 2 tablespoons whole buttermilk to ½ cup (4 fl oz/125 ml) heavy (double) cream, cover the container, and let it stand overnight at room temperature. If time is short, 2 tablespoons cider vinegar added to 1 cup (8 fl oz/250 ml) heavy cream at room temperature will thicken the cream within the hour.

Pays de la Loire

Saumon à la Crème au Muscadet

salmon in cream and muscadet sauce

Muscadet, a very dry white wine, is produced in a relatively small area in the westernmost point of the Loire Valley, where the Loire River reaches the Atlantic at Nantes. The salmon, of course, comes from the river.

4 tomatoes, peeled, seeded, and diced

2 shallots, diced

1½ cups (12 fl oz/375 ml) Muscadet or other dry white wine

1 teaspoon salt, plus more to taste

1 teaspoon freshly ground pepper, plus more to taste

3 tablespoons unsalted butter

6 center-cut salmon fillets, about 1½ lb (750 g) total weight, skin removed

⅔ cup (5 fl oz/160 ml) crème fraîche

1 teaspoon minced fresh chervil

1 teaspoon minced fresh chives

1 teaspoon minced fresh tarragon

❧ In a saucepan over medium heat, combine the tomatoes, shallots, wine, and ½ teaspoon each salt and pepper. Cook, stirring occasionally, until reduced by one-third, about 10 minutes. Remove from the heat and set aside.

❧ In a large frying pan over medium-high heat, melt the butter. When it foams, add the salmon fillets. Sear until golden, about 2 minutes, then turn and sear on the second side until golden and just opaque throughout, about 2 minutes longer. Sprinkle the salmon with the remaining ½ teaspoon each salt and pepper and transfer to warmed individual plates.

❧ Strain the tomato mixture through a fine-mesh sieve placed over a bowl, pressing against the pulp to extract all the juice. Stir in the crème fraîche, then taste and adjust the seasonings. Return to the saucepan over medium heat and cook, stirring, until the sauce thickens a bit, 2–3 minutes.

❧ Pour the sauce over the salmon and sprinkle with the chervil, chives, and tarragon. Serve immediately.

serves 6

Provence

Gigot d'Agneau à la Boulangère

leg of lamb with potatoes and onions

The most treasured lambs in France are those that have grazed either on salt marshes (thus becoming pré salé, *or "salt meadow" lamb), such as the vast area of the Landes that reaches northwest of Bordeaux, or on wild herbs, like the famous lamb of Sisteron in the Basses-Alpes. The meat, full of the flavors of the* terroir, *brings a premium price, so restaurants advertise its provenance on their menus. It may be served simply roasted with herbs or prepared with vegetables.*

In Provence, cooks traditionally prepare the lamb with potatoes and onions. Legend has it that a hundred years ago or so, when the wood-fired communal bread ovens were an integral part of life, the lamb and potatoes were cooked in the bread ovens once all the bread had been baked.

1 tablespoon unsalted butter

2½ lb (1.25 kg) baking potatoes, very thinly sliced

2½ lb (1.25 kg) large yellow onions, very thinly sliced

1½ cups (12 fl oz/375 ml) beef stock

1 bone-in leg of lamb, 5½–6 lb (2.75–3 kg)

1 tablespoon extra-virgin olive oil

1½ teaspoons dried herbes de Provence

½ teaspoon salt

¾ teaspoon freshly ground pepper

3 cloves garlic, cut into fine slivers

☙ Preheat an oven to 400°F (200°C). Using the butter, grease a baking dish large enough to hold the lamb and vegetables. Set aside.

☙ In a large saucepan over medium–high heat, combine the potatoes, onions, and beef stock and bring to a boil. Reduce the heat to low and simmer, uncovered, for 10 minutes to soften the potatoes.

☙ Using a slotted spoon, transfer the potatoes and onions to the prepared baking dish, spreading them evenly. Pour the stock over the vegetables and bake for 20 minutes.

☙ Meanwhile, prepare the lamb: Using a sharp knife, make 20–25 slits, each 1 inch (2.5 cm) deep, all over the meat. Rub the lamb all over with the olive oil, *herbes de Provence,* salt, and pepper. Insert the garlic slivers into the slits.

☙ When the vegetables have cooked for 20 minutes, remove from the oven, place the lamb on top of them, and return the dish to the oven. Reduce the oven temperature to 375°F (190°C) and bake until an instant-read thermometer inserted into thickest part of the leg away from the bone registers 125°–130°F (52°–54°C) for medium-rare, about 1 hour. If medium is desired, roast for another 15 minutes, or until the thermometer registers 135°–145°F (57°–63°C). Remove from the oven, cover loosely, and let stand for 15–20 minutes.

☙ To serve, transfer the lamb to a cutting board and carve into thin slices. Arrange the potatoes and onions on a warmed platter and top with the lamb slices. Pour over any juices captured during cooking. Scoop up some of the potatoes and lamb slices for each serving.

serves 6–8

The most treasured lambs in France are those that have grazed either on salt marshes or on wild herbs, with the meat taking on the full flavors of the terroir.

Pays de la Loire

Crabe à sa Beurre
aux Algues

crab with its butter and seaweed

Lunch at a brasserie in Angers, not far from the château that dominates the city, was my introduction to this dish. The crab came on a large oval dish that was lined with seaweed so fresh that it looked and smelled as if it had just been pulled from the sea. The crab body was broken to expose the sweet yellow crab butter, but the claws were intact. It was up to me to crack them open with the hinged tool delivered by the waiter. The meat was perfectly cooked, tender, and juicy sweet. With a glass of cold, crisp Muscadet and still-warm bread, it remains one of my fondest memories of France.

¼ *cup (2 oz/60 g) salt*

1 lemon, halved, plus 1 lemon, quartered

1 dried bay leaf

2 live crabs, about 2 lb (1 kg) each

several handfuls of fresh small-leaved seaweed, preferably dark amber kelp

♛ Fill a big pot two-thirds full of water. Add the salt, two lemon halves, and bay leaf and bring to a boil over high heat. Carefully drop in the crabs, bring to a boil again, and keep at a strong boil for about 20 minutes. Using tongs, remove the crabs and let cool.

♛ To clean each crab, break off each leg by twisting it at the joint closest to the body; set the legs aside. Place the crab rounded-side down and, using the heels of your hands, press down on each side of the shell until it cracks down the middle. Pull off each half shell, being careful to reserve the juices, then pry up the tail flap, pull it back, and twist it off. Turn the crab over and remove the spongy gills—"dead man's fingers"—and discard. Leave the yellowish mass of crab butter intact for scooping out at the table. Pinch the mouth and mandibles, pull off, and discard. Crack each segment of the legs and claws at the joint with a crab cracker, being careful not to crush the meat.

♛ Arrange the seaweed in beds on individual plates. Arrange a crab on top of each, forming it into as life-like a position as possible. Serve with a crab cracker, crab forks, and the lemon quarters.

serves 2

Normandie

Demoiselles de Cherbourg à la Crème

lobster in the style of cherbourg

This is a luxurious dish, but one that is well worth making. Demoiselle, I have been told, is the traditional name for a small lobster. The "lobster butter" and the roe, if any, combine to make a rich, complexly flavored sauce that you will want to scoop up every last bit of with shards of bread. Serve with brut Champagne or Meursault.

2 live lobsters, 1½–1¾ lb (750–875 g) each

½ teaspoon salt

¾ teaspoon freshly ground black pepper

3 tablespoons unsalted butter

3 tablespoons Calvados

3 tablespoons Lillet, sweet vermouth, or dry white wine

2 cups (16 fl oz / 500 ml) crème fraîche

3 egg yolks

2 teaspoons minced fresh tarragon

⅛ teaspoon cayenne pepper

⅛ teaspoon paprika

☙ Bring a large pot three-fourths full of water to a boil over high heat. Immerse the live lobsters in the water and cook them for 2 minutes, just long enough to kill them. Lift out with tongs and set on a work surface. When cool enough to handle, using kitchen shears, cut the lobsters in half lengthwise, and separate the halves. Remove the head sac and the small intestine in the center of the tail and discard. Using a small spoon, scoop out the yellowish green tomalley (the "butter") and the reddish black coral, or roe, if present, and reserve them in a bowl. Break the claws with a mallet or nutcracker just enough to crack them, being careful not to crush the meat.

☙ Sprinkle the lobster halves with the salt and black pepper. In a large frying pan over medium-high heat, melt the butter. When it foams, add the lobster halves, shell side down, and cook them for about 2 minutes, turning so that all sides of the shell are exposed to the butter. Turn the halves and cook, meat side down, for another 2 minutes, moving them around in the pan. Add the Calvados, carefully ignite it with a long match to burn off the alcohol, and let the flames subside. Add the Lillet, vermouth, or white wine and raise the heat to high. Boil until reduced by half, about 1 minute. Reduce the heat to medium, add the crème fraîche, and continue to cook until the lobster meat is cooked through and pulls away from the shell when lifted with a fork and the cream has thickened, 2–3 minutes.

☙ Meanwhile, add the egg yolks and the tarragon to the bowl containing the tomalley and the roe, if using, and whisk well.

☙ Using tongs, remove the lobster halves, letting the juices drain back into the frying pan. Arrange on a warmed platter or individual plates.

☙ Reduce the heat to low and whisk the egg yolk mixture into the pan juices. Whisk until thickened, being careful not to allow the mixture to boil, just a minute or two. Add the cayenne and the paprika.

☙ Spoon the sauce evenly over the lobster halves and serve immediately.

serves 4

Les Pyrénées et Gascogne

Lapin aux Pruneaux

rabbit roasted with prunes

Throughout France, rabbit, part of the basse-cour
*(barnyard) along with chickens, guinea hens, and
other small animals, plays a big part in the simple,
home-style country cooking that I love so much. I have
raised my own rabbits over the years, but eventually
I found it easier to buy them from someone else. The
lean, firm white meat is suited to a number of
preparations, and cooks in each region vary the dishes
according to the local* terroir. *Thus, rabbit with prunes
in Gascony, with cream in Normandy, with mustard in
Burgundy, and with olives in Provence.*

½ teaspoon minced fresh thyme

½ teaspoon minced fresh sage

½ teaspoon minced fresh rosemary

½ teaspoon pepper

*1 young rabbit, about 2½ lb (1.25 kg), cut into
8–10 serving pieces*

8–10 pitted prunes

8–10 slices bacon

♛ Preheat an oven to 350°F (180°C).

♛ In a small bowl, combine the thyme, sage, rosemary, and pepper and mix well. Rub each piece of
rabbit with the mixture. Place a prune alongside each
piece of rabbit, wrap them together with the bacon,
and fasten the bacon in place with a toothpick. Put
the wrapped rabbit pieces in a shallow roasting pan
just large enough to accommodate them.

♛ Roast, basting from time to time with the pan
juices, until the thickest rabbit pieces are tender
when pierced with the tip of a sharp knife and the
meat is opaque to the bone, 1–1¼ hours. Transfer to
a warmed platter and serve at once.

serves 4

Ile-de-France

Steak-frites

steak and french fries

*Steak-frites is found everywhere in France, from
the humblest workingman's café to the most elegant
restaurant. The very best steak I've ever eaten in
a restaurant came at the end of a long day of traveling
with my children, just the three of us. We had crossed
the channel from Dover and landed at Ostend, in
Belgium, and by the time we were in northern
France we all were very hungry and very tired. We
found only shuttered villages and closed cafés
everywhere until I noticed an open bar with a small
hotel sign in the window. We were shown a room
above the bar, but even though they served food, they
said they were finished for the night. Seeing our
crestfallen faces, and my six-year-old clinging to my
skirt, the young man directed us down a road and
around a few turns into what seemed a residential
neighborhood. Then I spotted the restaurant. Cars were
parked every which way around it, expensive cars.
I was afraid it would be beyond our slender budget,
but cheerily said, "Oh, this looks nice!" Taking each
child by the hand, I went in. It was calm and peaceful,
beautifully appointed with fresh flowers and a grill on
one wall near where we were seated. After a first course
of ham with cornichons, my daughter wanted the fresh
trout (one of her childhood favorites). My son and
I both had steak-frites, but what steak-frites! The
meat had been sprinkled with herbs kept in a basket
nearby, and then grilled over grapevine cuttings in
front of us. The frites appeared on a huge platter,
cooked to perfection. And, to our delight, we were
served sorbet between the main course and our desserts
of crème brûlée. The dinner was three times the price
of the hotel and worth every glorious moment.*

*Various cuts of meat are used in France, but one of
the juiciest and most popular is the entrecôte, or
rib-eye steak. French fries vary somewhat from place
to place, but they must always be crunchy on the
outside and light and fluffy on the inside. It is said
that the Belgians invented the best method of
cooking—deep-frying the potatoes twice to give them
the necessary crunchy crust—but I've yet to find
a Frenchman who agrees.*

---

4 or 5 russet or other baking potatoes

vegetable oil for deep-frying

1½ teaspoons salt, plus salt to taste

*4 rib or rib-eye steaks, each about ½ inch
(12 mm) thick*

2 tablespoons minced fresh thyme

1 teaspoon freshly ground pepper

⅓–½ cup (3–4 fl oz/80–125 ml) water

Peel the potatoes and slice them lengthwise
¼ inch (6 mm) thick. Stack the slices and cut again
lengthwise to form sticks ¼ inch (6 mm) wide. As
the potatoes are cut, slip them into a bowl of cold
water. When all of them are cut, let stand in the water
for 30–60 minutes. Just before cooking, drain the
potatoes and pat dry thoroughly.

In a deep-fryer or heavy, deep saucepan, pour in
vegetable oil to a depth of 4 inches (10 cm) and heat
to 350°F (180°C), or until a potato dropped into it
sizzles upon contact.

When the oil is ready, put about one-fourth of the
potatoes in a deep-frying basket and fry until the
potatoes develop a white crust but do not brown,
about 2 minutes. Transfer to paper towels to drain.
Repeat until all the potatoes are cooked. The second
frying can take place as much as 3–4 hours later, but
the potatoes should rest a minimum of 5 minutes
between the fryings. Do the second frying in batches
also, but cook slightly longer, up to 3 minutes, allowing the potatoes to form a golden crust slowly.
Transfer to paper towels to drain and sprinkle each
batch with a little salt.

Cook the steaks while the French fries are cooking: Sprinkle the steaks with the thyme and the
pepper. Sprinkle the 1½ teaspoons salt over the
bottom of a large frying pan, and place over high
heat for 1–2 minutes, or until a drop of water sizzles
upon contact. Place the steaks in the pan and cook,
turning once, for about 2 minutes on each side for
medium-rare. Transfer to a warmed platter. Still over
high heat, pour in the ⅓–½ cup (3–4 fl oz/80–125 ml)
water and deglaze the pan, stirring to dislodge any
browned bits from the pan bottom.

Pour the pan juices over the steaks and serve
immediately with the hot French fries.

---

serves 4

Cuisiner avec Vins et Eaux-de-Vie

Wine is a deeply treasured part of the French patrimony, and people are profoundly proud of the wines that each region, each village, and each vineyard produce. Wines—red, white, sweet, dry, and fortified—are part of every cook's pantry, like salt, pepper, herbs, butter, cream, and olive oil, and they are added with a practiced hand. What wine is used generally depends upon what is locally produced, and the taste of a dish will reflect the regional wine. You'll find wine is an essential ingredient in the making of soups, stews, and sauces. It is employed to deglaze pans, to poach fruit, and to make homemade aperitifs and *digestifs*. Distilled spirits—brandy, Cognac, Armagnac, and Calvados—are used with equal aplomb for the same purposes, although in lesser quantities. The spirits have the additional quality of being flammable because of their high alcohol content. The flaming burns off the alcohol, leaving behind the complex flavors of the spirits.

Champagne et Le Nord

Ris de Veau aux Champignons

sweetbreads with mushrooms

Sweetbreads, really thymus glands, are considered a delicacy by the French, who have a wonderful way with les abats, the innards of animals. Indeed, some of the most beloved dishes of the French table are made from kidneys, livers, and sweetbreads. The sauce created in this dish is especially succulent, so serve it with rice, noodles, or toast.

2 lb (1 kg) veal or calf sweetbreads

¼ cup (2 fl oz/60 ml) white wine vinegar

3 tablespoons unsalted butter

2 carrots, peeled and diced

2 shallots, minced

2 celery stalks, diced

2 tablespoons minced fresh flat-leaf (Italian) parsley

1 teaspoon minced fresh thyme

1 dried bay leaf

½ teaspoon freshly ground pepper

½ cup (4 fl oz/125 ml) dry white wine

½ teaspoon salt

16 white onions, each 1–1½ inches (2.5–4 cm) in diameter, peeled

½ lb (250 g) fresh mushrooms, brushed clean and quartered

❧ In a bowl, combine the sweetbreads with cold water to cover. Cover the bowl and refrigerate for 2 hours, changing the water several times. If the sweetbreads were purchased whole, they will need trimming. With the sweetbreads still in the water, using a knife, separate the two lobes, which are connected by a tube, and discard the tube. Drain the sweetbreads and return them to the bowl with fresh water to cover. Add the vinegar and let the sweetbreads soak for another 30 minutes. Then remove as much of the remaining filament as possible without the sweetbreads losing their shape.

In a frying pan over medium heat, melt the butter. When it foams, add the carrots, shallots, celery, parsley, thyme, bay leaf, and ¼ teaspoon of the pepper. Reduce the heat to low and cook, stirring, until the vegetables are soft but not browned, about 10 minutes. Add the wine, raise the heat to high, and boil until reduced by half, 3–4 minutes.

Sprinkle the sweetbreads with the salt and the remaining ¼ teaspoon pepper and place them in the frying pan, arranging them snugly in a single layer atop the vegetables. Baste them with the butter and vegetables, cover tightly, and cook, still over low heat, until they turn opaque and begin to release their juices, about 5 minutes. Turn the sweetbreads and baste them again. Replace the cover and cook for another 5 minutes to release the juices further. The sweetbreads will reduce considerably in size as they render their juices.

Add the onions to the pan. Butter a sheet of parchment paper and place, buttered side down, over the sweetbreads and onions. Cover and cook over very low heat until the onions are tender and nearly translucent, about 30 minutes. Remove the cover and lift the paper. Turn the sweetbreads and add the mushrooms. Replace the paper and the cover and cook until the sweetbreads are tender when pierced with the tip of a knife, about 15 minutes.

Using a slotted spoon, transfer the sweetbreads and vegetables to a platter. Discard the bay leaf. Raise the heat to high and boil to reduce the pan juices by half, 2–3 minutes. Meanwhile, cut the sweetbreads into slices ½ inch (12 mm) thick. Return the slices and the vegetables to the pan and cook just to warm them through, 1–2 minutes.

Transfer the sweetbreads and cooked vegetables and their juices to a warmed platter or shallow bowl and serve immediately.

serves 4

Languedoc

Lapin Grillé à la Moutarde

mustard-grilled rabbit

Rabbit is one of my favorite meats, and this is a superbly simple and delicious way to serve it. I was inspired to try my own version after buying a grilled rabbit from a rotisserie in Louviers. Be sure to request that the liver, heart, and kidneys be left intact, as they will gently steam inside the cavity as the rabbit cooks and emerge succulent and delicately scented with herbed mustard. To accompany the rabbit, you might choose braised carrots with dill (page 171) and creamy mashed potatoes.

1 rabbit, about 2½ lb (1.25 kg), preferably fresh and with liver, heart, and kidneys intact

½ cup (4 oz / 125 g) Dijon mustard

4 cloves garlic, minced

1 tablespoon extra-virgin olive oil

1 tablespoon minced fresh tarragon

2 tablespoons minced fresh flat-leaf (Italian) parsley

¼ teaspoon salt

1 teaspoon freshly ground pepper

❧ Prepare a fire in a charcoal grill with a cover.

❧ Thread a skewer across and down the rib flaps of the rabbit to close the cavity. In a small bowl, combine the mustard, garlic, olive oil, tarragon, parsley, salt, and pepper to make a paste. Using a spatula, spread the paste all over the rabbit.

❧ When the coals are hot, push them to the sides of the fire pan and place a large drip pan in the bottom of the grill. Oil the grill rack and place the rabbit on it directly over the drip pan. Grill, uncovered, for 15 minutes. Cover the grill, leaving both the bottom and top air vents open, and grill the rabbit for 15 minutes longer. Remove the lid and, if necessary, add more coals to maintain the heat at 375°–400°F (190°–200°C). Turn the rabbit over and replace the cover. Continue to cook until the meat is opaque throughout at the thickest part of the leg and saddle, about 30 minutes.

❧ Transfer the rabbit to a cutting board. Using kitchen shears or a knife, cut the rabbit into pieces. Arrange on a warmed platter and serve hot.

serves 4

Île-de-France

Brochettes de Rognons, Foie, et Lardons

kidney, liver, and bacon kabobs

When I think of street food in France, these kabobs always come to mind, along with crepes, gaufres (waffles), and now, Vietnamese spring rolls. At fairs of any size, there is always someone grilling these kabobs and handing them out, each stick wrapped in a napkin. Mustard is available on the side, but I like them plain, flavored by the bacon and thyme.

1 lb (500 g) veal liver, about ½ inch (12 mm) thick

6 lamb kidneys

4 slices thick-cut bacon, cut into 1-inch (2.5-cm) pieces

1 teaspoon salt

1 teaspoon freshly ground pepper

1 teaspoon fresh thyme leaves

❧ Prepare a fire in a grill, or preheat a broiler (griller). Soak 24 wooden skewers in water to cover for about 15 minutes.

❧ Cut the liver into 1-inch (2.5-cm) pieces. If the kidneys are encased in fat, trim away the fat with a sharp knife and discard it. Slice the kidneys ¼ inch (6 mm) thick. Drain the skewers. Thread the liver alternately with kidney and bacon onto the skewers. Sprinkle with salt, pepper, and thyme.

❧ Place the skewers on the grill rack or slip under the broiler and grill or broil until browned on the first side, 2–3 minutes. Turn and cook for another 1–2 minutes. The liver should be still slightly pink and soft inside, the kidney cooked through but just barely, and the bacon partially crisped.

❧ Transfer to a warmed platter and serve at once.

serves 8

Le Sud-Ouest

Bifteck Marchand de Vin

steak with shallot–red wine sauce

On a cold spring day in Paris many years ago, I met an old friend at La Muette metro stop at noon. She took me off down the busy street to a very Parisian restaurant where we were ushered to one of the very best tables. We had oysters with a glass of Champagne, followed by bifteck marchand de vin *and a velvety Bordeaux. It was a wonderful lunch, and I cannot see the words* bifteck marchand de vin *without experiencing again my delight that day.*

2 rib steaks, ½–¾ inch (12 mm–2 cm) thick

½ teaspoon salt

1 teaspoon freshly ground pepper

2 teaspoons minced fresh thyme

2 tablespoons unsalted butter

¼ cup (1½ oz/45 g) minced shallots

⅓–½ cup (3–4 fl oz/80–125 ml) dry red wine

fresh flat-leaf (Italian) parsley

꙳ Trim the steaks of excess fat. Pat them dry and sprinkle with the salt, pepper, and thyme, pressing the seasonings into both sides. Heat a heavy, nonstick frying pan over medium-high heat. Add 1 table-spoon of the butter. When it has melted and is near sizzling, put the steaks in the pan and sear them, turning once, for 3–4 minutes on each side for medium rare; the timing will depend upon the thickness of the steaks and the desired amount of doneness. Keep the heat high, but do not let the fat burn. Test for doneness by cutting into one of the steaks. When they are ready, transfer them to a warmed platter and cover loosely with aluminum foil while you prepare the sauce.

꙳ Pour off all but 1 tablespoon of the pan juices. Return the pan to medium heat and add the shallots. Sauté until translucent, 2–3 minutes. Add the wine and deglaze the pan, stirring to dislodge any browned bits on the bottom. Cook until the wine is reduced by half and the mixture has thickened, 2–3 minutes. Stir in the remaining 1 tablespoon butter.

꙳ Pour the hot sauce over the steaks, garnish with the parsley, and serve immediately.

serves 2

Bourgogne et Le Lyonnais

Poulet Demi-Deuil

chicken in partial mourning

I first ate this extraordinary dish at a small hotel in Valensole, in Haute Provence, but its origin is in Lyons. The name comes from the black layer of truffles tucked between the skin and flesh of the breast, which is visible through the skin. For many years, it has been traditional to wear black when mourning the loss of a family member, and certainly fifty years ago, even twenty years ago, one would see many elderly French women dressed entirely or partially in black. Thus, the chicken might be said to be demi-deuil, or in partial mourning, as the truffles cast their color only around the breast, like a cloak. Traditions have changed, of course, and today far fewer people abide by the rule of wearing black to signal bereavement. The classic rendition includes filling the cavity with a bread-and-sausage stuffing, but I was served it without. You can prepare this dish with mushrooms—cèpes are especially good—but, of course, the flavor will be quite different.

1 oz (30 g) fresh black truffles

1 chicken, about 3½ lb (1.75 kg)

1 teaspoon salt

1 teaspoon freshly ground pepper

5 carrots, peeled

3 large leeks, including 2 inches (5 cm) of the green

1 yellow onion stuck with 2 whole cloves

1 turnip, peeled

1 celery stalk

3 fresh flat-leaf (Italian) parsley sprigs

3 fresh thyme sprigs

1 tablespoon unsalted butter

1 tablespoon heavy (double) cream

☙ If you have found the truffles yourself or have bought them directly from a truffle hunter, you will need to clean them. Rinse them with cold water and gently brush away the dirt with a fine-bristled brush, then dry with paper towels. Slice the truffles ⅛ inch (3 mm) thick.

☙ Rinse the chicken and pat dry. Insert your fingers between the skin and the flesh of the chicken breast, gently working your way all the way to the thighs and being careful not to tear the skin. Slip the truffle slices beneath the skin, positioning them to make an attractive pattern. Rub the chicken inside and out with ½ teaspoon each of the salt and pepper.

☙ Place the chicken in a large, heavy pot and add water to cover by 2 inches (5 cm). Add the carrots, leeks, onion, turnip, celery, parsley, thyme, and the remaining ½ teaspoon each salt and pepper. Place over medium-high heat and bring to a boil. Reduce the heat to low and simmer, uncovered, until the chicken is tender and the juices run clear when the thickest part of the thigh is pierced with the tip of a knife, about 1¼ hours.

☙ Using two large wooden spoons, lift the chicken from the pot and set aside. Using a slotted spoon or tongs, lift out the carrots, leeks, onion, turnip, celery, and parsley. Discard the cloves from the onion. Put the vegetables in a blender or food processor and add the butter and cream. Purée until smooth. Taste and adjust the seasonings.

☙ To serve, spoon the warm puréed vegetables onto a warmed serving platter and carefully place the chicken on top. To carve the chicken, remove it to another platter.

serves 4

Languedoc

Poussins Farcis aux Abricots et Figues Sèches

young chickens with apricot-fig stuffing

Apricots and figs, fresh or dried, are beloved fruits of the Mediterranean. They go well with the regional herbs, as you will see here. Rubbing the chickens inside and out with resinous rosemary and sage before roasting subtly flavors the meat and makes a good companion to the savory sweetness of the stuffing, which is also flavored by herbs.

4 young chickens or Cornish hens, 1–1¼ lb (500–625 g) each

1 teaspoon salt

2 teaspoons freshly ground pepper

¼ cup (⅓ oz/10 g) minced fresh sage

¼ cup (⅓ oz/10 g) minced fresh rosemary

STUFFING

4–5 cups (8–10 oz/250–315 g) sliced or cubed two-day-old baguette, pain au levain, or any combination of coarse country breads

1 tablespoon unsalted butter

½ large yellow onion, minced (about 1 cup/ 6 oz/185 g)

1 clove garlic, minced

2 cups (16 fl oz/500 ml) boiling water

½ cup (3 oz/90 g) chopped dried figs

½ cup (3 oz/90 g) chopped dried apricots

3 tablespoons minced fresh rosemary

3 tablespoons minced fresh thyme

1 teaspoon salt

2 teaspoons freshly ground pepper

GLAZE

½ cup (5 oz/155 g) apricot jam

2 tablespoons Banyuls vinegar or balsamic vinegar

fresh rosemary sprigs

❦ Preheat an oven to 400°F (200°C).

❦ Rinse the birds and pat dry. Rub inside and out with the salt and pepper, then with the sage and rosemary. Discard the herbs, or for a stronger impression, leave some of the herbs clinging to the skin or tucked under the skin.

❦ To make the stuffing, place the bread in a large bowl and set aside. In a small saucepan over medium heat, melt the butter. Add the onion and garlic and sauté until translucent, 3–4 minutes. Add the boiling water and pour the mixture over the bread. Turn the bread to soak all the pieces. Let stand until the bread is cool enough to handle and the water has been absorbed, 10–15 minutes. Using your hands, squeeze the bread, breaking it down until a thick paste forms. Add the dried figs and apricots, rosemary, thyme, salt, and pepper, and continue squeezing to incorporate them into the paste.

❦ Spoon the stuffing into the cavities using ⅓–½ cup (3–4 oz/80–125 g) per bird. Do not pack the cavities too full. Gently slip your fingers between the skin and the meat of the breast to make a pocket, and tuck some of the stuffing under the skin as well. Tie the legs together with kitchen string and tuck the wings under the breasts.

❦ Place the birds, breast sides up, on a rack in a roasting pan. Roast the birds for 25 minutes.

❦ While the birds are roasting, prepare the glaze: In a small saucepan over low heat, combine the jam and the vinegar and heat, stirring occasionally, until a syrup forms, 3–4 minutes.

❦ Remove the birds from the oven and, using a pastry brush, coat them with the glaze. Return to the oven and roast until the juices run clear when the thickest part of the thigh is pierced with the tip of a knife, about 25 minutes longer.

❦ Remove the birds from the oven, garnish with rosemary sprigs, and serve.

serves 4

Birds, stuffed and then roasted, are filled with what is at hand: bread, prunes, and walnuts in Gascony, dried apricots in the south, truffles in the Périgord and Haute Provence.

Languedoc

Cassoulet

Cassoulet is a defining dish in Languedoc, from Toulouse in the southwest to Carcassonne standing guard over the plains reaching to Spain to Castelnaudary just past the Gard River. Each of these cities has its own version of the dish, but so do smaller villages and individual families. Some use lamb, others only pork. Confit of goose is a requirement in some households, partridges in others.

In essence, layers of white beans that have been slowly cooked with herbs are interspersed with layers of different cooked meats, thoroughly moistened with the cooking juices of both, topped with a final layer of bread crumbs, and then baked until a thick crust forms and the juices bubble beneath. It is a time-consuming dish to make, and one to satisfy a large group of hearty eaters.

BEANS

3½ cups (1½ lb/750 g) dried white beans such as Great Northern, preferably from a recent harvest

½ lb (250 g) fresh pork rind

1 lb (500 g) lean pork belly

bones reserved from pork loin (see below)

2 yellow onions, thinly sliced

4 cloves garlic, chopped

8 fresh flat-leaf (Italian) parsley sprigs

4 fresh thyme sprigs

2 bay leaves

6 peppercorns

3 whole cloves

1 teaspoon salt

3½ qt (3.5 l) water

PORK LOIN

1½–2 lb (750 g–1 kg) boneless pork loin, bones reserved, tied

1 teaspoon salt

1 teaspoon freshly ground pepper

1 teaspoon fresh thyme leaves

1 teaspoon minced fresh rosemary

2 tablespoons rendered pork, duck, or goose fat or olive oil

1 yellow onion, minced

4 cloves garlic, minced

1 lb (500 g) tomatoes, peeled and chopped

1 bottle (24 fl oz/750 ml) dry white wine

LAMB

2 tablespoons rendered pork, duck, or goose fat or olive oil

2 lb (1 kg) boneless lamb shoulder, cut into 2-inch (5-cm) cubes

1 yellow onion, minced

2 cloves garlic, minced

3 fresh thyme sprigs

½ teaspoon salt

½ teaspoon freshly ground pepper

1 bottle (24 fl oz/750 ml) dry white wine

4 Toulouse or other well-seasoned pure pork sausages

TOPPING

1½ cups (6 oz/185 g) coarse dried bread crumbs

2 tablespoons chopped fresh flat-leaf (Italian) parsley

½ cup (4 oz/125 g) rendered pork, duck, or goose fat, melted

❧ To prepare the beans, pick them over, discarding any stones or misshapen beans. Rinse the beans and drain. Place in a large saucepan with cold water to cover by 3 inches (7.5 cm). Bring to a boil over high heat. Reduce the heat to low and simmer, uncovered, until softened and swollen, about 30 minutes.

❧ Meanwhile, in a saucepan, combine the pork rind and pork belly with water to cover by 3 inches (7.5 cm). Bring to a boil over high heat, reduce the heat to medium, and cook for 20 minutes. Drain and rinse under cold running water. Drain again and cut the rind into ½-inch (12-mm) cubes.

❧ When the beans are ready, drain and place in a large pot. Add the pork rind, pork belly, bones from loin, onions, garlic, parsley, thyme, bay leaves, peppercorns, cloves, salt, and the 3½ qt (3.5 l) water. Bring to a boil over high heat, reduce the heat to low, and cook, uncovered, for about 1 hour.

❧ While the beans are cooking, prepare the pork loin: Rub the pork loin all over with the salt, pepper, thyme, and rosemary. In a heavy pot over medium-high heat, warm the fat or olive oil. When hot, add the pork loin and brown on all sides, turning as necessary, about 8 minutes. Add the onion and garlic and cook, stirring, for 1–2 minutes. Add the tomatoes and 1½ cups (12 fl oz/375 ml) of the wine, reduce the heat to low, cover, and cook until the meat is tender, about 1 hour.

At the same time, prepare the lamb: In a heavy pot over medium-high heat, warm the fat or olive oil. When hot, add the lamb and brown on all sides, turning as necessary, about 8 minutes. Add the onion, garlic, thyme, salt, and pepper and mix well. Pour in the wine, cover, reduce the heat to low, and simmer until the meat is tender, about 1½ hours.

When the pork loin is ready, using tongs, remove it from the pan and add it to the beans. Add the remaining 1½ cups (12 fl oz/375 ml) wine to the pork juices in the pan and deglaze the pan over high heat, stirring to dislodge any browned bits from the pan bottom. Boil until the wine is reduced by half. Pour the juices into the beans.

When the lamb is ready, using a slotted spoon, transfer it to the pot holding the beans, reserving the lamb juices. Add the sausages to the beans and cook over medium-low heat until the juices from the sausages run clear, about 30 minutes.

Preheat an oven to 375°F (190°C).

Using tongs, remove the pork loin, pork belly, and sausages from the beans and place on a cutting board. Cut them into slices about ½ inch (12 mm) thick

and set aside on a plate. Using the slotted spoon, transfer the lamb to the same plate.

Select a 3½–4-qt (3.5–4-l) baking dish or oven-proof saucepan. Using the slotted spoon, scoop out enough beans to form a layer about 1 inch (2.5 cm) deep in the bottom of the baking dish or saucepan.

Top the beans with a layer of the mixed meats. Repeat the layers until all the meats are used, ending with a layer of beans. Ideally, you will have 2 layers of meat. Spoon the reserved juices from the lamb over the beans, and add enough bean broth just to cover the beans. Top evenly with the bread crumbs and the parsley, then pour the melted fat over the top.

Bake until a crust forms, about 15 minutes. Using a large kitchen spoon, break through the crust and spoon the juices that lay beneath it over the top. Bake for another 15 minutes until a second crust forms. Break the crust and spoon over the juices again. Bake for a final 15–20 minutes until the crust forms again.

Serve hot directly from the dish or pan, making sure a variety of meats is included in each serving.

serves 10–12

LES LEGUMES

*The kitchen garden
and the open-air
market are the
hallmarks of French
seasonal cooking.*

FOR MANY YEARS I operated a business that imported French vegetable seeds to the United States, so it should come as no surprise that I have a deep love of French vegetables and all the wonderful ways in which they are cooked. In France, vegetables are treated with the same care and respect given to all other foods. They are also accorded the same sense of pride in *produits du terroir* that is bestowed upon fruits, cheeses, and meats. The dual traditions of the *potager* and the *marché,* the kitchen garden and the open market, have resulted in the *cuisine du potager* and the *cuisine du marché,* together the hallmarks of seasonal cooking.

If you pass a French kitchen garden or market garden in springtime, you are likely to see a stand of fava (broad) beans, their long, waxy pods dangling beneath the leaves and the tops of the plants sporting masses of white blossoms with velvety black throats. In the same garden you would no doubt find radishes, the long scarlet ones tipped with white that, outside of France, are called French breakfast radishes, a name, no doubt, the result of the French custom of eating the young, tender root vegetables with a slice of buttered bread at midmorning. The fat, hollow tops of spring onions will wave in the breeze, next to thick, redveined beet leaves and furry, serrated turnip leaves. Elsewhere in the gardens spring lettuces and dark green spinach plants will be bursting with new growth.

If you visit an open market at the same time, you'll see many of the same vegetables, but in a different setting. Here, when the vendors pass them the scales, the customers eagerly fill them with fresh fava beans, asparagus tips, or spinach leaves. Bunches of radishes, washed sparkling clean, will be lined up in picturesque pyramids, their succulent white roots beckoning you to sample them. The best of these items have been brought by *maraîchers,* local and regional market growers who, in traditional fashion, harvest their own crops, load them into little Renault and Citroën vans, and sell them in the markets in the surrounding villages and cities. When the market closes at

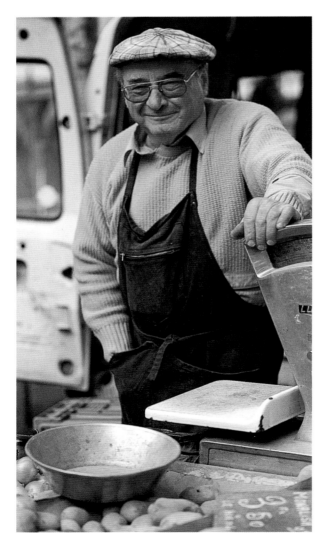

noon, they pack up any wares that are left, have a drink at a café and maybe lunch at a local restaurant, then head home to repeat the process the next day.

As you travel from region to region, and market to market, you'll see that regional vegetable specialties abound. In Brittany and neighboring Normandy, the globe artichokes seem to be the symbol of the area. They are huge, nearly the size of cannonballs, with thick, meaty stems and rounded, notched leaves, and they taste as good as they look. In Provence, you will see much smaller globes with a more tapered leaf. Even more distinctive are the violet artichokes called Violette de Provence. These are considerably smaller than the variety from Brittany, about the size of a large lemon, and are often sold on long, edible stems, bundled together by the count and tied with twine. Eating them raw, dipped in aioli or a vinaigrette, is a wonderful springtime diversion. Cabbages are the pride of Alsace, and in the north you'll find salsify and Belgian endive (chicory/witloof). In the south, in summertime, the shelling beans, sweet peppers (capsicums), and eggplants (aubergines) supply the necessary ingredients for regional dishes like *soupe au pistou* and ratatouille.

A number of national and international seed companies have offices in France. Vilmorin, established in 1789, is the oldest, not only in France, but in the world. Yet it is the smaller regional companies that produce and sell seeds for vegetables that are indigenous to the area or are improved selections from old heirloom strains. J. P. Gautier et Fils is one such company. When I was first sent there by an English seedman who regularly dealt with them, the company was located in one of the old, sprawling eighteenth-century houses in the tiny town of Eyragues, just a short distance from Saint-Rémy. The owner, M. Gautier, was the son of the founder and a very charming Provençal gentleman of perhaps sixty. He escorted me and my partner around his processing plant, pointing out the various machines, carefully crafted models from the early 1900s, that sorted the crop seeds from the chaff and the weed seeds.

When we went into the vast buildings, once a series of barns, where the seeds were stored, it was full of the sweet aroma of carrot and fennel. He showed us the experimental stations outside the town, we visited market growers of melons and lettuces, and then he took us to lunch in Saint-Rémy at a little restaurant where everyone knew him. We see each other occasionally now, and although I miss the old buildings, I know he is pleased with his large, modern facility. I still buy Laury escarole (Batavian endive), a fine oak-leaf lettuce named Cocarde, Musqué de Provence pumpkin, and several selections of leek from him. They perform splendidly in my Mediterranean climate in California.

Throughout France, potatoes are important in the diet, and the wide range of varieties attest to their popularity. In late summer and early fall, *potagers* and market gardens have masses of solid green leaves dotted here and there with early blossoms. The people know their potatoes and grow different varieties for different uses. In the supermarkets you find them bagged

Left top: Artichokes, ubiquitous in Provence, range from large, green, violet-tinged ones with substantial fleshy bases to small, dark brown buds that require greater effort, but yield a sweeter reward. **Left middle:** Eggplants (aubergines) are prevalent in Languedoc-Roussillon, where *aubergines au gratin à la catalane*—eggplant stuffed with its own pulp, onion, olive oil, bread, parsley, and garlic—and *aubergines à la nîmoise*—eggplant topped with ham, olive oil, bread crumbs, and garlic—are local favorites. **Left bottom:** The humble potato inspires countless refined and rustic preparations: mashed with fresh cheese in *la truffade,* combined with salt cod in *brandade de vendredi,* or sliced and baked with cabbage and pork. **Above:** The traditional ball game of *boules,* or *pétanque,* similar to Italian bocce, is especially popular among older gentlemen in the south.

Above: In the Loire Valley, the romantic fifteenth-century Château d'Ussé, with its white turrets and fanciful setting, inspired author Charles Perrault's *Sleeping Beauty.* **Near right:** Lettuce abounds in market gardens in the south, where innumerable types of different color, leaf shape, and flavor thrive in the mild Provençal climate. **Far right top:** The brilliant purple flush of the artichoke plant's thistles announce the presence of the globelike edible bud. **Far right middle:** Selecting olives can be a challenge in France, where there are a wealth of choices: green, black, purple, and white; large and small; dry and firm; pulpy and juicy. **Far right bottom:** Vine-ripened tomatoes, popular throughout France, are particularly prevalent in Provençal cooking, where any dish described as *à la provençale* comes with the promise of tomatoes, garlic, and olive oil.

with a color-coded label announcing their varietal names and which ones are best for sautéing, which for boiling, and which for baking. One friend, in a hurry, picked up a bag of boiling potatoes when she wanted baking. She spent a good deal of time at dinner apologizing for her potato gratin, explaining she had used the wrong potatoes, which dissolved instead of holding their sliced shape. It was certainly delicious, with its crisp crunch and soft, creamy potatoes, but it wasn't precisely what she had wanted.

My French neighbors Maurice and Françoise grow a goodly plot of potatoes each year, dig them in late summer or early fall, then store them in their *cave* to use through June or even July of the next year. One year I dug potatoes with them and thoroughly enjoyed myself. First, Maurice came through with the tractor, loosening the plants. Then Françoise, assorted children, and I followed behind with big, heavy-duty plastic buckets. We dug down with our hands into the loosened dirt to find the potatoes, becoming excited when an especially large one was discovered, or when a group of four or five, still attached to its leafy tops, was unearthed. Any funny-shaped ones we set aside to show off and laugh over later. At my home in California, I grow several varieties of potato, partly for the sheer pleasure of digging them up months later.

Although the French have a strong interest in both the cultivation and consumption of vegetables, there is not a French vegetarian tradition. Nonetheless, many dishes are vegetarian or nearly so. I think this is partly because meat was a luxury for so many years and remains quite expensive, and also because people had their own *potagers*. A *potager,* unlike an American harvest garden, which is planted in spring and harvested in summer, is a year-round kitchen garden in which one is both planting and harvesting throughout the calendar. It is a custom that ensures there will always be something fresh from the garden, something at its peak of quality. In French homes especially, I have noticed that the main course is often a seasonal vegetable gratin followed by a salad. In fall, it might be a pumpkin

gratin; in winter, potatoes; in spring, beets or artichokes; and in summer, shelling beans or eggplant. The dish is carefully made with the freshest vegetables, milk or stock, and herbs, and finished with a topping of local cheese and perhaps buttered bread crumbs. I have also been offered, both in restaurants and in homes, a dish of fresh pasta dressed with olive oil and vegetables. One favorite is made with squash blossoms and black olives, another with shelling beans and wilted escarole. The combinations, using only fresh vegetables and pantry staples, are varied and countless.

Vegetables are also braised in wine, in cider, in eau-de-vie, and in beer, depending upon the local products. In the Auvergne or the Dordogne, they are combined with chestnuts, while in Provence they are paired with pine nuts or almonds. Creamed vegetables, buttered vegetables, and vegetables simply well seasoned with herbs and their blossoms are central to the French table.

In many vegetable dishes, meat plays the role of a seasoning element. *Jambon cru* is especially popular, as it adds a salty component along with a little fat. Thin slices might be used to wrap heads of Belgian endive before they are sauced and baked, stirred into a pot of tender *petits pois,* or used in stuffings for zucchini (courgettes), turnips, or even mushrooms. All kinds of sausages play a similar role, appearing in egg dishes, as ingredients in stuffings for vegetables, or in sauces for pasta or rice.

Thus, there is no doubt that vegetables are an important part of every meal in France, whether used in salads or soups, served as first courses, or treated as main courses or side dishes. The tradition of *cuisine du potager* and *cuisine du marché* is the source of the fine cooking with seasonal fresh ingredients that I love about French culinary custom, and forms the base that is responsible for the best of the country's regional fare. Often simple, rarely pretentious, the local table is always good.

Left top: Gothic architecture flourished in the thirteenth century, as exemplified by this church in the Champagne region. **Left bottom:** A classic straw market basket hangs on the door of a Beaune home, ready for use. **Below top:** Cabbages and leeks appear in numerous recipes, especially those for the soups traditionally made in the Ile-de-France, such as *potage parisien* (vegetable soup), *potage Parmentier* (thick potato soup), and *potage bonne femme* (potato and leek soup). **Below bottom:** *Potagers,* kitchen gardens found throughout France, provide a supply of fresh vegetables and herbs year-round.

Provence

Asperges et Artichauts aux Olives Noires et Parmesan

sautéed asparagus and artichokes with black olives and parmesan

In Provence and elsewhere in southern France, asparagus and artichokes are in season at the same time, stacked high next to each other in the markets or growing side by side in the potager. *They can be sautéed together for either a side dish or a first course.*

2 lemons, halved

8 small artichokes

2 tablespoons extra-virgin olive oil

1 lb (500 g) tender green asparagus spears, woody ends removed and cut into 1-inch (2.5-cm) lengths

2 cloves garlic

2 fresh thyme sprigs

1 bay leaf

8 salt-cured black olives

¼ cup (1 oz/30 g) shaved Parmesan cheese

☙ Have ready a large bowl of water to which you have added the juice of 1 lemon. Working with 1 artichoke at a time, cut off the stem near the base. Pull back and snap off the first layer of leaves. Slice off the upper third of the artichoke. Rub the cut surfaces with a lemon half. Continue to pull back and snap off layers of the leaves until you reach the tender, pale inner yellow leaves. Cut off any remaining tough leaf tips. Rub with a lemon half. If the choke in the center has developed any prickly tips, scoop them out with the edge of a spoon. If it is only furry, leave it, as it will be edible after cooking. Depending upon their size, cut the artichokes lengthwise into 4 or 6 pieces, and drop them into the lemon water. When ready to begin cooking, drain and pat dry.

☙ In a heavy ovenproof pan over medium heat, warm the olive oil. Add the artichokes, asparagus, garlic, thyme, and bay leaf and sauté until the artichokes and asparagus glisten, 2–3 minutes. Cover, reduce the heat to low, and cook, stirring occasionally, until tender, 5–6 minutes. Uncover, add the olives, and cook, stirring, until the artichokes are tender and slightly golden, 2–3 minutes longer. Transfer to a warmed serving bowl and top with the Parmesan cheese. Serve warm.

serves 4

Franche-Comté et Les Alpes

Gratin Dauphinois

potato gratin

Dauphiné, one of the ancient provinces of France, today is incorporated into the governmental departments of the Hautes-Alpes, Isère, and the Drôme. This potato dish is a classic of the region. Of course, there are many versions of this wonderful gratin, which makes an ideal accompaniment to meats, but this one is quite straightforward and easy to prepare. The main thing to keep in mind is the thinner the potato slices, the better they will melt together to form a distinctive texture.

1 clove garlic

4 tablespoons (2 oz/60 g) unsalted butter

2 lb (1 kg) waxy boiling potatoes such as Red Rose, White Rose, or Bintje, peeled, if desired, and cut into slices ⅛ inch (3 mm) thick

1 teaspoon salt

½ teaspoon freshly ground pepper

⅛ teaspoon ground nutmeg

¼ lb (125 g) Beaufort or Gruyère cheese, shredded

1 cup (8 fl oz/250 ml) milk

☙ Preheat an oven to 425°F (220°C).

☙ Rub a shallow baking dish with the garlic and grease heavily with 1 tablespoon of the butter. Spread half of the sliced potatoes in the prepared baking dish. Sprinkle with half each of the salt, pepper, nutmeg, and cheese. Cut 2 tablespoons of the butter into small bits and use to dot the surface. Spread the remaining potatoes on top and sprinkle them with the remaining salt, pepper, nutmeg, and cheese. Cut the remaining 1 tablespoon butter into small bits and use them to dot the top.

☙ In a small saucepan over medium-high heat, bring the milk just to a boil. Pour the milk over the potatoes, sliding a knife between the edges of the pan and the potatoes to help the milk run underneath.

☙ Bake until the milk is absorbed and a golden brown crust forms, 35–45 minutes. The timing depends upon how thinly the potatoes are sliced. Serve immediately directly from the dish.

serves 6

Pays de la Loire

Asperges au Beurre d'Estragon

asparagus with tarragon butter

Asparagus is surely one of the quintessential French vegetables. In the markets in spring, you can find white asparagus in sizes from pencil-thin to nearly as thick as a fist next to green asparagus tips anchored by slender stalks. White asparagus, whose fibrous stems must be peeled, has a decidedly bittersweet taste. Green asparagus, in contrast, is quite sweet. Both varieties are grown and then harvested by cutting the stalk beneath the ground with special asparagus knives. Different varieties, not growth habit, account for the difference in color and taste. Certain varieties have been developed that are amenable to being grown beneath the ground, and they thus become blanched from the lack of chlorophyll. This simple butter-and-herb treatment is delicious with white or green asparagus. If you are using the former, you will need to cook them longer, especially if they are thick.

1 lb (500 g) asparagus spears

3 tablespoons unsalted butter, at room temperature

1 tablespoon minced fresh tarragon

❧ Gently bend each asparagus spear near the bottom of the stem until the woody end snaps off. If using white asparagus, peel the stalks with a vegetable peeler. Place the spears in a steamer rack over boiling water, cover, and steam until just tender when pierced with a fork, 3–4 minutes for green asparagus or 15–20 minutes for white asparagus (depending upon thickness). If using green asparagus, the color should still be bright green. Remove the asparagus from the steamer and rinse briefly under cold running water to halt the cooking. Drain and set aside.

❧ In a bowl, mix together the butter and tarragon until creamy.

❧ Arrange the still-warm asparagus on a platter and spread the butter over them. Serve immediately.

serves 4

Franche-Comté et Les Alpes

Tartiflette

sautéed potatoes with reblochon cheese

Reblochon, a raw cow's milk cheese that benefits from AOC standing, dates from the thirteenth century. At that time, the authorities levied a tax on the amount of milk produced each day. In order to avoid having to pay the whole amount, the peasants in the area around the town of Thônes would only partially milk their cows. Then once the collectors left, they quickly began milking again, and from this second milking they made a cheese. Reblaca means "stealing" in the dialect of the area, and so, the story goes, reblochon was the cheese made from "stolen milk."

The cheese is made in a wheel about ten inches (25 cm) in diameter that develops a bright orange crust. When quite ripe—it is aged a minimum of three weeks—it is supple and bendable, with an interior that is meltingly creamy. This is the stage at which it must be for making tartiflette. *The round is cut in half crosswise to make two rounds, and the two rounds are layered with cooked potatoes and onions, then the whole is baked until the cheese melts. It is a hearty alpine dish that needs to be washed down with one of the local wines, such as the red Mondeuse, and followed by a green salad.*

1 tablespoon unsalted butter

1 tablespoon extra-virgin olive oil

3 lb (1.5 kg) waxy boiling potatoes such as Belle de Fontanay, Yellow Finn, White Rose, or Red Rose, peeled and cut into ½-inch (12-mm) cubes

½ teaspoon salt

2½ yellow onions, cut into slivers ¼ inch (6 mm) thick

¼ cup (1½ oz/45 g) lardons or bacon strips, each about 1 inch (2.5 cm) long by ¼ inch (6 mm) wide

½ teaspoon freshly ground pepper

½–⅔ cup (4–5 fl oz/125–160 ml) crème fraîche

1 whole ripe reblochon cheese

❦ Preheat an oven to 375°F (190°C).

❦ In a large, deep, ovenproof frying pan over medium heat, melt the butter with the olive oil. When the butter foams, add the potatoes and sauté until they begin to turn golden, 10–15 minutes. Sprinkle with the salt and add the onions and lardons or bacon strips. Cook, turning occasionally and making sure nothing is sticking, about 10 minutes longer. Cover, reduce the heat to low, and cook until the potatoes are thoroughly tender, 7–10 minutes longer. Stir in the pepper.

❦ Remove half of the potatoes and onions to a deep plate. Pour one-half of the crème fraîche evenly over the potatoes remaining in the frying pan. Cut the cheese in half horizontally to make 2 rounds. If desired, scrape away a little of the orange crust, as it has a strong flavor, or if you like, leave it intact. Place 1 round, cut side down, on the potatoes in the frying pan. Cover this with the potatoes from the deep plate to make a second layer. Pour the remaining crème fraîche evenly over the top, and place the second cheese round, cut side down, on this layer.

❦ Bake until the cheese has melted into the potatoes, about 15 minutes. Serve immediately directly from the frying pan, scooping out the portions with a serving spoon or spatula.

serves 4–6

Noix

Hazelnuts (filberts), walnuts, almonds, and, of course, chestnuts are an important part of the regional cooking wherever they are grown. They are crushed to make oil, ground to make flour, and used in various stages of ripeness. Green walnuts, gathered before the inner shell has formed, are used to make the popular aperitif *vin de noix* in Haute Provence, Gascony, and Savoy. Near Grenoble, a major walnut-producing area, along with the region around Bordeaux, a small percentage of the walnut crop is harvested early when the nuts are mature, yet still soft. Considered a specialty, they have a slightly green taste and are spread onto slices of buttered bread. Throughout the year, mature walnuts are incorporated into sweet and savory dishes, and walnut mustard is a specialty in the Dordogne.

Green almonds, ripened only to the stage when the kernel is fully formed beneath the furry green covering but the shell is still soft, are cracked open and eaten with salt at aperitif time. The mature nuts are ground, slivered, or chopped and cooked in pastries and sweets. They are used to thicken and flavor sauces, especially in the south, just as hazelnuts are in the alpine regions.

Chestnuts are steeped in sugar syrup for *marrons glacés,* cooked whole to use in stews, and made into purées for use in confections. Yet, the first thought that comes to mind when I think of chestnuts is of the chestnut braziers on city street corners during winter, and of the vendors who wrap the hot nuts in cones of newspaper for selling to passersby.

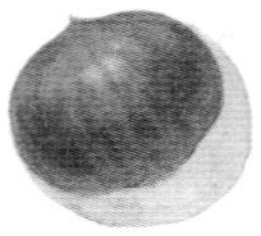

Provence

Fèves aux Fleurs de Thym

sautéed fava beans with thyme blossoms

One of the best things about spring and early summer in the potager *is the harvest of fava beans. When you combine them with the lavender thyme blossoms that bloom during the same months in Provence, you have a dish so delicious, so satisfying, that nearly all else pales beside it. I leave the young beans unpeeled, just as my neighbors do, because I too like the characteristic, slightly bitter taste and crunchiness of the skins. Older fava beans should be peeled, however. Immerse the shelled beans in a small saucepan of boiling water and blanch for twenty seconds. Drain and, when cool enough to handle, slip off the skins.*

2 tablespoons extra-virgin olive oil
2 cloves garlic, minced
2 lb (1 kg) very young fava (broad) beans, shelled
½ cup (4 fl oz/125 ml) water
2 tablespoons fresh thyme blossoms
scant ½ teaspoon salt
½ teaspoon freshly ground pepper

In a heavy saucepan over medium heat, warm the olive oil. Add the garlic and sauté just until the garlic softens, 1–2 minutes. Add the fava beans and sauté, stirring, until the skins begin to pop and change color, 4–5 minutes. Add the water, thyme blossoms, salt, and pepper. Reduce the heat to low, cover, and cook until the beans are tender and the water has evaporated, 5–6 minutes.

Transfer to a warmed serving dish and serve immediately.

serves 4

Alsace-Lorraine

Chou Rouge aux Pommes et Genièvre

red cabbage with apples and juniper

This simple cabbage dish is a superb accompaniment to pork chops, sausage, or pork roast. The apples contribute their sweetness, the juniper imparts a taste of the forest, and the vinegar gives a hint of acidity.

1 head red cabbage, about ¾ lb (375 g)

4 apples such as Granny Smith, Gala, or Golden Delicious

3 tablespoons unsalted butter

1 red (Spanish) onion, minced

3 juniper berries

¼ cup (2 fl oz/60 ml) red wine vinegar

¼ cup (2 fl oz/60 ml) chicken stock

½ teaspoon salt

½ teaspoon freshly ground pepper

1 teaspoon minced fresh chives

♛ Cut the cabbage in half and remove the core. Place the halves, flat sides down, on a cutting board and slice thinly. Set aside. Halve and core 2 of the apples, then cut them, leaving them unpeeled, into 1-inch (2.5-cm) cubes. Set aside.

♛ In a heavy saucepan over medium heat, melt the butter. Add the onion and sauté until translucent, 2–3 minutes. Add the cubed apples and sauté until slightly softened, 3–4 minutes longer. Add the cabbage and the juniper berries and sauté until the cabbage is glistening and the color has lightened, 5–6 minutes. Add the vinegar and deglaze the pan, stirring to dislodge any bits clinging to the bottom. Add the stock, salt, and pepper and bring to a boil. Reduce the heat to low, cover, and simmer until the cabbage is pale pink and tender, about 15 minutes.

♛ While the cabbage is cooking, peel, halve, and core the remaining 2 apples, then grate on the large holes of a handheld shredder-grater. At the end of 15 minutes, remove the cabbage from the heat and stir in three-fourths of the grated apple. Transfer to a warmed serving bowl, top with the remaining grated apple and the chives, and serve.

serves 4 or 5

Languedoc

Girolles à la Crème

chanterelles with crème fraîche

Chanterelles, known as girolles *in France, are apricot-colored, horn-shaped mushrooms that grow in association with conifers and oaks. They are considered one of the finest mushrooms and are used in gratins, pasta dishes, and savory tarts, or simply sautéed in olive oil or butter with garlic and parsley. Chanterelles grow abundantly in many regions of France, but they are especially popular in Languedoc and Provence.*

1 lb (500 g) fresh chanterelle mushrooms, brushed clean

2 tablespoons unsalted butter

1 tablespoon extra-virgin olive oil

¼ teaspoon salt

1 teaspoon minced garlic

1 tablespoon minced fresh flat-leaf (Italian) parsley

¼ teaspoon freshly ground pepper

½ cup (4 fl oz/125 ml) crème fraîche

🦪 Cut large mushrooms through the stem ends into halves or quarters, but leave smaller ones whole.

🦪 In a frying pan over medium heat, melt the butter with the olive oil. When the butter foams, add the mushrooms and salt. Turn a time or two, then cover and cook, shaking the pan from time to time, until the mushrooms have released some of their juices and are lightly browned, about 10 minutes.

🦪 Add the garlic, parsley, and pepper and cook, uncovered, stirring occasionally, until the mushrooms are glistening and have rendered more of their juices, 1–2 minutes longer. Add the crème fraîche, raise the heat to medium-high, and cook, stirring, until the cream thickens and blends with the juices, 1–2 minutes longer.

🦪 Transfer the mushrooms and their sauce to a warmed serving bowl and serve immediately.

serves 3 or 4

Champagne et Le Nord

Gratin de Betteraves aux Lardons

beet gratin with lardons

In many French markets, beets are found precooked, sold alongside the fresh vegetables, ready to be peeled and used right away. Most potagers, especially those in the north, have a healthy planting of beets, and the sturdy roots, as well as the leaves, are used in numerous dishes. In this hearty dish, thick-cut bacon can be substituted for the lardons.

3 lb (1.5 kg) beets

1½ lb (750 g) baking potatoes such as russet

½ cup (3 oz/90 g) lardons, each about 1 inch (2.5 cm) long and ¼ inch (6 mm) thick

4 tablespoons (2 oz/60 g) unsalted butter

¾ cup (3 oz/90 g) shredded Beaufort or Gruyère cheese

1 teaspoon salt

1 teaspoon freshly ground pepper

1 tablespoon minced fresh rosemary

1 cup (8 fl oz/250 ml) heavy (double) cream

¾ cup (6 fl oz/180 ml) milk

⅓ cup (¾ oz/20 g) fresh bread crumbs

If the beet greens are intact, trim them off, leaving about ½ inch (12 mm) of the stems; reserve the greens for another use. Place the beets in a saucepan, add water to cover, and bring to a boil over high heat. Reduce the heat to medium-low, cover, and cook until tender, about 1 hour. At the same time, place the potatoes in a saucepan with water to cover and bring to a boil over high heat. Reduce the heat to medium, cover, and cook until tender when pierced, 45–50 minutes.

Drain the beets and potatoes, keeping them separated. When cool enough to handle, peel them and cut into slices ¼ inch (6 mm) thick. Set aside separately. Preheat an oven to 350°F (180°C).

In a frying pan over medium heat, sauté the lardons until translucent, 3–4 minutes. Using a slotted spoon, transfer to paper towels to drain.

Using 1 tablespoon of the butter, grease a 2½-by-8-by-10-inch (6-by-20-by-25-cm) gratin dish. Arrange a layer of half the beet slices in the prepared dish. Sprinkle with one-half of the lardons, and then

with one-third each of the cheese, salt, pepper, and rosemary. Cut the remaining 3 tablespoons butter into small bits and use 1 tablespoon to dot the top. Cover with a layer of all the potato slices. Sprinkle with the remaining lardons and half each of the remaining cheese, salt, pepper, and rosemary. Dot with 1 tablespoon of the butter. Add a final layer of beets and top with the remaining cheese, salt, pepper, and rosemary. Pour the cream and milk over all. Top evenly with the bread crumbs and dot with the remaining 1 tablespoon butter.

Bake until the sauce is bubbling and the top is golden brown, 30–40 minutes. Remove from the oven, cover loosely with aluminum foil, and let stand for 10 minutes. Serve directly from the baking dish.

serves 8

Le Sud-Ouest

Courgettes Chaudes aux Noix et Roquefort

warm zucchini with walnuts and roquefort

When the Roquefort cheese is crumbled over the warm zucchini, it melts and mingles with the walnut oil just enough to make the sauce. It can be served as a first course, but it also makes a fine accompaniment to fish or chicken.

3 zucchini (courgettes), thinly sliced

3 tablespoons walnut oil

1 teaspoon red wine vinegar

½ teaspoon freshly ground pepper

2 oz (60 g) Roquefort cheese

¼ cup (1 oz/30 g) walnuts, coarsely chopped

Place the zucchini slices on a rack in a steamer over boiling water, cover, and steam until just tender, about 3 minutes.

Transfer the zucchini slices to a bowl, pour the walnut oil and vinegar over them, and then sprinkle with the pepper. Crumble the cheese over the warm zucchini and turn the slices. Add half of the walnuts and turn again. Sprinkle with the remaining walnuts and serve immediately.

serves 4 or 5

Le Centre

Navets Farcis

stuffed turnips

Turnips remain popular in France, where they are given a number of respectable treatments. This dish was inspired by a similar one I had in the Berry. The more mature the turnips, the more peppery they will taste, an appealing flavor that will permeate the stuffing.

4 large turnips, about ⅓ lb (155 g) each

scant 1 teaspoon sugar

1 lb (500 g) bulk pork sausage

¼ cup (1¼ oz/37 g) finely chopped hazelnuts (filberts)

¼ cup (1½ oz/45 g) dried currants

1 tablespoon minced fresh sage

❀ Preheat an oven to 350°F (180°C). Slice off the upper one-fourth of each turnip and reserve. Using a melon baller or a small spoon, scoop out the center of each turnip, leaving a shell about ½ inch (12 mm) thick. Reserve the flesh.

❀ Bring a large saucepan three-fourths full of water to a boil over high heat. Add the turnip shells and the sliced-off upper portions. Parboil until half-cooked, 6–7 minutes. Drain and set aside.

❀ Mince half of the scooped-out turnip flesh. (Reserve the remaining flesh for another use or discard.) Sprinkle a scant ¼ teaspoon of the sugar over the inside walls of each turnip. In a bowl, combine the minced turnip, sausage, hazelnuts, currants, and sage and mix well.

❀ Put the turnip shells in a baking dish that is just large enough to hold them snugly. Fill each shell with the stuffing, heaping it about 1 inch (2.5 cm) above the rim of the turnip. Pour water into the baking dish to a depth of ½ inch (12 mm) and put the dish in the oven.

❀ Bake until the stuffing is cooked and browned and the skin of the turnip can be easily pierced, 1¼–1½ hours. Place the tops on the stuffed turnips during the last 10 minutes of cooking, if desired.

❀ Transfer to a warmed platter or individual plates and serve immediately.

serves 4

Les Marchés en Plein Air

For me, the outdoor markets, *les marchés en plein air,* are France's greatest attraction. I can date my life by the open markets I've been in and by what I saw and did or didn't buy. I am still haunted by things I've wanted to purchase and eat or cook, but couldn't: the baby eels in Perpignan on a Saturday in spring, the magnificent venison roast at a market near Châteauroux in the Berry, mushrooms as big as my fist in Dijon.

It is impossible for me to pass up a market, no matter how impractical it might be. Quickly I find a parking spot, usually at a distance from the stalls unless I am there before nine. Grabbing a basket I keep handy in the car, I head out at a brisk pace for the brightly colored umbrellas and awnings that signal the market's riot of seductive sights and smells. It's easy to while away the morning walking up and down the rows of vendors, inspecting the fruits, vegetables, herbs, spices, charcuterie, cheeses, and sundry items.

Everywhere in France, the open market is an integral part of life, a place where locals meet, chat, and, above all, avail themselves of the incredible bounty of their land and people. Saturday and Sunday markets are especially lively, because many people are off work. By noon crowds have begun to gather at the cafés that invariably border a part of the market. Families and friends meet at a favorite café to have an aperitif and watch the shoppers swirl by. Sometimes, the aperitif turns into a simple lunch, a pâté sandwich perhaps, or, if the tables are part of a brasserie or bistro, a *plat du jour, steak-frites,* or a plate of oysters. Slowly the market decamps, the streets are swept, and by two o'clock there is little trace of the whirl of activity, food, and fragrance that makes up French outdoor markets.

Provence

Poivrons Rôtis

roasted red peppers

In Haute Provence, my neighbor's mother, whom everyone called Mémé, an affectionate term for grandmother, was of Italian peasant stock from Calabria. She had beautiful olive skin, a head of magnificent, thick, pure white hair, and the kind of profile beloved by Renaissance painters. A terrible flirt, even at eighty, she charmed everyone, including my husband. When he first met her, we had been invited to her daughter's home for dinner. The first course was homemade charcuterie and olives, but Mémé leaned over toward my husband, touched his hand briefly, and said she was going to get him something special, something she herself had made. Off she went to the kitchen, a bulky figure in black, her legs bowed, but full of grace nonetheless. She returned with a bowl of roasted red peppers in olive oil with garlic and thyme and set it in front of my husband. A small, possessive smile crossed her face as she did. They were indeed delicious, and although roasted red peppers are a classic of Provence, hers seemed especially good. The peppers can also be roasted over a charcoal fire.

> 5 meaty red bell peppers (capsicums)
> 2 cloves garlic, halved
> 4 fresh thyme sprigs
> ¼ teaspoon salt
> ¼ teaspoon freshly ground pepper
> ¼ cup (2 fl oz/60 ml) extra-virgin olive oil

❦ Preheat a broiler (griller). Arrange the peppers on a broiler pan and slip under the broiler. Broil (grill), turning as needed, until blackened and blistered on all sides. Remove the peppers from the broiler, drape loosely with aluminum foil, and let cool for 10 minutes, then peel away the skins. Gently pull or cut out the stems. Make a single lengthwise slit in each pepper and remove the seeds and ribs. Slice the peppers lengthwise into quarters.

❦ Place the peppers in a glass or ceramic bowl or jar and add the garlic, thyme, salt, and pepper. Pour in the olive oil and turn to coat the peppers evenly.

❦ Serve warm or at room temperature. The peppers will keep, covered, in the refrigerator for up to a week. Bring to room temperature before serving.

serves 4

Provence

Choux Brocolis à l'Ail

broccoli with olive oil and grated garlic

I had never eaten broccoli cooked this way until I had dinner one fall evening with two of my neighbors in Provence, both of Italian origin. For the first course, Françoise brought to the table a big bowl of broccoli cut that afternoon from their potager. It had been cooked until it was limp and rather olive green. She took several cloves of garlic and grated them over the top, then sprinkled the broccoli with olive oil. It was sublime. Since then, I have made it many times, offering it both as a side dish and as a first course.

> 1½ lb (750 g) broccoli
> 3 cups (24 fl oz/750 ml) water
> 1 teaspoon salt, plus salt for passing
> ¼ cup (2 fl oz/60 ml) extra-virgin olive oil
> 6 cloves garlic
> pepper mill for passing

❦ Cut off and discard the tough ends of the broccoli stalks. Cut each stalk lengthwise into quarters or thirds, cutting through the florets and stems.

❦ In a saucepan over medium-high heat, combine the broccoli, water, and 1 teaspoon salt and bring to a boil. Cover, reduce the heat to low, and cook until the broccoli has lost its bright green color and has become soft and tender, 15–20 minutes.

❦ Drain the broccoli and transfer to a warmed serving bowl. Pour the olive oil over it and, using a grater, grate on about half the garlic. Serve immediately. Pass the remaining garlic, along with the grater, and salt and pepper at the table.

serves 4

The custom of the potager, with planting and harvesting throughout the calendar, ensures there will always be something fresh from the garden.

Provence

Salade de Tomates

tomato salad

It isn't summer in Provence unless there is some sort of tomato salad at least once a day, if not twice. Sometimes the tomatoes will be sliced, other times quartered. The salad might include anchovies, green peppers (capsicums), fresh or aged goat cheese, onions, cucumbers, or olives. It is an ideal accompaniment to grilled fish and chops, or makes a fine first course on its own.

6 ripe tomatoes, thinly sliced

2 tablespoons minced red (Spanish) onion

½ teaspoon salt

½ teaspoon freshly ground pepper

¼ cup (⅓ oz/10 g) minced fresh basil

3 tablespoons extra-virgin olive oil

1 tablespoon red wine vinegar

☗ Arrange the tomato slices on a platter. Sprinkle with the red onion, salt, and pepper, and scatter the basil over the top. Drizzle with the olive oil and the vinegar. Serve immediately.

serves 4–6

Pays de la Loire

Concombres Sautés à l'Aneth

sautéed cucumbers with dill

Although we think of dill as a northern European herb, it is also used in France, albeit only infrequently. Cucumbers have a larger Gallic profile, probably having taken root in French soil sometime in the fourteenth century, following their considerable popularity in the gardens of the ancient Romans and their descendants.

This is a wonderful preparation to accompany fish of all kinds, either served alongside in a scoop or spread beneath as a bed. The cucumbers soften and absorb a little of the broth as they cook, while the dill enhances their flavor and that of the fish.

2 cucumbers

1 teaspoon unsalted butter

¼ teaspoon salt

¼ teaspoon freshly ground white pepper

¼ cup (2 fl oz/60 ml) chicken stock

2 tablespoons chopped fresh dill

☗ Peel the cucumbers, then cut them in half crosswise. Cut again lengthwise and scrape out the seeds with a spoon. Cut crosswise into slices ¼ inch (6 mm) thick.

☗ In a frying pan over medium heat, melt the butter. When it foams, add the cucumbers, salt, and pepper and sauté for 1 minute. Add the stock and continue to cook until the cucumbers are soft and translucent, 2–3 minutes longer. Stir in the dill and remove from the heat.

☗ Transfer to a warmed serving dish and serve immediately.

serves 4

Alsace-Lorraine

Carottes à l'Aneth

braised carrots with dill

To me, it is imperative to have braised carrots with veal or beef stews, along with either buttered noodles or potatoes, because the sweetness of the carrots brings all into balance. They make an excellent side for other meats and fish as well. Other herbs may be used instead of the dill, such as thyme, rosemary, or sage, but in smaller amounts.

The wild carrot had been known for centuries in France, but it was employed primarily for medicinal purposes. It wasn't until the eighteenth century, after the French seed house of Vilmorin-Andrieux undertook the selection and breeding of carrots for vegetable production for the market growers, that today's fleshy orange root became the standard.

Carrots, both raw and cooked, are much appreciated in France, and they have become one of my favorite vegetables, especially when given a simple treatment with herbs.

6 carrots, cut into slices ¼ inch (6 mm) thick

2 cups (16 fl oz/500 ml) water

½ cup (4 fl oz/125 ml) chicken stock

1 teaspoon salt

1½ tablespoons unsalted butter

½ teaspoon freshly ground pepper

3 tablespoons minced fresh dill

❦ In a saucepan, combine the carrots, water, stock, and ½ teaspoon of the salt. (If using salted stock, use less salt.) Bring to a boil over medium-high heat, reduce the heat to low, and simmer until the carrots are nearly tender, about 10 minutes. Remove from the heat and drain well.

❦ Return the carrots to the saucepan and add the butter, the remaining ½ teaspoon salt, and the pepper. Cover and cook over the lowest heat until the butter is nearly absorbed, about 5 minutes.

❦ Transfer to a warmed serving bowl, stir in the dill, and serve immediately.

serves 4

Champignons Sauvages Grillés à l'Ail et Persil

grilled wild mushrooms with garlic
and parsley

*In France, hunting for wild mushrooms is a national
pastime, and in fall, when the mushrooms follow the
first rains, they appear on menus in various forms,
including in stews, stuffed as first courses, sautéed as
accompaniments, and sometimes just simply grilled, one
of my favorite preparations. Sanguins, which are firm
textured with a concave cap and faintly orange flesh,
are what I prefer for grilling.*

*Like the French, I love to go mushroom hunting, and
over the years I have learned to identify a number of
species. When I find ones I am not sure about, I take
them to the local pharmacist, who identifies them
for me. It is a service that all French pharmacies offer.*

*16 fresh mushrooms such as cèpe, chanterelle, or
sanguin*

*3 tablespoons extra-virgin olive oil, plus more
for drizzling*

½ teaspoon salt

½ teaspoon freshly ground pepper

4 cloves garlic, minced

*¼ cup (⅓ oz / 10 g) minced fresh flat-leaf
(Italian) parsley*

✤ Prepare a fire in a charcoal grill, or preheat a
broiler (griller). Trim off the stem end from each
mushroom and brush away any dirt or leaves with
a stiff brush. Put the mushrooms in a bowl with the
3 tablespoons olive oil, salt, pepper, half of the garlic,
and half of the parsley. Turn to coat well. Mix together the remaining garlic and parsley; set aside.

✤ When the coals are medium-hot, oil the grill rack
or, if the mushrooms are small, a hinged grill basket.
Place the mushrooms, stem sides down, on the rack
or in the basket. Grill until lightly golden on the first
side, 3–4 minutes. Turn, top with the remaining garlic and parsley, and drizzle with a little oil. Grill until
golden, 3–4 minutes longer. If using a broiler, cook
the mushrooms, stem sides down, on a broiler pan
about 3 inches (7.5 cm) from the heat source as
directed for the charcoal grill.

✤ Transfer to a warmed platter and serve hot.

serves 3 or 4

Le Potager

No matter where you travel in France, you'll find *potagers*. These year-round kitchen gardens, like the open markets, are the source of the fresh vegetables and herbs that make even the simplest French food exquisite. Freshly dug potatoes, just-picked *haricots verts,* shiny firm eggplants (aubergines), crisp, white heads of cauliflower, slender green asparagus stalks, and solid, purple-topped turnips all commonly travel from the *potager* to the table in a matter of hours.

The gardens aren't large. Their purpose is to supply the kitchen on a daily basis with fresh vegetables, and they succeed admirably. *Potagers* are so important in French life that they are often detailed in deeds. My own deed includes *"un jardin potager avec droit à un puits, un sol de 96 centiares,"* that is, "a kitchen garden with the rights to a well, 96 square meters of ground." Even as late as the mid-twentieth century, having a potager was considered necessary in many parts of France to ensure fresh vegetables of good quality throughout the year. The tradition continues to be strong, as I verify with every French visit and sojourn.

Terrines de Légumes au Coulis de Framboise

layered terrines with raspberry sauce

This makes an elegant first course or a light main course. The distinct flavor of each vegetable is retained in this colorful layered dish, while at the same time delivering a harmonious whole. Raspberry sauce, slightly tart, brings out the sweetness in the vegetables. Other choices for the same treatment are spinach and asparagus. Port can be used in place of the vin doux.

1 lb (500 g) celery root (celeriac), peeled and cut into slices ⅜ inch (1 cm) thick

1 lb (500 g) young, sweet carrots, peeled and quartered lengthwise

1 lb (500 g) peas, shelled

1 whole egg, plus 2 egg yolks

1 cup (8 fl oz/250 ml) heavy (double) cream

¼ cup (2 oz/60 g) unsalted butter

RASPBERRY SAUCE

½ cup (2 oz/60 g) fresh raspberries

2 tablespoons sugar

½ cup (4 fl oz/125 ml) vin doux *such as Banyuls or Beaumes-de-Venise*

⅓ cup (3 fl oz/80 ml) raspberry vinegar

❦ Bring a saucepan three-fourths full of water to a boil over high heat. Add the celery root, reduce the heat to medium, and cook until very tender when pierced with a fork, about 15 minutes. Drain well and set aside.

❦ At the same time, bring another saucepan three-fourths full of water to a boil over high heat. Add the carrots, reduce the heat to medium, and cook until very tender when pierced with a fork, 5–7 minutes. Drain well and set aside.

❦ Bring a third small saucepan three-fourths full of water to a boil over high heat. Add the peas, reduce the heat to medium, and cook until very tender when pierced, 5–7 minutes. Drain well and set aside.

❦ Purée each vegetable separately in a blender, rinsing the blender container between uses and putting the purées in separate bowls. Each purée should measure about 1½ cups (12 fl oz/375 ml).

In a separate bowl, whisk together the whole egg, egg yolks, and cream just until blended. Spoon ¼ cup (2 fl oz/60 ml) of the egg mixture into each of the vegetable purées. Stir each until well mixed.

Preheat an oven to 350°F (180°C). Using the butter, heavily grease 2 terrines each 6 inches (15 cm) long and 3¼ inches (8 cm) wide (or use small loaf pans of the same size).

Fill a pastry (piping) bag fitted with a plain tip with the puréed carrots and squeeze an even layer of carrots into each terrine, filling each vessel about one-third full. Using a clean pastry bag, repeat the process, first with the puréed peas, filling the middle one-third of each terrine, and then with the celery root, filling the top one-third.

Place the terrines in a large, ovenproof pot with a tight-fitting lid. Carefully pour water into the pot to reach about ½ inch (12 mm) below the tops of the terrines. Remove the terrines from the pot and bring the water to a boil over high heat. Remove the pot from the heat, put the terrines back into the pot, and cover tightly.

Bake until the mixture is firm to the touch, 50–60 minutes. Remove the terrines from the pot and let stand for 10–15 minutes.

Meanwhile, make the raspberry sauce: In a saucepan over medium heat, combine the raspberries, sugar, *vin doux,* and vinegar. Cook, stirring, until the sugar thoroughly dissolves, 4–5 minutes. Remove from the heat and pour through a fine-mesh sieve placed over a bowl, pressing it through with the back of a spoon.

To unmold, invert a serving plate on top of a terrine. Holding the plate and terrine firmly together, turn them over so the plate is on the bottom. Shake the terrine and lift it off. Repeat with the other terrine. To serve 4, cut each terrine in half and, using a spatula, transfer each half to another plate.

To serve, spoon the raspberry sauce around each serving.

serves 2–4

Le Centre

Galettes de Potiron

pumpkin pancakes

There are two main varieties of French pumpkins. In the north, Rouge vif d'Etampes, a beautiful, flattened, bright red pumpkin named for the city of Etampes in the Ile-de-France, is grown, while in the south, Musqué de Provence, a huge, deeply lobed, buff-colored pumpkin with fine, dense flesh and very hardy skin, is found in the fields. In the markets, Musqué de Provence is sold by the slice. The red pumpkin has lighter flesh and thinner skin, but both store well. Use a pie pumpkin here, or substitute a butternut or Hubbard squash. Serve the pancakes alongside roasted meats such as duck or pork.

1-lb (500-g) piece pumpkin (see note)

2–3 tablespoons light cooking oil

2 yellow onions, minced

⅔ cup (3½ oz/105 g) all-purpose (plain) flour

2 eggs

¼ cup (2 fl oz/60 ml) crème fraîche

½ teaspoon salt

½ teaspoon freshly ground pepper

1 teaspoon fresh thyme leaves

2 tablespoons unsalted butter

❦ Scrape out any seeds and fibers from the piece of pumpkin and peel away the skin. Using a handheld shredder-grater, coarsely grate the pumpkin. Set aside. In a frying pan over medium heat, warm 1 tablespoon of the oil. Add the onions and sauté until translucent, 2–3 minutes. Set aside.

❦ In a bowl, whisk together the flour, eggs, crème fraîche, salt, pepper, and thyme. Add the grated pumpkin and the sautéed onions. Mix well.

❦ In a frying pan over medium heat, melt the butter and 1 tablespoon of the remaining oil. When the butter foams, drop a heaping tablespoon of the pumpkin mixture into the frying pan for each pancake, spacing them about 2 inches (5 cm) apart. Flatten and smooth each mound to make a pancake a generous ¼ inch (6 mm) thick. Cook, turning once, until golden on both sides, about 8 minutes total. Transfer to a warmed platter and keep warm. Repeat, adding oil to the pan, if needed. You should have about 8 pancakes in all. Serve immediately.

serves 4

Champagne et Le Nord

Beignets de Salsifis

salsify fritters

Salsify, also known as oyster plant, is one of those old-time, somewhat-forgotten vegetables—les légumes oubliés—that are making a comeback in French kitchens. It is a winter-hardy root, popular particularly in the north where the cold months can be severe, and during World War II it provided the sustenance, along with Jerusalem artichokes, for many families. Consequently, it became associated with poverty and bad times and fell into disfavor. Lately, however, its delicate oysterlike flavor and fine texture are being rediscovered in restaurants and homes.

4–5 cups (32–40 fl oz/1–1.25 l) water

3 tablespoons cider vinegar

5 tender salsify roots, ½ lb (250 g) total weight

vegetable oil for deep-frying

¾ cup (4 oz/125 g) all-purpose (plain) flour

½ teaspoon salt

1 cup (8 fl oz/250 ml) ice water

❦ Combine the water and vinegar in a non-aluminum saucepan. Using a vegetable peeler, scrape away the skin of the salsify roots. Rinse them, cut crosswise into 2-inch (5-cm) lengths, then quarter lengthwise to make thin sticks. Immediately immerse in the vinegar water to prevent discoloration.

❦ If the salsify roots are very young and tender, they now can be patted dry, dipped in batter, and fried. If they are mature, parboil them first in their vinegar water for 8–10 minutes, drain, and pat dry.

❦ In a deep-fat fryer or deep, heavy frying pan, pour in vegetable oil to a depth of 2 inches (5 cm) and heat to 350°F (180°C), or until a dab of batter dropped into it puffs and sizzles upon contact.

❦ While the oil is heating, in a large bowl, whisk together the flour and salt, and then whisk in the ice water. Dip the salsify pieces, 4 or 5 at a time, into the batter, and then slip them into the hot oil. Fry until golden brown and cooked through, 2–3 minutes. Using a slotted spoon, transfer to paper towels to drain. Place on a paper towel–lined plate in a warm oven until all have been fried.

❦ Arrange on a platter and serve hot.

serves 4–6

Le Sud-Ouest

Haricots Flageolets aux Herbes

flageolet beans with bay and winter savory

Flageolet beans are a French national treasure. They are a small, kidney-shaped shelling bean that is used both fresh and dried. The flavor is mild, the texture smooth and meaty. They may be white or green, as there are several varieties, including the much-appreciated heirloom Chevrier Vert.

Roast leg of lamb is, for many French families, incomplete without flageolet beans, and I am prone to agree. There is something about these luscious legumes, cooked with herbs, that marries perfectly with the lamb and its juices. The beans can be served to accompany other dishes as well, however, such as roast pork, veal, or beef or grilled chops. If you should be fortunate to have fresh flageolet beans, by all means, use them. Simply reduce the cooking time to about twenty minutes, or until the beans are just tender.

2 cups (about 1 lb/500 g) dried flageolet beans

2½ qt (2.5 l) water

1 teaspoon salt

2 dried bay leaves

4 fresh winter savory sprigs, each about 6 inches (15 cm) long

½ teaspoon freshly ground pepper

❧ Rinse the beans and drain. Place in a large saucepan and add the water and salt. Let stand for 5 minutes. Remove and discard any beans that float to the surface.

❧ Add the bay leaves and winter savory sprigs and bring to a boil over medium-high heat. Cover partially, reduce the heat to low, and simmer until the beans are thoroughly tender to the bite, about 2 hours. Discard the bay and herb sprigs.

❧ Transfer the beans to a warmed serving dish, sprinkle with the pepper, and serve immediately.

serves 4–6

Le Centre

Gratin de Poireaux

leek gratin

Leeks are such an important element for the
potager *and the market garden alike that French
seed companies have developed many season-specific
varieties. One type is planted in fall, another in
summer, and still another in spring to ensure a year-
round crop. Traveling through France, you will almost
always see a substantial row of leeks in the* potagers,
*even in the very cold climates, as a number of cold-
resistant varieties have been developed. Home cooks
use leeks as a base for soups and stocks, braise them as
a vegetable accompaniment, and steam and serve them
with olive oil or bake them into gratins for a main
course or a substantial side dish.*

*In this gratin, the leeks are first minced and sautéed
before being combined with a sauce—in this instance,
one enriched with goat cheese and* jambon cru.
*Another version can be made using whole leeks, steam-
ing them, and then laying them snugly in a buttered
gratin dish before spooning the sauce over them.*

*Either style of gratin is an excellent candidate for
baking in individual ramekins, which make an
elegant presentation.*

*4 tablespoons (2 oz / 60 g) plus 1 teaspoon
unsalted butter*

1 tablespoon extra-virgin olive oil

*6 large leeks, white part and 2 inches (5 cm) of
the green, minced*

2 tablespoons all-purpose (plain) flour

½ teaspoon salt

½ teaspoon freshly ground black pepper

¼ teaspoon cayenne pepper

¾ cup (6 fl oz / 180 ml) milk

¼ lb (125 g) fresh soft goat cheese

*2 tablespoons chopped fresh flat-leaf (Italian)
parsley*

2 oz (60 g) thinly sliced jambon cru *or
prosciutto, minced*

2–3 tablespoons grated Cantal cheese

✜ In a large frying pan over medium heat, melt
1 tablespoon of the butter with the olive oil. When
the butter foams, add the leeks and sauté until
translucent, about 5 minutes. Remove from the heat
and set aside.

✜ Preheat an oven to 375°F (190°C). Using the
1 teaspoon butter, generously grease a shallow 1-qt
(1-l) baking dish.

✜ In a heavy saucepan over medium heat, melt
2 tablespoons of the butter. When it foams, remove
the pan from the heat and whisk in the flour, salt,
black pepper, and cayenne pepper to form a paste.
Return the pan to medium heat and slowly whisk in
the milk in a steady stream. Reduce the heat to low
and stir until there are no lumps. Simmer the sauce,
stirring occasionally, until it thickens enough to coat
the back of a spoon, 12–15 minutes. Stir in the goat
cheese and continue to cook until the cheese is
incorporated, 1–2 minutes.

✜ Stir the leeks, parsley, and *jambon cru* or prosciutto
into the sauce. Spoon the mixture into the prepared
baking dish. Top evenly with the Cantal cheese. Cut
the remaining 1 tablespoon butter into small bits and
use to dot the surface.

✜ Bake until a crisp, golden crust forms on top,
20–30 minutes. Serve hot directly from the dish.

serves 4–6

Languedoc

Fenouil Braisé

braised fennel

Fennel is one of the great Mediterranean vegetables used throughout southern France in salads, braises, sautés, and gratins. It has a pleasing licorice flavor and a firm, crunchy texture when raw, like that of celery, but once cooked it becomes pleasantly soft. Here it is braised and then gratinéed for an excellent side dish, or in larger amounts, a main course.

4 fennel bulbs

1 tablespoon extra-virgin olive oil

1 clove garlic, minced

3 tomatoes, coarsely chopped

1 teaspoon minced fresh thyme

½ teaspoon salt

½ teaspoon freshly ground pepper

¼ cup (1 oz/30 g) coarse dried bread crumbs

1 tablespoon unsalted butter, cut into bits

2 tablespoons chopped fresh basil

☙ Cut off the stems and feathery tops and any bruised outer stalks from the fennel bulbs. Halve the bulbs lengthwise. Cut the halves lengthwise into slices ½ inch (12 mm) thick.

☙ Preheat an oven to 450°F (230°C).

☙ In a frying pan over medium heat, warm the olive oil. Add the garlic and sauté until lightly golden, 1–2 minutes. Add the fennel slices and sauté until they become slightly golden, 10–12 minutes. Add the tomatoes, thyme, salt, and pepper and continue to cook, uncovered, until the tomatoes soften slightly, about 5 minutes. Cover, reduce the heat to low, and cook for another 5 minutes. Raise the heat to medium and cook until the tomatoes have thickened into a sauce and the fennel is very tender and soft, about 5 minutes longer.

☙ Transfer the fennel mixture to a small gratin dish. Sprinkle evenly with the bread crumbs, dot with the butter, and top with half the basil. Bake until the top is browned, about 15 minutes.

☙ Remove from the oven, sprinkle with the remaining basil, and serve directly from the dish, scooping out portions with a large spoon.

serves 4

À la Recherche de Légumes Verts dans la Nature

Wild greens, long gathered by the rural French, are still part of local tradition. It is a lucky diner indeed who is offered a salad or omelet of foraged greens. Wild dandelion, purslane, the young, tender shoots of red poppies, fennel, and bitter chicory are among the culinary treasures that might be used. Other favorites are arugula (rocket), borage, and nettles (cooked only). In late winter and early spring the wild leeks and garlic that grow in the vineyards might be included as well. Borage and nettles can be treated in much the same way as you would treat other mild greens—blanching, steaming, or sauté-ing them. Once cooked, they can be seasoned with cream, shallots, or onions, spiced with a little nutmeg or lemon juice.

Salads are the most popular use for dandelion, where even the root is scraped and cleaned, then minced and added to the vinaigrette. A salad of pure dandelion may be bit overpowering for all except aficionados of its bitter flavor, so it is sometimes mixed with a variety of lettuces (see page 57). Toasted nuts, lardons, and chopped or poached eggs are the usual garnishes.

Wild fennel, both its branches and its feathery leaves, are an important component in Mediterranean fish soups and *grillades,* where its pungent licorice flavor mixes with the sweetness of the seafood. Wild leeks, thin as a grape tendril, are a special treat when steamed and then lightly drizzled with a vinaigrette.

Amateur foragers, alas, should never set out on a search (*une recherche*) for greens without a knowledgeable forager in tow.

Le Sud-Ouest

Pommes de Terre Rôties aux Herbes Variées

roasted potato halves with herb sprigs

Potatoes, in any form, are a good choice to accompany nearly any dish. This preparation looks especially appealing because the different herb sprigs make a varied pattern on top of the potatoes. Having an herb garden, which many French people do, makes putting together this dish as simple as walking out the door and snipping a few herbs.

4 or 5 russet or other baking potatoes, unpeeled, cut in half lengthwise

3 tablespoons extra-virgin olive oil

8–10 assorted herb sprigs such as rosemary, thyme, winter savory, marjoram, and sage in any combination, each about 2 inches (5 cm) long

2 teaspoons salt

☙ Preheat an oven to 375°F (190°C).

☙ Put the halved potatoes in a bowl and pour the olive oil over them. Turn or rub them with your hands until they are well coated with the oil. Place the potatoes, cut sides up, on a baking sheet, and press an herb sprig onto each half. Sprinkle with the salt.

☙ Bake until a golden crust has formed on the cut surface and the potato is tender clear through when pierced with the tip of a knife, about 45 minutes. Remove from the oven and place, herb side up, on a platter. Serve hot.

serves 4

My French neighbors plant a goodly plot of potatoes each year, dig them in late summer or early fall, then store them in their cave to use through June or even July of the next year.

Le Sud-Ouest

Pipérade

basque-style scrambled eggs

This classic egg-and-pepper dish from the Basque country can be served any time of day—breakfast, lunch, or dinner. Part of its characteristic seasoning comes from a special local pepper grown in the fields around the town of Espelette, in the Pyrenees only half an hour inland from Biarritz. You will know you are in Espelette when you see the facades of buildings hung with strings of drying red peppers, les piments d'Espelette. The narrow peppers are about three inches (7.5 cm) long, and once dried are roasted, then ground. The ground pepper is rubbed into the surface of hams and is used to season many dishes, including the famed poulet à la basquaise and pipérade.

2 tablespoons extra-virgin olive oil

1 large yellow onion, minced

1½ green bell or Bull's Horn peppers (capsicums), seeded and cut lengthwise into strips ¼ inch (6 mm) wide

1½ red bell or Bull's Horn peppers (capsicums), seeded and diced

6 tomatoes, peeled, seeded, and coarsely chopped

1 clove garlic, minced

½ teaspoon sugar

¼ teaspoon salt

¼ teaspoon freshly ground black pepper

5 eggs, lightly beaten

½ teaspoon ground piment d'Espelette or ¼ teaspoon cayenne pepper

☙ In a frying pan over medium heat, warm the olive oil. Add the onion and sauté until translucent, 2–3 minutes. Add the green and red peppers and sauté until they begin to change color and become slightly limp, 3–4 minutes. Cover and cook until soft and limp, 3–4 minutes longer. Add the tomatoes, garlic, sugar, salt, and black pepper. Stir, then cover, reduce the heat to low, and cook until the tomatoes have thickened somewhat, 20–25 minutes.

☙ Using a fork, stir the eggs and the ground red pepper into the tomato-pepper mixture. Continue to stir until the eggs form soft curds, 2–3 minutes.

☙ Spoon onto a warmed platter or individual plates and serve at once.

serves 4

Pays de la Loire

Echalotes Caramélisées

ramekins of caramelized shallots

Commercial shallot fields are found in the Loire Valley around Angers. The shallots are planted in holes punched in the black plastic covers that warm the field rows in early spring. After harvest in summer, they are kept in well-ventilated storage sheds and shipped all over the world during the next twelve months. Shallots are naturally sweet, so they make excellent candidates for braised dishes and are a superb accompaniment to roast meats and fowl and to vegetable gratins.

7 tablespoons (3½ oz / 105 g) unsalted butter

1 lb (500 g) large shallots, peeled but left whole

1 tablespoon minced fresh thyme

½ teaspoon salt

½ teaspoon freshly ground pepper

1½ tablespoons sugar

¼ cup (2 fl oz / 60 ml) dry red wine such as Merlot or Burgundy

☙ Preheat an oven to 350°F (180°C). Using 1 table-spoon of the butter, grease 4 ramekins 1½ inches (4 cm) in diameter and 1½ inches (4 cm) deep.

☙ In a frying pan just large enough to hold the shallots in a single layer, melt the remaining 6 table-spoons (3 oz/90 g) butter over medium heat. Add the shallots, reduce the heat to low, and cook, turn-ing often, until slightly golden, about 5 minutes. Cover tightly and cook, turning, until a deeper gold, 3–4 minutes. Add the thyme, salt, and pepper, re-cover, and cook until lightly browned and barely soft, 3–4 minutes longer. Pour off all but 2 tablespoons of the butter. Sprinkle with the sugar and cook, stirring, until the shallots are caramelized and a thick syrup has formed, 3–4 minutes. Add the wine, raise the heat to medium-high, and deglaze the pan, stirring to dis-lodge any browned bits stuck to the pan bottom, 1–2 minutes longer. Divide the shallots and syrup among the ramekins. Place on a baking sheet.

☙ Bake until golden brown and very tender, about 15 minutes. Remove from the oven and let cool for about 5 minutes before serving.

serves 4

Pays de la Loire

Epinards à la Crème aux Oeufs Durs

creamed spinach with hard-boiled eggs

In spring and fall, spinach is sold in France's open markets in bulk. Because the iron-rich vegetable has such a high water content, a single pound (500 g) of fresh leaves is reduced to a mere handful or two when cooked, certainly inadequate for spinach lovers like the French—and me.

8 qt (8 l) water

1 tablespoon salt

3–4 lb (1.5–2 kg) spinach, stems removed

3 tablespoons unsalted butter

1 shallot, minced

½ teaspoon salt

½ teaspoon freshly ground pepper

1 cup (8 fl oz/250 ml) heavy (double) cream

6 hard-boiled eggs, peeled and halved lengthwise

In a large pot, bring the water to a boil over high heat. Add the salt and spinach, pressing the spinach down into the water with a spoon. When the water returns to a boil, cook the spinach until just tender, about 2 minutes. Pour into a colander, then rinse with cold water to halt the cooking. Using your hands, squeeze the spinach dry. Chop coarsely and set aside.

In a frying pan over medium heat, melt 2 tablespoons of the butter. When it foams, add the shallot and sauté until translucent, 1–2 minutes. Add the spinach and cook, stirring, until the spinach has lost all of its moisture, about 5 minutes. Reduce the heat to low, add the salt and pepper, and stir in ½ cup (4 fl oz/125 ml) of the cream. Bring to a simmer and cook, stirring occasionally and gradually adding the remaining ½ cup (4 fl oz/125 ml) cream, until the mixture is thick and creamy, 10–15 minutes. Stir in the remaining 1 tablespoon butter.

To serve, spoon the spinach onto a warmed platter or shallow baking dish and arrange the egg halves down the middle. Serve immediately.

serves 6

Cuisiner avec Fromage

When you cook with cheese (*cuisiner avec fromage*), you can bring a complexity of flavors to a dish with a single ingredient. The great range of tastes and textures present in the myriad of French cheeses—nearly 400 recognized varieties—form a vast pantry available to the French cook. Since many of the cheeses are local, you'll find different types being used for a vegetable gratin in the Auvergne than you'll find in the Basque country or in Gascony or in Quercy.

Goat's milk cheese, of which the French consume more than any other European country, is excellent for cooking because the butterfat and solids don't separate when heated, unlike many cow's milk cheeses. Soft fresh goat cheese melts to make a creamy liaison for stuffings or a smooth sauce or topping. Hard cheeses are typically grated and added at the end of cooking.

Le Sud-Ouest

Cèpes Farcis
stuffed cèpes

Cèpes, Boletus edulis, *are the royalty of the mushroom world, greatly esteemed for their firm texture, aromatic flesh, and intense flavor. During the fall, hunters seek them in the forests from the Dordogne to the Basses-Alpes. In a good year, a sizable number of full baskets can be amassed by a single individual.*

They are often presented stuffed, to accompany a main dish such as roast duck, veal, or pork or for serving as a first course. The stuffing can be used for other mushrooms as well, although the unique flavor of the cèpes will be absent.

8 fresh cèpe mushrooms, about 1 lb (500 g) total weight, brushed clean

3 oz (90 g) thinly sliced jambon cru *or prosciutto, minced*

2 oz (60 g) roulade, *pancetta, or bacon, minced*

1 egg, lightly beaten

2 tablespoons fresh goat cheese

1 clove garlic, minced

1 shallot, minced

2 tablespoons minced fresh flat-leaf (Italian) parsley

1 teaspoon fresh thyme leaves, minced

½ teaspoon freshly ground pepper

2 tablespoons extra-virgin olive oil

❀ Preheat an oven to 400°F (200°C).

❀ Remove the stems from the mushrooms and mince them. In a bowl, combine the minced stems, *jambon cru* or prosciutto, *roulade* (or pancetta or bacon), egg, goat cheese, garlic, shallot, parsley, thyme, and pepper. Mix well to form a stiff paste.

❀ Rub the mushroom caps with all but 1 teaspoon of the olive oil. Using a small spoon, stuff each mushroom cap to heaping with the minced-stems mixture. Place, stuffed side up, in a baking dish just large enough to accommodate them without crowding. Drizzle the remaining 1 teaspoon oil evenly over the tops. Bake until the cheese melts, the stuffing is lightly browned, and the mushroom caps can be easily pierced with the tip of a knife, 20–25 minutes.

❀ Transfer to a warmed serving platter and serve.

serves 4

Ile-de-France

Coeurs de Céleri Braisés

braised celery hearts

Long, slow cooking in chicken stock transforms celery hearts to a velvety texture and both intensifies and mellows their flavor. The tender hearts have long been a favorite in central and northern France, although I associate them with rather old-fashioned Parisian restaurants. They make a superb accompaniment to any roast meat.

4 celery bunches

2 tablespoons unsalted butter

2 tablespoons extra-virgin olive oil

1 bay leaf

½ teaspoon freshly ground pepper

¼ teaspoon salt

1 cup (8 fl oz/250 ml) chicken stock

✿ Remove the tough outer stalks from each celery bunch (reserve for another use or discard), leaving only the tender stalks of the heart. Trim the rough edges of the celery base where the outer stalks have been removed, but keep the base intact. Quarter each celery heart lengthwise.

✿ In a large frying pan over medium heat, melt the butter with the olive oil. When the butter foams, add the celery pieces, arranging them in a single layer and alternating the base ends with the tops to fit them snugly. Sauté, turning once, until glistening and slightly limp, 2–3 minutes. Reduce the heat to low and add the bay leaf, pepper, and salt. Cover tightly and cook until the celery has begun to brown slightly, about 10 minutes. Uncover, pour in the stock, re-cover, and cook until the celery is tender and cuts easily with a fork, about 10 minutes longer.

✿ To serve, place on a warmed platter along with some of the stock.

serves 4

Champagne et Le Nord

Salsifis à la Crème

salsify in cream

The delicately flavored salsify and its near-relative, the black-skinned scorzonera, are long-growing, cold-hardy root vegetables that are planted in summer for harvest in winter or the following spring. Salsify, sometimes called poor man's asparagus or oyster plant (the latter due to its slightly glossy appearance when cooked, a look likened to oysters), is a fine candidate for this treatment in cream, as its flavor can be overpowered by the robust ingredients favored in the south, such as garlic and olive oil.

2 tablespoons cider or white wine vinegar or fresh lemon juice

10 salsify roots, about 1 lb (500 g) total weight

1 teaspoon salt

3 tablespoons unsalted butter

3 tablespoons heavy (double) cream

1 teaspoon fresh lemon juice

1 tablespoon chopped fresh flat-leaf (Italian) parsley

⅛ teaspoon ground nutmeg

✿ Fill a large bowl three-fourths full of water and add the vinegar or lemon juice. Using a vegetable peeler or paring knife, scrape away the skin from the salsify roots. Rinse the salsify and cut into pieces 2 inches (5 cm) long. Quarter the pieces lengthwise to make thin sticks. As they are cut, drop them into the bowl of water to prevent discoloring.

✿ Bring a saucepan three-fourths full of water to a boil over high heat, then add the salt. Drain the salsify and add to the boiling water. Reduce the heat to medium and cook until tender when pierced with the tip of a knife, 20–30 minutes. The younger and more tender the salsify, the less cooking time it will require. Drain well.

✿ In a frying pan over medium heat, melt the butter. When it foams, add the salsify and cook, stirring, until lightly golden, 3–4 minutes. Add the cream, lemon juice, parsley, and nutmeg. Cook, stirring, until the salsify is well coated with the cream, about 1 minute longer.

✿ Transfer to a warmed serving dish. Serve at once.

serves 4

Le Centre

Lentilles aux Carottes et Céleri-Rave

lentils with carrots and celery root

Puy is famous for its tiny green lentils, called lentilles du Puy. *These small, deep green legumes, also known as French lentils, hold their shape during cooking longer than the more common brown lentils, and I think they have a finer flavor as well. Here, they are seasoned with* roulade, *a salt-and-spice-cured bacon similar to Italian pancetta.*

2 oz (60 g) sliced roulade *or* pancetta, *cut into strips 1 inch (2.5 cm) long by ¼ inch (6 mm) wide*

1 tablespoon extra-virgin olive oil

1 yellow onion, chopped

2 cloves garlic, minced

3 small carrots, peeled and diced

½ celery root (celeriac), peeled and diced

2 cups (14 oz/440 g) small green lentils, picked over and rinsed

8 cups (64 fl oz/2 l) water

1 teaspoon salt

2 fresh bay leaves or 1 dried bay leaf

1½ teaspoons freshly ground pepper

1 tablespoon minced fresh thyme

☙ In a heavy saucepan or soup pot over medium-low heat, warm the *roulade* or pancetta pieces until they begin to release their fat. Add the olive oil, onion, and garlic and sauté until translucent, 3–4 minutes. Add the carrots and celery root and sauté until just beginning to soften, 1–2 minutes. Add the lentils and stir until they glisten, 1–2 minutes. Then add the water, salt, and bay leaves, raise the heat to medium-high, and bring to a boil. Reduce the heat to low, cover, and simmer until the lentils are soft but still hold their shape, about 30 minutes. If necessary, continue to simmer, uncovered.

☙ Add the pepper and thyme and discard the bay leaves. Taste and adjust the seasonings. Serve at once.

serves 4–6

Champagne et Le Nord
Gratin de Chicons

gratin of belgian endive

Belgian endive was discovered in Belgium around 1850. The stories of its discovery vary, but all agree that it was by accident. A farmer had, by chance, put some chicory roots in his basement or compost pile in the fall, then found a few weeks later that they had produced tender white shoots that were slightly bitter. It was a fresh, leafy vegetable in winter when few fresh vegetables were available, so it wasn't long before other farmers in Belgium and northern France began to produce this exotic specimen. In the summer, the farmers grew endives in their fields, where they produced large, bitter, dark green leaves. In the fall, the leaves were cut to within an inch of the crown, then the roots were dug up and stored in cellars or in trenches filled with sand, where later they produced the pale ivory heads known as chicons. *Today, the production is done hydroponically on a large scale in special forcing sheds.* Chicons *are one of the most popular vegetables in the north of France, in the regions of Pas de Calais and Flanders, where dozens of treatments have been devised. I like them all, whether in salads, braised, in gratins, and even grilled.*

8 heads Belgian endive (chicory/witloof)

3½ tablespoons unsalted butter

3 tablespoons all-purpose (plain) flour

½ teaspoon salt

¼ teaspoon ground nutmeg

⅛ teaspoon cayenne pepper

1 cup (8 fl oz/250 ml) milk

¼ cup (1 oz/30 g) grated Parmesan cheese

¼ lb (125 g) thinly sliced jambon cru or prosciutto, cut into slivers

2 tablespoons shredded Emmentaler or Comté cheese

1½ teaspoons freshly ground black pepper

❧ Preheat an oven to 375°F (190°C).

❧ Using a small, sharp knife, core each endive by cutting an inverted V out of the base. Set the cored endives aside.

❧ In a saucepan over medium heat, melt 2 tablespoons of the butter. When it begins to foam, remove the pan from the heat and whisk in the flour, salt, nutmeg, and cayenne pepper until a paste forms. Return the pan to medium heat and gradually whisk in the milk in a steady stream. Reduce the heat to low and stir until there are no lumps. Simmer the sauce, stirring occasionally, until it becomes thick enough to coat the back of a spoon, about 15 minutes. Stir in the Parmesan cheese and continue to cook just until the cheese melts into the sauce, 2–3 minutes longer. Remove from the heat.

❧ Using 1 tablespoon of the butter, grease the bottom and sides of a shallow baking dish just large enough to hold the Belgian endives snugly. Arrange the Belgian endives in the dish and top with the slivers of *jambon cru* or prosciutto. Pour the sauce over the top. Cut the remaining ½ tablespoon butter into small bits and dot the surface, then scatter the Emmentaler or Comté cheese evenly over the top.

❧ Bake until the endives are tender when pierced with a knife tip and the surface has formed a bubbly, slightly golden crust, 25–30 minutes.

❧ Remove from the oven and sprinkle with the black pepper. Serve hot directly from the dish.

serves 4–6

Alsace-Lorraine

Chou Farci

whole stuffed cabbage

Although preparing, stuffing, and cooking a whole cabbage might seem daunting at first, it is really quite easy and the results are impressive. Stuffed cabbage is a typical dish in northern France, and especially in Alsace, where cabbages are an important part of the local agricultural economy and show up in many of the region's traditional dishes.

1½ cups (12 fl oz/375 ml) chicken stock

¾ cup (5 oz/155 g) long-grain white rice

1 large green or Savoy cabbage, 5–6 lb (2.5–3 kg)

2 tablespoons plus 2 teaspoons salt

¼ cup (2 oz/60 g) unsalted butter

½ yellow onion, minced

½ cup (3 oz/90 g) chopped prunes

¾ lb (375 g) fresh white mushrooms, brushed clean and minced

2 teaspoons freshly ground pepper

½ teaspoon ground cumin

1½ lb (750 g) bulk pork sausage

¼ cup (2 fl oz/60 ml) heavy (double) cream

STOCK

8–10 cups (2–2½ qt/2–2.5 l) water

¼ cup (2 fl oz/60 ml) white wine vinegar

1 yellow onion, quartered

6 fresh tarragon sprigs

6 peppercorns

4 whole cloves

1 teaspoon salt

❀ In a saucepan over medium-high heat, bring the chicken stock to a boil. Add the rice, return to a boil, cover, reduce the heat to very low, and cook until tender and the stock is absorbed, about 20 minutes.

❀ Meanwhile, trim the cabbage of the tough outer leaves that it will have if coming from the garden or a farmers' market. Place in a large soup pot or stockpot and add water to reach halfway up the sides of the cabbage. Add 2 tablespoons salt, cover, and bring to a boil over high heat. Reduce the heat to medium and cook, covered, for 15 minutes.

❀ Line a large bowl with a 24-inch (60-cm) square of cheesecloth (muslin), allowing the excess to drape over the edge. Lift the cabbage out of the pot, transfer it to the cheesecloth-lined bowl, and let stand until cool enough to handle, about 15 minutes. Gently unwrap the leaves one by one until you reach the tightly wrapped center, which will be just a little larger than a fist. Using a sharp knife, cut through the center at its base, being careful not to tear the unwrapped leaves. It may take several cuts to succeed. Remove the center and set aside. Cut away any excess core to ensure a substantial cavity. Set the cabbage aside.

❀ Chop the removed center of the cabbage. In a large frying pan over medium heat, melt the butter. When it foams, add the onion and sauté until translucent, 2–3 minutes. Add the chopped cabbage and the prunes, reduce the heat to medium-low, cover, and cook until the cabbage has thoroughly wilted, reducing its volume by half, 6–8 minutes. Remove the cover and stir in the mushrooms. Raise the heat to medium and sauté for 3–4 minutes. The mushrooms should be softened but not mushy. Stir in the remaining 2 teaspoons salt, the pepper, and the cumin. Transfer to a large bowl.

❀ In another frying pan over medium heat, crumble the sausage and cook, stirring occasionally, until no longer pink but not yet browned, 6–7 minutes. Using a slotted spoon, transfer to paper towels to drain briefly, then add the sausage to the cabbage mixture along with the rice and the cream. Stir and compact the mixture until it feels like a soft paste.

❀ Fill the cabbage cavity with the cabbage-sausage mixture, rounding it a bit on top. Starting from the innermost leaf, rewrap the cabbage. When the last leaf is folded over, gather up the four corners of the cheesecloth and tie them together with kitchen string to hold the cabbage in shape during cooking.

❀ To make the stock, in the soup pot or stockpot, combine the water, vinegar, onion, tarragon, peppercorns, cloves, and salt. Add the wrapped cabbage and place over medium-high heat. Bring to a boil, then reduce the heat to low, cover, and cook until the cabbage and its stuffing are thoroughly heated, 1–1½ hours, depending upon the weight of the cabbage. Carefully lift the cabbage out of the stock and place in a bowl. Discard the stock. Let the cabbage stand for 1 hour before serving.

❀ To serve, transfer to a platter or a shallow bowl. Untie the cheesecloth and slide it from beneath the cabbage. Cut into wedges. Serve at room temperature.

serves 10–12

Bretagne

Artichauts aux Crevettes

artichokes with shrimp

In Brittany, the huge, round Camus variety of artichoke is used for this dish. It is meaty, intensely flavorful, and, because of its size, an excellent candidate for stuffing with savory mixtures.

4 large globe artichokes

1 teaspoon sea salt

4 teaspoons Dijon mustard

1 teaspoon extra-dry vermouth

½ cup (4 fl oz / 125 ml) mayonnaise, homemade or purchased

1 teaspoon minced fresh rosemary

½ teaspoon table salt

½ teaspoon freshly ground pepper

1 lb (500 g) bay shrimp or other small cooked shelled shrimp

1½ tablespoons minced fresh flat-leaf (Italian) parsley

⚜ Trim off the stem of each artichoke even with the bottom and snap off any damaged outer leaves. Put the artichokes in a large pot and add water to a depth of 4 inches (10 cm). Sprinkle with the sea salt and bring to a boil over high heat. Cover, reduce the heat to low, and simmer until the base of the artichokes can be readily pierced with the tines of a fork, about 45 minutes. Using tongs, transfer the artichokes to a colander and invert to drain. Let cool.

⚜ Cut off the upper one-fourth of each artichoke and discard the prickly trimmings. Using a spoon, scoop out the center leaves and the furry choke from each artichoke to create a bowl. Wrap in plastic wrap and chill for about 2 hours.

⚜ In a bowl, combine the mustard and vermouth and stir until well blended. Add the mayonnaise, rosemary, table salt, and pepper and stir to combine. Add all but 12 of the shrimp and turn gently to coat evenly. Fill the center of each artichoke, dividing the mixture evenly. Rewrap in plastic wrap and chill for at least 1 hour or for up to 3 hours.

⚜ Garnish each artichoke with 3 of the reserved shrimp and sprinkle with the parsley. Serve chilled.

serves 4

Sel Marin

In France, the ancient practice of gathering salt from the sea (*sel marin*) continues. *Le sel de Guérande,* harvested from the salt basins in the area of Guérande in Brittany, is made up of medium-to-large, irregularly shaped crystals, grayish ivory and still slightly moist from the sea. Sometimes called *sel gris* because of its color, the salt has a light, briny taste. Sea salt is also gathered from the salt basins of Ile de Ré, off the Atlantic coast near La Rochelle, and in Provence from the basins of the Camargue and Aigues-Mortes.

The most valued of all the natural sea salts is *fleur de sel,* which forms on the surface of the sea only on certain very dry, hot days when the wind is blowing in a particular fashion. It is scraped up by hand using a special raking tool called a *lousse.* The tiny crystals of *fleur de sel* are very fine and delicate, as is its flavor.

LES DESSERTS

Dessert can range
from a lone apple,
peeled at the table,
to a tall and glamorous
chocolate confection.

NO MATTER HOW SIMPLE or how elaborate a French meal might be, dessert is an essential part. Something sweet, as the French like to say, brings closure to the *repas*. This is usually followed by a *café express* or, if an evening meal, perhaps a tisane, an herbal infusion such as *tilleul* (linden) or *menthe* (mint). For more elaborate meals, fruit is a course in itself, offered after cheese and before a sweet, but often a bowl of fruit, especially at home, is served as the dessert. Thus a dessert can range from a lone apple or orange, peeled at the table, to glamorous confections of chocolate and intricate cream-filled pastries. Between the two extremes are fruit puddings, cakes, tarts, fresh cheeses and honey, cookies, ice creams, and sorbets.

Everywhere in France, in every region, city, town, and village, one finds that happy French institution, the *pâtisserie*. Virtually every day of the year, pastry shops supply the more ornate creations that few French men or women make at home. They don't need to. They can be assured of a fine cake or tart from the *pâtisserie*, made with top-quality eggs, cream, chocolate, sugar, and fruit, that will satisfy the desire for a delectable and beautiful dessert.

Walking the streets of any French town or city is a call to pause before the windows of the many *pâtisseries*, as each one seems to compete with the next in an effort to entice with layered *millefeuilles*, brilliantly colored fruit *tartes* and *tartelettes*, and dark, intense-looking chocolate *gâteaux*, some decorated with paper-thin slices of chocolate or masses of chocolate curls. Impossibly light puff pastries, dusted with confectioners' (icing) sugar and nuts and filled with voluptuous creams, come in flavors of coffee, chocolate, vanilla, and almond. More demurely stand the stolid pudding cakes, cut into squares that surreptitiously hide dried plums or raisins. A variety of cookies is always on hand as well, the smaller ones sold by weight, the larger ones by the piece.

Sometimes the *boulangerie* and the *pâtisserie* are one and the same, especially in small villages like mine. Along a far wall stand the breads, in a glass counter the pastries. On Saturday and Sunday mornings, when nearly

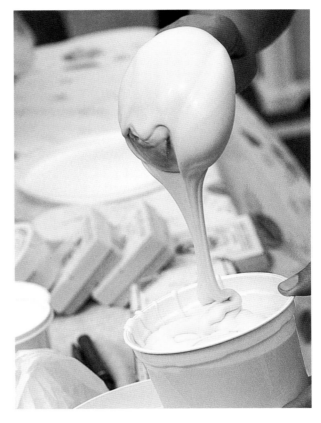

Preceding spread: Almost too beautiful to eat, plump, luscious berries are used in many ways, from sorbets to tarts to liqueurs. Of course, they are also exquisite eaten simply out of hand. **Left:** A young boy gazes longingly at the treats on display in a pastry shop window in Paris. **Above top:** A row of statuesque cypress trees, once painted by Claude Monet, stands tall in the hills of Provence, near the town of Bonnieux. **Above bottom:** Norman cows are great producers of milk, resulting in a rich local cuisine that incorporates generous amounts of cream, butter, and crème fraîche.

Above: The Arc de Triomphe, commissioned by Napoleon to commemorate the fallen of past wars, is visible from the Place de la Concorde, a magnificent square punctuated by a pink granite obelisk that once stood in the Temple of Rameses II in Luxor.

everyone in the village is either having *des invités* for lunch or dinner or is invited to someone else's home, people come early to get the best pick of the desserts, if they haven't ordered ahead. On holidays, my little *boulangerie-pâtisserie* makes stunning cakes, decorated in a style worthy of a city pastry shop. I once bought a chocolate cake there to take to a friend who had invited me for lunch. Thin, delicate cake layers were spread with a light filling of raspberry jam. The whole had been iced with chocolate and beautifully decorated with rings of glazed raspberries. The cake was only about eight inches (20 cm) in diameter, but it was at least six inches (15 cm) tall, and left all twelve of us happily satiated.

When I think of dessert in France, I think primarily of two things: sweets from the *pâtisserie* and fruit. Even more than a love and respect for elegant pastries, the French have an incredibly deep appreciation and enthusiasm for seasonal fruits. They are aware that the fruit's moment is brief and fleeting, its appearance limited by time and circumstance, and that locally produced, perfectly ripe fruits are available for only a short period each year. So, a bowl or tart of strawberries, just picked in May from a Savoyard strawberry patch, will have pride of place for dessert. It will relinquish its place to the wild berries in summer and to the pome fruits in fall. The pattern is repeated all over France, varying only with the ripening times and varietal nuances of each region.

In summertime in southern France, there seem to be few desserts to compete with a perfectly ripe melon. For nearly twenty-five years, my neighbor Maurice has been growing what many consider to be the best melons in the Haute Var. He still has the same customers from the surrounding village, as well as the German, Dutch, English, and French *estivants,* the summer vacationers, who have discovered his melons and keep returning to him for more during their holiday. At the open market, he will have people lined up three and four deep at his table—no umbrellas, nothing fancy, just a table, melons, and a scale—while other melon vendors wait for customers. Usually Françoise, his wife, does the selling, and over the years I have

Left: A raspberry grower admires the vibrant color and lingering fragrance of her crop. **Above top:** The Jardin des Tuileries, designed by André Le Nôtre in the seventeenth century, provides a welcome haven from the clamor of Parisian streets—a perfect spot for a stroll, a picnic, a long embrace. **Above middle:** Many French goat cheeses are entitled to an *Appellation d'Origine Contrôlée* label, guaranteeing they were made in a certain place according to a specific method, an indication of high quality. **Above bottom:** A sign beckons cheese lovers to sample the fresh products available nearby.

Below: In France, the first cherries of the season ripen near the small town of Céret, a center of Catalan culture with a mild Mediterranean climate that nurtures the local grapes as well. **Below bottom:** *Crêperies,* bars, and shops fill the center of Rennes, a lively Breton town that was founded by the Gauls and later colonized by the Romans. **Right:** The fruit trees of Provence—peach, apricot, cherry, quince—flower in early spring. Within a few months, their fruits are proudly displayed at the local markets.

helped her, but the customers are demanding. They want a Charentais melon that will be perfectly ripe for next day's dinner, plus one for lunch that day. I had to learn from Françoise to choose a correct specimen for the different occasions. For a same-day lunch, the fruit should be slightly cracked at the bottom, exuding its aroma that announces its honeyed flesh is ready to be savored right away. Left until the next day, it would be over-ripe. For a next-day dinner, the melon should not be cracked, but show a hint of yellow in the greenish rind, indicating its peak is near. For travelers wanting to take some home with them, journeying to far away places such as Paris, Frankfurt, or Brussels, we'd recommend a Boule d'Or or other variety of melon, one not as fragile as the Charentais.

Fruit-based desserts comprise the majority of homemade fare in France, with *clafoutis,* tarts, poached fruits, and fruit pastries among the favorites. One of the things that makes baking with fruit so easy there is that puff pastry, *pâte brisée,* and plain pie pastry are readily available in supermarkets, even those in the small towns. The rolled-up rounds of dough need only to be unfolded. Nothing is easier than unwinding a spool of puff pastry onto a baking sheet, topping it with fresh peaches, plums, berries, or apples that have been tossed with sugar and flour, dotting the fruit with butter, and then folding the edges up around the filling to form a rustic tart. It bakes quickly and comes to the waiting table still warm, golden, and crisply puffed, rich with the season's flavor. For a fancier presentation, a pastry dough is fitted into a tart pan before being filled with rounds of citrus or wedges of plums or nectarines.

Of course, not all desserts are fruit based. Among the most popular home and restaurant desserts are creams and puddings, such as chocolate mousse, crème caramel, and crème brûlée. It is in the cake category that regional specialties shine, primarily in the *pâtisseries.* One finds such delicacies as the *tarte tropezienne* of the Var, a sugar-topped brioche cake split in half and filled with a pastry cream lightly flavored with almond, or the famous

gâteau Basque, a wonderfully dense cake filled with *crème pâtissière* or cherry jam. Brest has its specialty, a cake made of *pâte à choux* in the shape of a wheel, topped with sugar and almonds, and filled with cream. The people of Languedoc favor their local chestnut cake, while those of Alsace have *Kugelhopf,* an almond-and-raisin cake.

Sometimes a very fresh cheese, such as petit-suisse, fromage frais, or a day-old goat cheese, is served as dessert, along with sugar, honey, or jam. A very special treat for everyone is handmade ice cream from a *glacerie,* scooped up from the open cardboard or plastic buckets on display in the freezer and packed into an insulated carton for the trip home. You can always tell the season by the names chalked up on the board: fresh strawberry ice cream in spring, peach in summer, walnut and almond in fall.

Most exotic of all, though, are the grand chocolate shops, *les chocolateries,* that can be found in French cities. Here reside some of

the most skilled artisans in France, the *choco-latiers* who make candies according to time-honored traditions. At one such shop in Angers, a town I used to visit on business every year, I always bought chocolates for my mother. She was a true lover of chocolates, but never, she said, had she ever tasted anything like the ones I carried back to her in the shimmering gold box, tied with gold ribbon. She hoarded them, allowing herself one, or maybe two, every night for a final bit of dessert, along with her coffee, which is indeed when chocolates are usually offered in France, at the very end of a meal.

Pâtisseries, glaceries, and *chocolateries,* shops that offer irresistible sweets to take home, are as intrinsic to the French landscape as *boulangeries* and charcuteries, those other institutions that provide the French cook with fine, freshly made products for the daily table. Or should one want to cook, custards and puddings and fresh fruit desserts are the most likely choices for the essential sweet finish to the meal.

Left top: The hills of Grasse, the perfume center of France, are blanketed with stands of fragrant lavender. **Left bottom:** *Tilleul,* the blossoms and leaves of the linden tree, are used to make an infusion much enjoyed by the French. **Below top:** Bayonne, in the Basque country, is famous for chocolate. It arrived there with Spanish Jews fleeing the Inquisition and was for a long time a luxury, served first as a beverage flavored with cinnamon and clove and then later in pieces with bread, quince preserves, and sheep's milk cheese as a midafternoon pick-me-up. **Below bottom:** Le Flore en l'Ile, one of the most famous cafés in Paris, boasts a breathtaking view of Notre Dame, just across the water.

Alsace-Lorraine

Babas au Rhum

rum and orange babas

Babas ostensibly were named after Ali Baba, the hero of A Thousand and One Nights. *It was reportedly the favorite book of Stanislas Leszczyński of Lorraine, the former king of Poland (his daughter married Louis XV) and the inventor of the sweet. Babas are cakes, either small or large, that are soaked in a sugar-and-rum syrup until saturated and spongy. There are, as usual, many versions, but this one is adapted from my mother's recipe.*

Three things are especially important in making babas: the rising temperature must be very warm, you must continue to work with the very, very sticky dough until it becomes elastic, and both the cakes and the syrup must be warm when you pour the syrup over them.

DOUGH

3 tablespoons granulated sugar

¼ cup (2 fl oz/60 ml) warm water

2½ teaspoons (1 package) active dry yeast

3 tablespoons milk

5 tablespoons (2½ oz/75 g) unsalted butter

2½ cups (12½ oz/390 g) all-purpose (plain) flour, sifted

2 large eggs

¼ teaspoon salt

SYRUP

¾ cup (6 oz/185 g) granulated sugar

1½ cups (12 fl oz/375 ml) water

1 tablespoon fresh orange juice

⅓ cup (3 fl oz/80 ml) dark rum

TOPPING

1 cup (8 fl oz/250 ml) heavy (double) cream

2 tablespoons confectioners' (icing) sugar

½ teaspoon vanilla extract (essence)

2 tablespoons finely julienned orange zest

☗ To make the dough, in a small bowl, combine 1 tablespoon of the sugar and the water. Sprinkle the yeast over the water and put in a very warm place (80°–100°F/27°–38°C) until the mixture has more than doubled in size, about 10 minutes.

☗ In a small saucepan over medium heat, combine the milk and 4 tablespoons (2 oz/60 g) of the butter and heat until the butter melts. Set aside.

☗ Sift the flour again into a bowl and make a well in the center. Add the eggs, salt, the remaining 2 tablespoons granulated sugar, the yeast mixture, and the warm (not hot) milk mixture. Beat with a whisk until blended. The dough will be so sticky that it cannot yet be kneaded in the traditional sense. Instead, using your hands and leaving the dough in the bowl, pull it high and slap it back into the bowl. Continue doing this until it becomes so elastic you can pull it into ropes without it tearing, about 5 minutes. Gather the dough into a ball, cover the bowl with a damp kitchen towel, put in a very warm place, and let the dough rise until doubled in size, 1½–2 hours. Gently roll the edges of the dough over the center and push the dough down.

☗ With the remaining 1 tablespoon butter, grease 6 baba cups or standard muffin cups. Divide the dough equally among the cups, filling each one-third full. Cover with a damp kitchen towel and again put in a very warm place to rise for about 1 hour. The dough should be just peeking over the rims. While the dough is rising, position a rack in the upper third of an oven and preheat to 375°F (190°C).

☗ Meanwhile, make the syrup: In a saucepan over medium-high heat, bring the granulated sugar and water to a boil, stirring to dissolve the sugar. Add the orange juice and cook, stirring, until a thick syrup forms, 4–5 minutes. Let cool slightly, then stir in the rum. Keep warm.

☗ Remove the kitchen towel and place the cups in the oven. Bake until the babas are nicely golden and pull away from the sides of the cups, about 15 minutes. Remove from the oven, let stand for 10–15 minutes, then unmold them. Set upright on a rack.

☗ To soak the babas in the syrup, poke them all over with a wooden skewer. Put them in a shallow baking dish and spoon the syrup over them. As it drains into the dish, spoon it over again. Let stand for 4–5 minutes, then spoon it over again. Repeat several times until the babas are soft and spongy. Put a rack on a baking sheet and place the babas on the rack. Let drain until they stop dripping, then transfer the babas to another plate or dish, cover, and refrigerate for at least several hours or for up to 24 hours.

☗ To make the topping, beat the cream until soft peaks form. Add the confectioners' sugar and the vanilla and beat until stiff peaks form.

☗ To serve, place the babas on individual plates. Spoon the topping onto each baba and sprinkle with the orange zest. Serve at once.

serves 6

Provence

Compote de Sanguines

blood oranges in honey compote

The blood oranges that appear in winter throughout France come primarily from North Africa and Israel. I had never seen a blood orange until moving to Provence, where they were quite common, even in small village épiceries. I fell in love with them, not only for their berrylike flavor, but also for their intense, exotic color, which is shown off in this simple compote. Serve with hard almond cookies for dipping into the juice.

4 blood oranges

1 cup (8 fl oz/250 ml) water

½ cup (6 oz/125 g) honey such as acacia, millefleur, or orange blossom

2 whole cloves

☸ Remove the zest in large pieces from 3 of the blood oranges and set aside. Working with 1 orange at a time and using a small, sharp knife, cut a slice off the top and bottom to expose the flesh. Thickly slice off the peel in strips, cutting around the contours of the fruit to expose the flesh. Cut each orange crosswise into rounds ¼ inch (6 mm) thick. Remove any seeds. Place in a bowl, cover, and set aside.

☸ In a heavy saucepan over medium heat, combine the water and honey. Cook, stirring often, until blended. Add the cloves and three-fourths of the orange zest. Reduce the heat to low and simmer, uncovered, until a thin syrup forms and the flavors are blended, about 1 hour.

☸ Strain the syrup through a fine-mesh sieve placed over a pitcher. Discard the contents of the sieve, including the zest. Pour the syrup over the sliced oranges. Cover and let stand at room temperature for at least 1 hour. If not serving immediately, refrigerate for up to 24 hours before serving. Spoon the oranges and syrup into small bowls. Cut the reserved zest into julienne and garnish the oranges just before serving.

serves 4

Normandie

Pommes Sautées

sautéed apples with calvados

*This farm-style dessert is rich with the flavor
of the Norman countryside.*

¼ cup (2 oz / 60 g) unsalted butter

2 lb (1 kg) firm, sweet apples such as Golden
Delicious, Gala, or Reinette, peeled, cored, and
cut lengthwise into slices ¼ inch (6 mm) thick

3 tablespoons confectioners' (icing) sugar

2 tablespoons Calvados

In a large frying pan over medium heat, melt the
butter. Add the apple slices, sprinkle with the sugar,
and sauté until lightly golden, 3–4 minutes. Turn and
sauté until lightly golden on the second side, 2–3
minutes longer. Pour on the Calvados and ignite
with a match. Let the flames subside. Transfer to
warmed individual plates and serve.

serves 4

Franche-Comté et Les Alpes

Fromage Frais au Miel

fresh cheese and mountain honey

*Whenever some version of cheese and honey appears
in front of me on a dessert menu anywhere in
France, I order it. I have never been disappointed.*

1 small day-old cheese fresh from the mold, made
from cow's or goat's milk

2–3 tablespoons full-bodied honey such as
chestnut, linden, or lavender

Put the unmolded cheese in a bowl, spoon the
honey over it, and serve.

serves 1

Miel

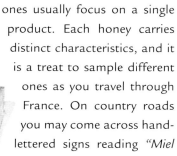

Wherever you go in the French countryside, you are likely to find locally produced honey, or *miel*. In spring and summer, beehives dot orchards, forests, meadows, and fields, and the bees feed on whatever is blooming. Once a particular bloom is over, that honey is gathered and the bees are set elsewhere to feast on another nectar. Small producers may depend upon three or four different kinds of honey, while larger ones usually focus on a single product. Each honey carries distinct characteristics, and it is a treat to sample different ones as you travel through France. On country roads you may come across hand-lettered signs reading *"Miel à vendre ici,"* or "Honey for sale here." It is well worth stopping, as chances are it will be farmhouse honey made the old-fashioned way by small producers.

Honey turns up in a variety of guises on the French table. You will find it spread on the morning *tartines,* used in such savory dishes as roast duck (see page 93) or chicken as a glaze, and added to sweets of all kinds. A truly extraordinary dessert is an utterly simple one: a stream of mountain honey spooned over fresh cheese (see page 209).

Provence

Glace au Miel de Lavande

lavender honey ice cream

Although fields of cultivated lavender are common today in Provence, wild lavender was gathered commercially until the late 1940s. Here, its aromatic blossoms are combined with honey, another significant product of the region, to make an ice cream that is lusciously rich.

3 cups (24 fl oz/750 ml) heavy (double) cream

1 cup (8 fl oz/250 ml) milk

½ cup (6 oz/185 g) lavender, orange blossom, or clover honey, plus honey for serving

½ cup (3½ oz/105 g) firmly packed brown sugar

1 teaspoon dried lavender blossoms

1 piece vanilla bean, 2 inches (5 cm) long

¼ teaspoon salt

4 egg yolks

¼ teaspoon ground cloves

❦ In a heavy saucepan over medium–high heat, combine the cream, milk, ½ cup (6 oz/185 g) honey, brown sugar, lavender blossoms, vanilla bean, and salt. Bring to a boil, stirring often until the sugar dissolves completely.

❦ In a bowl, whisk the yolks until they are lemon colored. Slowly whisk about 1 cup (8 fl oz/250 ml) of the hot cream mixture into the yolks. Now, whisk the yolk mixture into the hot cream mixture. Continue to cook, stirring constantly, until the mixture thickens enough to coat the back of a spoon, 5–6 minutes. Do not allow it to boil. Remove from the heat and let cool to lukewarm. Pour through a fine-mesh sieve placed over a bowl, discarding the lavender and vanilla bean. Stir in the cloves.

❦ Freeze in an ice cream maker according to the manufacturer's directions. Scoop into small bowls and drizzle with honey.

makes about 1 qt (1 l)

Provence

Glace à la Fenouil

candied fennel ice cream

I confess to being a lover of fennel in all its forms, but I had my doubts when offered candied fennel ice cream at a restaurant school outside of Avignon. One spoonful and all my doubts disappeared.

CANDIED FENNEL

2 cups (1 lb/500 g) sugar

2 cups (16 fl oz/500 ml) water

1 fennel bulb, trimmed and finely diced

ICE CREAM

3 cups (24 fl oz/750 ml) heavy (double) cream

1 cup (8 fl oz/250 ml) milk

1 cup (8 oz/250 g) sugar

1 tablespoon fennel pollen (optional)

¼ teaspoon salt

4 egg yolks

1 piece vanilla bean, about 2 inches (5 cm) long

❀ To make the candied fennel, in a heavy saucepan over medium-high heat, bring the sugar and water just to a boil, stirring until the sugar dissolves. Boil until a thin syrup forms, 3–4 minutes. Add the fennel and reduce the heat slightly to keep at a gentle boil. Cook, stirring occasionally, until the fennel has absorbed much of the syrup and has become somewhat golden, about 20 minutes. Using a slotted spoon, transfer the fennel to a sieve to drain.

❀ To make the ice cream, in a heavy saucepan over medium-high heat, combine the cream, milk, sugar, fennel pollen, if using, and salt. Bring just to a boil, stirring until the sugar dissolves. Meanwhile, in a bowl, whisk the egg yolks until they are lemon colored. Slowly whisk about 1 cup (8 fl oz/250 ml) of the hot milk mixture into the yolks. Now, whisk the yolk mixture into the hot milk mixture. Continue to cook, stirring constantly, until the mixture thickens enough to coat the back of a spoon, 3–4 minutes. Do not allow it to boil. Add the vanilla bean, remove from the heat, and let cool to lukewarm. Pour through a fine-mesh sieve placed over a bowl, discarding the vanilla bean.

❀ Freeze in an ice cream maker according to the manufacturer's directions. When firm, stir in the candied fennel, reserving 1 tablespoon for garnish. Scoop into small bowls. Garnish with the reserved fennel.

makes about 1 qt (1 l)

Normandie

Sablés de Caen

butter cookies

These buttery shortbread cookies are found all over France today, but their origins are in butter-rich Normandy, where they are enjoyed by children (and adults) for the four o'clock goûter, or teatime.

½ cup (4 oz/125 g) unsalted butter, at room temperature

6 tablespoons (3 oz/90 g) sugar

⅛ teaspoon salt

¼ teaspoon vanilla extract (essence)

1¼ cups (6½ oz/200 g) all-purpose (plain) flour

❀ Place the butter in a bowl. With a wooden spoon or an electric mixer, beat until creamy. Add the sugar, salt, and vanilla extract and continue to beat until fully incorporated. Add the flour and work it with your fingers just until incorporated. Gather the dough into a ball, wrap in plastic wrap, and refrigerate until well chilled, about 1 hour.

❀ Preheat an oven to 375°F (190°C). Line a baking sheet with parchment (baking) paper.

❀ Place the dough on a floured work surface and cover it with a piece of waxed paper or plastic wrap. Roll out the dough ¼ inch (6 mm) thick. Using a round cookie cutter 2 inches (5 cm) in diameter, cut out as many cookies as possible. Place them 1 inch (2.5 cm) apart on the prepared baking sheet. Gather together the scraps, roll out one more time, and cut out more cookies. Add them to the baking sheet.

❀ Bake until the edges are golden, 10–12 minutes. Transfer to a rack to cool completely. Store in an airtight container for up to 4 days.

makes about 18 cookies

Le Sud-Ouest

Fondant

flourless chocolate cake

I first ate this dense, bittersweet chocolate dessert, which tastes like chocolate truffles, in a bistro near Bayonne, one of France's old, notable chocolate-making centers. Sometimes I like to dust it with cocoa powder before serving.

1 egg yolk

⅓ cup (3 oz/90 g) sugar

6 tablespoons (3 fl oz/90 ml) milk

8 oz (250 g) bittersweet chocolate, chopped into small pieces

1 cup (8 oz/250 g) unsalted butter, cut into pieces, at room temperature

¼ cup (2 fl oz/60 ml) orange liqueur

In a medium saucepan, whisk together the egg yolk and sugar until a light lemon yellow, about 2 minutes. In a small saucepan, bring the milk to a boil. Whisking constantly, slowly pour the boiling milk into the egg mixture, then cook over medium heat, stirring constantly, until thick enough to coat the back of a spoon, 3–4 minutes.

Place the chocolate in a heatproof bowl and set over (not touching) barely simmering water in a saucepan. Slowly pour the hot milk mixture over the chocolate and stir until the chocolate melts, about 2 minutes. Add the butter and continue to stir until the mixture is creamy, 1–2 minutes. Remove from the heat and stir in the orange liqueur.

Pour the mixture into 2 loaf pans, each 6 inches (15 cm) long and 3¼ inches (8 cm) wide. Cover with plastic wrap and refrigerate until quite firm, at least 12 hours or for up to 24 hours.

To unmold, immerse the bottom of a pan in a basin of hot water for about 30 seconds. Slide a knife along the inside edge of the pan and invert a serving plate on top. Holding the plate and the pan firmly together, turn them over and lift off the pan. Repeat with the second pan.

Cut into thick slices to serve.

serves 6–8

Franche-Comté et Les Alpes

Bugnes

deep-fried pastries

These pastries appear in southern France, from the Basses-Alpes south into Provence and on through the southwest. They are called by various names, including bugnes in Savoy and merveilles in Provence and the southwest. They often have other names characteristic of a particular village, and in different areas they are made in different shapes. I was taught to make them by a woman who lives in the small alpine village of Les Allues. She calls them carquelins in the local dialect and shapes them with a slit in the middle through which the pastry is tucked. They are served by the thousands during village fêtes at Mardi Gras time, when platters and baskets of the golden pastries are passed about, heavily sprinkled with confectioners' sugar. Bugnes making is a perfect occasion to gather friends together, as it is a task best accomplished with several sets of willing hands.

3½ cups (17½ oz/545 g) all-purpose (plain) flour

½ cup (4 oz/125 g) granulated sugar

1½ teaspoons baking powder

¼ teaspoon salt

5 eggs

½ cup (4 oz/125 g) unsalted butter, melted and cooled

1 tablespoon canola or other light oil, plus oil for deep-frying

confectioners' (icing) sugar

❧ In a bowl, stir together the flour, granulated sugar, baking powder, and salt. Make a well in the center and add the eggs, butter, and 1 tablespoon oil. Working quickly with your fingertips, incorporate the flour into the wet ingredients to make a sticky dough. Keep working and kneading the dough in the bowl until it is no longer sticky and has become elastic, about 10 minutes.

❧ On a lightly floured work surface, shape the dough into a rectangle about 1 inch (2.5 cm) thick. Dust with a little flour, then fold lengthwise into thirds. Roll it out again into a rectangle about 1 inch (2.5 cm) thick. This time, fold it into thirds from a short side. Repeat 5 more times, working quickly. Then roll the dough out into a rectangle 1½ inches (4 cm) thick. Cover with a kitchen towel and let rest for 1 hour.

❧ Divide the dough into quarters. On the floured work surface, roll out each piece into a 6-by-14-inch (15-by-35-cm) rectangle a scant ¼ inch (6 mm) thick. Cut into strips ½–¾ inch (12 mm–2 cm) wide and 6 inches (15 cm) long. In the center of each strip, cut a lengthwise slit about 2 inches (5 cm) long. Fold one end of the strip through the slit. Alternatively, omit the slits and simply twist each strip to make a bowlike shape.

❧ In a deep frying pan or deep-fryer, pour in the oil to a depth of 4 inches (10 cm). Heat to 375°F (190°C) on a deep-frying thermometer, or until a piece of pastry dropped into the oil puffs immediately and turns golden. Drop in the pastries, a few at a time, and fry until puffed and golden, 1–2 minutes. Using tongs, turn and fry the other side until golden, about 1 minute longer. Using the tongs, transfer to paper towels to drain. Using a fine-mesh sieve, dust with lots of confectioners' sugar. Repeat until all the pastries are fried.

❧ Serve the pastries hot or at room temperature.

makes about 100 pastries; serves 8–10

Les Pyrénées et Gascogne

Gateau de Mûre

blackberry upside-down cake

In the mountains, summertime is wild berry time.
One August, when friends returned to Provence
after two weeks in the Pyrenees, they brought back not
only jars of berry jam that they had made but
also a bucket of fresh berries. We made a cake similar
to this one and ate it warm with double-vanilla
ice cream from a local glacier *(ice cream shop).*

⅓ *cup (3 oz/90 g) unsalted butter, plus*
1 tablespoon, melted and cooled

2 cups (1 lb/500 g) granulated sugar

1 pint (8 oz/250 g) blackberries

4 eggs

1 cup (5 oz/155 g) all-purpose (plain) flour

1 teaspoon baking powder

¼ *teaspoon salt*

❦ Preheat an oven to 350°F (180°C). Put the ⅓ cup (3 oz/90 g) butter in a 9- or 10-inch (23- or 25-cm) round baking dish with 2½-inch (6-cm) sides. Place in the oven to melt, about 5 minutes. Remove from the oven and add 1 cup (8 oz/250 g) of the sugar. Stir and return to the oven for 5 minutes, stirring once or twice, then remove from the oven. Spread the berries in a single layer on the sugar.

❦ Separate the eggs, putting the whites into a large bowl and the yolks into a smaller one. Whisk the 1 tablespoon melted butter into the yolks and set aside. In another bowl, sift together the flour, baking powder, and salt. Set aside. With an electric beater set on medium speed or with a whisk, beat the egg whites just until they form firm peaks. Do not overbeat. Fold the remaining 1 cup (8 oz/250 g) sugar into the egg whites, about one-fourth at a time. Then fold in the egg yolk mixture about one-fourth at a time. Finally, fold in the flour mixture about ¼ cup (1½ oz/45 g) at a time. Pour the batter over the berries and spread to cover evenly.

❦ Bake until a toothpick inserted into the center comes out clean, about 30 minutes. Let stand for at least 10 minutes before unmolding, then slide a knife along the inside edge of the dish. Invert a large plate over the top. Holding the plate and dish firmly together, turn them over and lift off the dish. Serve the cake warm, cut into wedges.

serves 6–8

Confitures

Confitures, delicious French preserves, jams, and jellies made from cherries, raspberries, quinces, blackberries, apricots, blueberries, plums, and other seasonal fruits, play nearly as important a role in dessert making as they do at the breakfast table, where they are spread onto bread and croissants. Thick preserves, such as apricot or cherry, are used to fill deep-fried pastries. Jellies are melted and thickened to glaze fruit tarts large and small. *Confitures* top fresh cheese and are spooned alongside ice cream and sweet *pain perdu.* In the *pâtisserie,* you'll find them hidden between layers of cakes and pooled atop cookies.

Many people still make a few jars of their favorite *confiture* at home, perhaps with fruit brought back from the August vacation in the mountains or countryside. They are brought out for special occasions— Christmas morning breakfast, out-of-town visitors—and the label begins the story: *confiture de figues sauvages, fait à Moustiers-Ste-Marie, août 1998* (wild fig jam, made at Moustiers-Ste-Marie, August 1998). The rest of the story—that is, where the figs were found and gathered, what the weather was like, who was along on the trip—is told over exclamations of how good the jam is.

Alsace-Lorraine

Tarte à la Rhubarbe et aux Fraises

rhubarb-and-strawberry tart

Rhubarb grows well in colder climates, and it is a much-looked-for seasonal specialty in such areas as Savoy and Alsace, where, along with strawberries, it is plentiful in late-spring and early-summer gardens.

6 rhubarb stalks, cut into slices about ½ inch (12 mm) thick (about 2¾ cups / 1¼ lb / 625 g)

1½ cups (12 fl oz / 375 ml) water

juice of 1 lemon

1 teaspoon grated lemon zest

1 vanilla bean, slit lengthwise and cut crosswise into thirds

¾ cup (6 oz / 185 g) firmly packed brown sugar

1 tablespoon all-purpose (plain) flour

1¼ lb (625 g) strawberries, hulled and halved

1 sheet frozen puff pastry, about 12 by 14 inches (30 by 35 cm) and ¼ inch (6 mm) thick, thawed in the refrigerator

1 tablespoon unsalted butter, cut into small bits

✾ In a large saucepan over medium-high heat, combine the rhubarb, water, lemon juice, lemon zest, and vanilla bean. Bring to a boil, reduce the heat to low, and simmer, uncovered, until the rhubarb is tender, about 15 minutes. Remove from the heat and let cool. Cover and chill for about 1 hour. Drain the rhubarb and discard the cooking juices.

✾ In a bowl, stir together the brown sugar and flour until well mixed. Add the drained rhubarb and mix well. Add the strawberries and turn them gently to incorporate fully.

✾ Preheat an oven to 375°F (190°C). On a lightly floured work surface, roll out the puff pastry to about 18 inches (45 cm) square. Trim off the corners to make a round. Transfer the pastry to an ungreased baking sheet. Heap the rhubarb mixture in the middle, dot with butter, and fold up the edges to create a free-form tart with the fruit visible in the center.

✾ Bake until the crust is golden brown and puffed, 20–25 minutes.

✾ Remove from the oven and serve hot, or transfer to a rack and serve warm or at room temperature.

serves 6

Pays de la Loire

Poires au Thé aux Epices

pears poached in tea with spices

The département of Anjou has long been a center of French pear production. The still-popular Doyenne du Comice variety was first grown in Angers, the capital, and many other famous pears were developed there as well. Reportedly, pears were a favorite of Louis XIV, and one of the pears of which he was reportedly fond, Louise Bonne, I have growing in my own small orchard, so I can attest to its melting, sweet flavor and velvety texture.

Remember, pears ripen better off the tree than on. If left on the tree, they become grainy. Choose pears that are firm and greenish with just a tinge of yellow developing, then put them in a bag in the cellar and let them ripen there, softening and turning yellow, so you can savor the true taste of a ripe fruit.

In this recipe, the pears contribute juice and flavor to the compote syrup, blending with the background tastes of Earl Grey and star anise. Serve these pears simply, on their own with a goodly amount of syrup and perhaps with a slice of blue cheese and another of walnut bread.

1 cup (8 fl oz/250 ml) dry white wine

1 cup (8 fl oz/250 ml) water

¾ cup (6 oz/185 g) sugar

2 tablespoons Earl Grey tea in a tea ball, or 2 Earl Grey tea bags

1 orange zest strip, 2 inches (5 cm) long

4 whole cloves

2 star anise

1 piece vanilla bean, 2 inches (5 cm) long

5 pears, peeled, halved or quartered lengthwise, and cored

❧ In a saucepan over medium-high heat, combine the wine, water, sugar, tea, orange zest, cloves, star anise, and vanilla bean and bring to a boil, stirring to dissolve the sugar. Boil until a light syrup forms, about 5 minutes. Remove from the heat and let stand for 15 minutes. Remove the tea ball or tea bags.

❧ Return the pan to medium heat and bring to just below a boil, then reduce the heat to low. Using a large spoon, slide the pear pieces into the liquid and poach them for 3–4 minutes. Turn them over and continue to poach just enough to soften the pears slightly, 2–3 minutes. To test for doneness, pierce with the tip of a sharp knife.

❧ Transfer the contents of the saucepan to a glass bowl. Let cool completely, then remove the orange zest, cloves, star anise, and vanilla bean, if desired. Cover and refrigerate to chill.

❧ The pears will keep for up to 5 days in the refrigerator. Serve in small bowls with some of the syrup spooned over the top.

serves 6–8

Bourgogne et Le Lyonnais

Mousse au Chocolat

chocolate mousse

Chocolate mousse is almost a synonym for French dessert. Unfortunately, one often finds poor imitations of the real thing in France and elsewhere. A good chocolate mousse is so rich, so chocolatey, that, as a friend says, one can only eat half of what would be a normal dessert portion. The styles range from gooey to firm. This version falls into the latter group. If you'd like, garnish it with chocolate shavings.

¼ lb (125 g) bittersweet chocolate, chopped into very small pieces

3 tablespoons unsalted butter, cut into small pieces

3 eggs

⅛ teaspoon salt

2 tablespoons confectioners' (icing) sugar

♕ Place the chocolate in a heatproof bowl. Set over (not touching) barely simmering water in a saucepan. Heat, stirring, until the chocolate melts, about 2 minutes. Add the butter and continue to stir until the butter melts and is incorporated, 30–60 seconds.

♕ Separate 1 egg, placing the white in a large bowl and adding the yolk to the chocolate. Quickly whisk in the yolk, fully incorporating it. Repeat with the remaining 2 eggs. Remove the bowl from over the saucepan and let cool to lukewarm.

♕ Add the salt to the egg whites. Using an electric mixer set on medium-high speed, beat the whites until they form stiff peaks, then beat in the confectioners' sugar. Using a rubber spatula, gently fold the egg whites into the chocolate, being careful not to deflate the whites.

♕ Spoon the mixture into a large bowl or individual glasses. Cover and refrigerate until very firm, at least 6 hours or for up to 24 hours. Serve well chilled.

serves 4

Fruits de Saison

Fruit is often served as dessert in France, a particularly healthful habit, and seasonal fruit desserts (*fruits de saison*) are considered highly desirable. In winter it might be oranges, apples, and dried fruits, and in spring cherries or apricots. Of course, in summer, the fruit bowl will be heaped with peaches, plums, nectarines, grapes, and melons. Come fall, figs and pears are the main attractions.

The home orchard, or *verger,* is the counterpoint of the *potager,* and whenever possible people will plant as many fruit trees as they can, even in small city backyards. It is considered a true luxury to be able to serve fresh fruit to guests from one's own trees. Failing that, people seek out the best of what is available from the local market.

In addition to being served on their own as desserts, fruits form the basis of many simple desserts. *Clafouti,* a cakelike pudding classically made with cherries, is also fashioned from apricots, peaches, figs, plums, or nectarines. A fruit *gratin,* in which halved or sliced fruit is put in a buttered gratin dish, then sparsely covered with a light batter and sugared, is one of the easiest desserts to put together, yet when it comes hot and fragrant to the table, it makes an elegant appearance.

Seasonal fruits such as peaches, cherries, or grapes can be used to fill crepes or to top pound cake or ice cream, and they are especially good if first poached in a sugar syrup flavored with a little vanilla. The best *pâtisseries* tempt everyone who passes them with their displays of exquisite tarts constructed of seasonal fruits, such as blackberries in spring, oranges and lemons in winter, and prune plums in fall.

Gratin de Pêches

peach gratin

Fruit gratins, which the French prepare often, are some of the easiest fruit desserts to make. Just enough thin, crepelike batter is used to hold the fruit together when it is sliced. All sorts of fruits can be used, from figs to berries to apricots. Serve the gratin on its own or with crème fraîche or ice cream.

1 teaspoon plus 1 tablespoon unsalted butter, cut into small bits

4 tablespoons (2 oz/60 g) sugar

¼ cup (2 fl oz/60 ml) milk

1 egg

⅛ teaspoon salt

¼ cup (1½ oz/45 g) all-purpose (plain) flour

2 lb (1 kg) peaches, peeled, halved, and pitted

2 tablespoons coarsely chopped almonds or walnuts

♕ Preheat an oven to 425°F (220°C). Using the 1 teaspoon butter, grease an 8- or 9-inch (20- or 23-cm) gratin dish or other shallow baking dish, then sprinkle it with 1 tablespoon of the sugar.

♕ In a bowl, whisk together the milk, egg, 1 table-spoon of the sugar, and the salt. Gradually whisk in the flour. Pour this creamy batter into the gratin dish and top with the prepared peaches. Sprinkle the remaining 2 tablespoons sugar and the nuts over the top and dot with the 1 tablespoon butter.

♕ Bake until the batter is set, the butter is melted, and the peaches are cooked through, 12–15 minutes. Remove from the oven and let stand for about 10 minutes, then serve.

serves 4–6

Le Sud-Ouest

Crêpes aux Coings
à l'Armagnac

crepes with armagnac-quince filling

*Crepes, paper-thin pancakes, seem to be synonymous
with France, and* créperies *abound throughout
the country. Most of them serve the pancakes in both
sweet and savory versions so that you can make a
complete meal of them, but some—especially the open-
air stands—serve only sweet crepes with butter
and sugar or a selection of jams. Raw quince are pale,
astringent, and flavorless. Once cooked, they
become a soft amber-rose and richly flavorful.*

CREPE BATTER

4 eggs

*1¾ cups (14 fl oz/430 ml) milk, or more if
needed*

⅓ cup (2 oz/60 g) all-purpose (plain) flour

1 teaspoon sugar

½ teaspoon salt

FILLING

3 tablespoons unsalted butter

*4 large quinces, peeled, cored, and cut lengthwise
into slices ¼ inch (6 mm) thick*

2 tablespoons sugar

¼ cup (2 fl oz/60 ml) water

2 tablespoons Armagnac

about ¼ cup (2 oz/60 g) unsalted butter

1 cup (8 fl oz/250 ml) heavy (double) cream

1½ tablespoons sugar

To make the crepe batter, in a large bowl, whisk together the eggs and 1¾ cups (14 fl oz/430 ml) milk until blended. Then, a little at a time, whisk in the flour, sugar, and salt to make a thin, lump-free batter. If, despite your best efforts, there are still lumps, strain the batter through a sieve lined with several thicknesses of cheesecloth (muslin). Cover and refrigerate for 2 hours.

To make the filling, in a frying pan over medium heat, melt the butter. When it foams, add the quince slices and cook until glistening, 1–2 minutes. Add the sugar and continue to cook until lightly browned on the first side, 2–3 minutes. Turn the slices and continue to cook until lightly browned on the second side, another 2–3 minutes. Add the water and continue to cook until the quince slices are tender, 2–3 minutes longer. Pour the Armagnac over the quinces and ignite with a match. When the flames subside, cover and keep warm until ready to serve.

Place a 12-inch (30-cm) frying pan, preferably nonstick, over medium-high heat. When a drop of water flicked into the pan sizzles and spatters, the pan is ready. Drop in 1 teaspoon butter. When it melts, tip the pan from side to side to coat the bottom evenly. If the batter seems too thick (it should be the consistency of heavy (double) cream), thin it by beating in a little milk. Then pour a scant ¼ cup (2 fl oz/60 ml) of the batter into the pan, quickly tipping and rotating the pan to coat the bottom evenly. Pour off any excess. In a very short time, only about 30 seconds, bubbles will begin to appear on the surface and the edges will begin to dry and pull away from the pan sides. Using a spatula, turn over the crepe and cook just a moment longer on the other side. Transfer to a plate, stacking as you go, and cover to keep warm. Repeat until all the batter has been used, adding more butter as needed. You should have about 16 crepes.

In a bowl, using an electric mixer set on high speed, beat the cream until it begins to thicken, about 2 minutes. Slowly add the sugar, while continuing to beat until soft peaks form.

To serve, place 1–1½ tablespoons of the quince in the center of a crepe. Fold the crepe in half, and then into quarters. Place on an individual plate. Repeat until all the crepes are filled and folded, placing 2 crepes on each plate. Top each crepe with a spoonful or two of whipped cream. Serve at once.

serves 8

It is considered a true luxury to be able to serve guests fresh fruit from one's own trees. Failing that, hosts seek out the best of what is available from the local market.

Le Centre

Clafouti aux Cerises

cherry custard cake

Clafouti, *a custardlike pudding thick with locally grown tart, dark cherries, originated in Limousin, in the center of France. The delectable dish has been taken up all over the country, however, and not only are different varieties of cherries used, but different fruits as well. The cherries are typically left unpitted, so be sure to warn your guests if you stick to tradition.*

1½ teaspoons unsalted butter

1 cup (8 fl oz/250 ml) milk

¼ cup (2 fl oz/60 ml) heavy (double) cream

⅔ cup (3½ oz/105 g) all-purpose (plain) flour, sifted

3 eggs

¼ cup (2 oz/60 g) granulated sugar

1 tablespoon vanilla extract (essence)

¼ teaspoon salt

4 cups (1 lb/500 g) stemmed sweet or tart cherries, pitted if desired

1 tablespoon confectioners' (icing) sugar

❧ Preheat an oven to 350°F (180°C). Using the butter, grease a 9- to 10-inch (23- to 25-cm) round baking dish. In a bowl, combine the milk, cream, flour, eggs, granulated sugar, vanilla, and salt. Using an electric mixer set on medium speed, beat until frothy, about 5 minutes.

❧ Pour enough of the batter into the prepared baking dish to cover the bottom with a layer about ¼ inch (6 mm) deep. Put the dish in the preheated oven for 2 minutes, then remove it. Cover the batter with a single layer of the cherries. Pour the remaining batter over the cherries. Return to the oven and bake until puffed and browned and a knife inserted into the center comes out clean, 30–35 minutes.

❧ Dust the top of the *clafouti* with confectioners' sugar. Serve warm.

serves 6–8

Le Sud-Ouest

Pouding au Pain aux Fruits Secs

bread pudding with currants and apricots

I have always admired the French way of treating leftover bread as a pantry item. Just because it is no longer fresh doesn't mean it has lost its value, but rather that it has been transformed, like milk to cheese or grapes to wine, into something else valuable. In desserts, stale bread is used primarily in puddings and for pain perdu (page 242), while in savory dishes it might be used in a stuffing for vegetables, fish, or birds, as a final topping for gratins, or for any dishes to be finished with a crunchy topping.

In bread puddings, the final result depends upon the kind of bread you use. If it is a sturdy, chewy country-style bread, the pudding will be light and airy, almost soufflélike, as such bread holds its structure, allowing for air between the crumbs. If the bread is dense and soft, the pudding will be dense as well. Both styles are good. I associate this particular version with southwestern France, with its vast stretches of apricot orchards.

½ cup (3 oz/90 g) dried currants

1 cup (6 oz/185 g) dried apricots, coarsely chopped

⅓ cup (3 fl oz/80 ml) rum

3 tablespoons unsalted butter

4–6 cups (32–48 fl oz/1–1.5 l) milk

4 eggs

1 teaspoon vanilla extract (essence)

½ teaspoon salt

1¼ cups (10 oz/315 g) sugar

10–12 slices day-old bread, each about 1 inch (2.5 cm) thick (see note)

☙ In a bowl, combine the currants and apricots. Pour the rum over them and let soak at room temperature overnight until nicely plumped.

☙ Preheat an oven to 375°F (190°C). Using 1 tablespoon of the butter, generously grease a 5-by-9-by-3-inch (13-by-23-by-7.5-cm) loaf pan or other 2-qt (2-l) baking dish.

☙ Pour the milk into a large bowl. Use about 4 cups (32 fl oz/1 l) if you are using a fine-textured bread, and about 6 cups (48 fl oz/1.5 l) if you are using a coarser, drier bread. Whisk in the eggs, vanilla, salt, and all but 6 tablespoons (3 oz/90 g) of the sugar. Drain the fruits, reserving the liquid. Stir the liquid into the milk mixture.

☙ Make a layer of bread in the bottom of the prepared pan. Set aside 1 tablespoon each of the currants and the apricots. Sprinkle the bread layer with one-third of the currants and apricots. Pour over one-fourth of the milk mixture. Repeat twice, pushing the layers down as you go and ending with a layer of bread followed by the last of the milk. Toss the reserved currants and apricots with the remaining 6 tablespoons (3 oz/90 g) sugar and sprinkle the mixture over the top. Cut the remaining 2 tablespoons butter into small bits and use to dot the top.

☙ Bake until a knife inserted into the center comes out clean, about 45 minutes. Remove from the oven and serve hot or warm, scooping it out into bowls.

serves 6

Le Sud-Ouest

Soufflé aux Pruneaux à l'Armagnac

prune and armagnac soufflé

Soufflés are traditional desserts throughout France, and you will often find that a particular region has a special version that calls for its local products. The presence of prunes and Armagnac identify this as a specialty of Gascony.

½ lb (250 g) pitted prunes

1 cup (8 fl oz/250 ml) warm water

2 tablespoons Armagnac

1½ tablespoons unsalted butter

1½ teaspoons plus 6 tablespoons (3 oz/90 g) granulated sugar

7 egg whites

⅛ teaspoon salt

confectioners' (icing) sugar

❧ In a bowl, combine the prunes, warm water, and 1 tablespoon of the Armagnac. Let stand at room temperature overnight until nicely plumped.

❧ The next day, preheat an oven to 350°F (180°C). Using the butter, generously grease an 8-inch (20-cm) soufflé dish. Sprinkle with the 1½ teaspoons sugar, then rotate the mold to coat the bottom and sides evenly.

❧ Drain the prunes, reserving 2 tablespoons of the liquid. In a blender, combine the prunes, the reserved liquid, and the remaining 1 tablespoon Armagnac. Process until a thick purée forms. Set aside.

❧ In a large bowl, combine the egg whites and salt. Using an electric mixer set on medium-high speed, beat until soft peaks form. Gradually beat in the 6 tablespoons (3 oz/90 g) granulated sugar until stiff peaks form. Using a rubber spatula, fold in the prune purée, a little at a time, being careful not to deflate the egg whites. Pour into the prepared dish.

❧ Bake until puffed above the rim, about 20 minutes. Remove from the oven and, using a fine-mesh sieve, dust the top of the soufflé with confectioners' sugar. Serve immediately.

serves 6

Digestifs

Just as aperitifs are the prelude to a meal, a *digestif* is the conclusion, its purpose to aid in digestion, a distinctly pleasurable assistance. Sometimes it is taken with an after-dinner coffee, but more often it follows it.

Unlike aperitifs, *digestifs* are usually products of distillation, either of wine or of fruits, and virtually all the regions of France have their own specialties. No doubt the most well-known is Cognac, distilled from wine in the area around the city of Cognac in Charentes. Not far away, in Gascony, Armagnac is the *digestif* of choice, made, like Cognac, from distilled wine. Marc, which is made by distilling the grape skins, stems, and seeds left behind after pressing grapes for wine, has its regional aficionados, and you can find *marc de Bourgogne, marc de Champagne, d'Auvergne, d'Alsace*—the list goes on and on. Calvados, a specialty of Normandy, is made from distilled apple juice and pulp. One can readily find eaux-de-vie of raspberries, pears, and other fruits made by first fermenting the fruit, then distilling it, which is a different process than that used for marc, although both can be quite good.

All the *digestifs,* with their complex flavors, are excellent in cooking, where they are frequently ignited, burning off the alcohol but leaving the flavor.

Ile-de-France

Tartelettes aux Fruits

berry tartlets

Rows of fruit tarts, shaped like diamonds, little boats, and scalloped rounds, are presented like glittering multicolored jewels in the windows of pâtisseries all over France. Pastry shops in obscure villages, industrial centers, resort communities, commuter towns, and elegant cities all bake and display beautiful tarts made of fresh fruits sitting atop a layer of crème pâtissière. They are not tricky to make, just time-consuming. To make a large tart, substitute a ten-inch (25-cm) tart pan for the smaller molds.

PASTRY DOUGH

2 cups (10 oz/315 g) all-purpose (plain) flour

1 teaspoon salt

½ cup (4 oz/125 g) plus 3 tablespoons chilled unsalted butter, cut into ½-inch (12-mm) chunks

6 tablespoons (3 fl oz/90 ml) ice water

PASTRY CREAM

1 cup (8 fl oz/250 ml) milk, plus 1 tablespoon (optional)

½ cup (4 oz/125 g) sugar

3 egg yolks

⅓ cup (2 oz/60 g) all-purpose (plain) flour

1 tablespoon unsalted butter, at room temperature

1½ teaspoons vanilla extract (essence)

½ cup (5 oz/155 g) red currant jelly

1½ cups (6 oz/185 g) blueberries

1½ cups (6 oz/185 g) raspberries

❦ To make the pastry dough, in a large bowl, stir together the flour and salt. Using a pastry blender or 2 knives, cut in the butter until pea-sized balls form. Add the ice water 1 tablespoon at a time while turning the dough lightly with a fork and then with your fingertips. (Do not overwork the dough, or it will become tough.) Gather the dough into a ball (it will be a little crumbly), wrap in plastic wrap, and refrigerate for 15 minutes.

❦ Preheat an oven to 425°F (220°C).

❦ Divide the dough into quarters and roll out 1 piece at a time, keeping the others refrigerated. On a floured work surface, roll out the first piece of dough a scant ¼ inch (6 mm) thick. Place a 2-inch (5-cm) round or other shape mold face down on the dough and, using a knife, cut out the same shape ½ inch (12 mm) larger than the mold. Continue until as much dough as possible has been used. Slip a knife or icing spatula under each cutout and gently press into a mold, trimming the edges as needed. Gather together the dough scraps and roll out again. Cut out as many shapes as possible, but do not rework the scraps a second time. Continue until all the dough has been used and the molds lined. Cut out a piece of parchment (baking) paper for each mold and use to line the molds. Fill the lined molds with pie weights or dried beans.

❦ Bake for 10 minutes, then lift out the weights and paper. With a fork, prick the bottoms of the tarts, return to the oven, and bake until golden, 4–5 minutes longer. Let cool completely on a rack.

❦ To make the pastry cream, pour the 1 cup (8 fl oz/250 ml) milk into a large saucepan and place over medium heat until small bubbles form along the edges of the pan. Meanwhile, in a large bowl, using an electric beater set on medium speed, beat together the sugar and egg yolks until lemon colored. Beat in the flour to form a thick paste. When the milk is ready, gradually pour it into the sugar mixture, beating constantly. When the warm milk is thoroughly incorporated, pour the mixture back into the saucepan and bring to a boil over medium-high heat, beating continuously. When the mixture thickens, after 1–2 minutes, immediately remove it from the heat and whisk vigorously until very thick, about 1 minute. Whisk in the butter and vanilla. Let cool slightly. If the pastry cream thickens too much to spread upon cooling, add the 1 tablespoon milk and whisk until smooth.

❦ In a saucepan over low heat, warm the jelly, stirring until melted. Remove from the heat. Pour just enough of the warm melted jelly into a cooled pastry shell to glaze the bottom, tipping the mold from side to side to coat evenly. Continue until all the pastries are glazed, reheating the jelly gently if needed to thin it.

❦ Spoon enough of the pastry cream over the glaze in each shell to make a layer ¼–⅓ inch (6–9 mm) thick. Cover the cream layer with the blueberries and raspberries. Spoon just enough glaze over the berries to coat them. Cover and refrigerate for at least 1 hour or for up to 12 hours.

❦ Let the tartlets stand at room temperature for 15–20 minutes before serving.

serves 12

Figues Rôties
à la Crème Fraîche

oven-roasted figs with crème fraîche

When figs are roasted or grilled, their natural sugars begin to caramelize slightly, and their already sweet taste takes on a deeper, richer flavor. Here that heightened intensity is further enhanced by the addition of a little crème fraîche. Any fig variety may be used as long as the fruits are very ripe and soft. My favorite, however, is the small, nearly black Violette de Bordeaux, which tastes like sweet berry jam.

1 teaspoon unsalted butter

16 very ripe figs

2 tablespoons granulated sugar

1 teaspoon fresh lemon juice

½ cup (4 fl oz/125 ml) crème fraîche

1 tablespoon grated lemon zest

1 tablespoon firmly packed brown sugar

❦ Preheat an oven to 400°F (200°C). Using the butter, grease a shallow roasting pan just large enough to hold the figs.

❦ Place the figs in the prepared pan and turn them once or twice to coat with the butter. Sprinkle with the granulated sugar.

❦ Bake just until the figs are cooked through, 10–12 minutes. Remove from the oven, drizzle with the lemon juice, and let stand for 5 minutes.

❦ Divide the figs among warmed dessert plates. Serve hot, garnished with a little crème fraîche, lemon zest, and brown sugar.

serves 8

The French have a deep appreciation and enthusiasm for seasonal fruits. They know that the fruit's moment is brief and fleeting.

Une Partie Intégrante du Repas

Few things are more representative of French eating habits than the cheese course, which follows the savory courses and precedes fruit or dessert. It is an integral part (*une partie intégrante*) of even the simplest meal. I've eaten in cafeterias on autoroutes and in cities, and I always have been surprised that the trays carried to the table have a component representing each course, including cheese. In some cases it is as simple as a wedge of foil-wrapped Camembert.

Whenever I have eaten in a French home, I have been offered cheese. Sometimes it is an elaborate presentation of several cheeses purchased for the occasion, while other times it is a single, perfectly ripe specimen. But most often it is simply the family's selection for the week. The plates are always changed and a clean knife and fork offered, even for the simplest cheese course. Whenever I have French visitors at my home in California, they are always grateful for my offering of a cheese course, saying how they have missed it during their travels and what an important part of the meal it is to them.

Tarte à la Tatin aux Coings

apple and quince tart

Tarte à la tatin, *an upside-down apple tart, takes on a new dimension in this version of the classic dish. Quinces and golden raisins are used in addition to the apples, and all the fruits are soaked overnight in a marinade of white wine, sugar, and vanilla before baking. The juices in the bottom of the dish, a combination of butter, sugar, and the juices from the fruit, caramelize to create a thick sauce that covers the top of the tart once it is turned out onto a plate.*

3 large or 6 small ripe quinces, peeled, cored, and cut lengthwise into slices ½ inch (12 mm) thick

4 large firm, sweet apples such as Golden Delicious, Reinette, or Gala, peeled, cored, and cut lengthwise into slices ½ inch (12 mm) thick

2 cups (16 fl oz/500 ml) Riesling or other fruity white wine

½ cup (4 oz/125 g) sugar

1 piece vanilla bean, 2 inches (5 cm) long

1 cup (6 oz/185 g) golden raisins (sultanas)

PASTRY

2 cups (10 oz/315 g) all-purpose (plain) flour

1 teaspoon salt

½ cup (4 oz/125 g) plus 3 tablespoons chilled unsalted butter

6 tablespoons (3 fl oz/90 ml) ice water

½ cup (4 oz/125 g) sugar

1 tablespoon unsalted butter

❧ In a large bowl, combine the quince and apple slices, wine, sugar, vanilla bean, and raisins. Stir to mix, then cover and let stand at room temperature for at least 4 hours or up to overnight.

❧ To make the pastry dough, in a large bowl, stir together the flour and salt. Cut off 1 tablespoon of the chilled butter and set aside. Cut the remaining butter into ½-inch (12-mm) chunks and add them to the flour mixture. Using a pastry blender or 2 knives, cut in the butter until pea-sized balls form.

Add the ice water 1 tablespoon at a time while turning the dough lightly with a fork and then with your fingertips. Do not overwork the dough, or it will become tough. Gather the dough into a ball (it will be a little crumbly), wrap it in plastic wrap, and refrigerate for 15 minutes.

❧ Preheat an oven to 375°F (190°C). Using the reserved 1 tablespoon butter, grease a 9- or 10-inch (23- or 25-cm) pie dish with 2- to 2½-inch (5- to 6-cm) sides. (Select a pie dish of clear glass, if possible, so that you can observe the syrup forming in the bottom of the dish.)

❧ Sprinkle the bottom of the prepared dish with ¼ cup (2 oz/60 g) of the sugar. Using a slotted spoon, lift the quince and apple slices and the raisins from the wine mixture. Arrange about one-third of the slices and raisins on the bottom of the prepared dish. Sprinkle on one-third of the remaining sugar. Repeat the layers twice. Cut the 1 tablespoon butter into small bits and use to dot the top evenly. Discard the wine mixture.

❧ On a floured work surface, roll out the dough into a round the same diameter as the baking dish and a scant ¼ inch (6 mm) thick. Drape the pastry around the rolling pin and transfer it to the pie dish. Unfold it and gently drop it over the fruit. Tuck the edges of the pastry down to the bottom of the dish. Any excess dough will form a rim. Prick the top with the tines of a fork.

❧ Bake until the crust is lightly golden and a thickened golden syrup has formed in the bottom of the dish, about 1 hour.

❧ Remove from the oven and let stand for 5 minutes. Slide a knife along the inside edge of the baking dish. Invert a serving platter on top of the dish. Holding the platter and the baking dish firmly together, turn them over so the plate is on the bottom. Lift off the dish. If a few fruit slices stick to the baking dish, gently remove them and place on the tart.

❧ Serve warm, cut into wedges.

serves 6–8

Le Centre

Flognard

plum custard cake

Various regions of France have a custardlike cake or flan, served either plain or with fruits. Prune plums are especially popular to use. In the Auvergne, the preparation is called flognard, *and is made with sliced local fruits such as pears or plums. In the Limousin, the custard cake is made with cherries and called* clafouti.

4½ tablespoons (2¼ oz/67 g) unsalted butter

¼ cup (1½ oz/45 g) all-purpose (plain) flour

¼ cup (2 oz/60 g) sugar

3 eggs

½ cup (4 fl oz/125 ml) milk

¼ teaspoon plum brandy or vanilla extract (essence)

6 red, purple, or green plums, pitted and cut into slices ¼ inch (6 mm) thick, or 12 prune plums, pitted and halved (about ¾ lb/375 g total weight)

Preheat an oven to 400°F (200°C). Using ½ tablespoon of the butter, heavily grease a 10-inch (25-cm) quiche dish or other shallow baking dish.

In a bowl, using a whisk or electric beater, beat together the flour, sugar, eggs, milk, and brandy or vanilla to make a thin batter. Beat vigorously for 1–2 minutes to incorporate air. Pour the batter into the prepared baking dish. Arrange the plums on top in a single, tightly packed layer. Cut the remaining 4 tablespoons (2 oz/60 g) butter into small bits and use to dot the top.

Bake until the top puffs up and the edges become a deep golden brown, about 30 minutes. Remove from the oven, cover loosely with aluminum foil, and let stand for about 5 minutes. It will deflate a bit.

Serve hot, warm, or at room temperature.

serves 4

Franche-Comté et Les Alpes

Fruits Rouges

red fruits in red wine

Fruits rouges, a classic French combination of red fruits, appears in jams, tarts, creams, and other desserts. This one, which reminds me of the mountains where my friends go to gather currants in the summer, is one of the simplest. If currants aren't available, you might substitute blackberries, or simply go without and increase the amount of strawberries and raspberries.

1½ cups (6 oz/185 g) strawberries, hulled

1½ cups (6 oz/185 g) raspberries

1 cup (4 oz/125 g) fresh currants, stemmed

1 tablespoon balsamic vinegar

1 cup (8 fl oz/250 ml) dry red wine such as Merlot or Burgundy

½ cup (2 oz/60 g) confectioners' (icing) sugar

2 tablespoons minced fresh mint

Cut large strawberries lengthwise into halves or quarters. If small, leave them whole. In a bowl, gently stir together the strawberries, raspberries, and currants. Sprinkle the vinegar, wine, and sugar over the top, then turn to mix well. Cover and refrigerate for several hours or for up to overnight.

To serve, spoon the chilled fruits into Champagne glasses or shallow bowls. Garnish with the mint and serve immediately.

serves 6–8

Fruit-based dishes comprise the majority of homemade dessert fare in France, with clafoutis, tarts, poached fruits, and fruit pastries among the favorites.

Franche-Comté et Les Alpes

Tarte aux Noix

walnut tart

In the region around Grenoble, where much of France's walnut crop is produced, it is not uncommon to see walnut pastries in the windows of pâtisseries. In this version, walnut liqueur, vin de noix, is used in the flavoring, but Cointreau or other orange liqueur makes a good substitute.

PASTRY

1½ cups (7½ oz/235 g) all-purpose (plain) flour

¼ cup (2 oz/60 g) granulated sugar

½ cup (4 oz/125 g) unsalted butter, cut into ½-inch (12-mm) chunks

1 egg

FILLING

2 tablespoons unsalted butter, melted and cooled

½ cup (3½ oz/105 g) firmly packed light brown sugar

2 eggs

¼ cup (2 fl oz/60 ml) walnut liqueur or Cointreau

1 teaspoon vanilla extract (essence)

1½ cups (6 oz/185 g) walnut halves, toasted

❦ Position a rack in the lower third of an oven and preheat to 350°F (180°C).

❦ To make the pastry, in a bowl, stir together the flour and granulated sugar. Add the butter and work it in with your fingertips until the mixture becomes crumblike. Add the egg and mix it with a fork. Press the dough evenly into an 11-inch (28-cm) tart pan with a removable bottom. Set aside.

❦ To make the filling, in a bowl, combine the melted butter, brown sugar, eggs, liqueur, and vanilla. Beat with a wooden spoon until blended. Stir in the toasted nuts. Pour the filling into the tart pan.

❦ Bake until the crust and the filling are golden brown, about 50 minutes. Transfer to a rack to cool until warm. Remove the pan rim and slide the tart onto a plate. Serve warm or at room temperature.

serves 12

Champagne et Le Nord

Sorbet au Champagne

champagne sorbet

This is a stylish way to finish a meal, as the flavor of Champagne is foremost. A drop or two of crème de cassis or other fruit liqueur might be added for color and flavor as well. Some good choices are pear, raspberry, and peach.

Only sparkling wines made in specified areas of Champagne under rigorous state-controlled regulations can legally bear the name Champagne, but for this sorbet other sparkling wines may be used. A particularly beautiful and flavorful sorbet may be made with a dry or brut rosé sparkling wine. For a festive preparation, garnish the sorbet with candied violets or rose petals, and serve in bowl-shaped Champagne glasses, the ones that were especially popular in the 1940s.

1 bottle (24 fl oz/750 ml) Champagne or sparkling wine

¼ cup (2 oz/60 g) sugar

♛ In a shallow metal bowl or pan, stir together the Champagne or sparkling wine and the sugar. Cover tightly with plastic wrap or aluminum foil and place in the coldest part of the freezer. Freeze, whisking every 30 minutes, until the mixture becomes firm and granular, about 4 hours.

♛ Once the mixture is granular, transfer it to a food processor or blender and process to break up the chunks. This will create a lighter texture.

♛ Put the mixture back in the shallow bowl or pan, cover with plastic wrap or foil, and refreeze until ready to serve. For optimum flavor, the sorbet should be served within 48 hours of being prepared.

♛ To serve, spoon into Champagne flutes, wine glasses, or other dessert dishes.

serves 4

Normandie

Galette de Pommes au Fromage

apple and goat cheese galette

One of the nice things about apples is that because a number of varieties store well, the fruit is in season from fall through spring. The French have made good use of this bounty, and consequently dishes incorporating apples are abundant and inventive. This one uses soft goat cheese and a light custard.

1 sheet frozen puff pastry, about 12 by 14 inches (30 by 35 cm) and ¼ inch (6 mm) thick, thawed in the refrigerator

¼ lb (125 g) fresh goat cheese

½ cup (4 oz / 125 g) plus 2 tablespoons sugar

1 egg

½ cup (4 fl oz / 125 ml) heavy (double) cream

¼ teaspoon vanilla extract (essence)

2 large apples such as Granny Smith, Gala, or Golden Delicious, peeled, cored, and cut lengthwise into slices ¼ inch (6 mm) thick

♛ Preheat an oven to 375°F (190°C).

♛ Unfold the sheet of puff pastry. Using a sharp knife, trim off the corners to make a round about 12 inches (30 cm) in diameter. Transfer the pastry to an ungreased baking sheet. Pinch the edges up to form a generous ¼-inch (6-mm) rim.

♛ In a bowl, whisk together the goat cheese, the ½ cup (4 oz / 125 g) sugar, the egg, cream, and vanilla until a smooth paste forms. Spread the paste evenly over the bottom of the pastry. Arrange the apple slices in a concentric circle on top. Sprinkle the 2 tablespoons sugar evenly over the apples.

♛ Bake until the pastry is puffed and browned and the apples are lightly golden, about 30 minutes. Remove from the oven, cover loosely with aluminum foil, and let stand for about 10 minutes.

♛ Serve the galette warm or at room temperature, cut into wedges.

serves 6

Quelques Fromages Assortis

There are several ways to compose a classic platter for a cheese course. The simplest is an offering of five to seven cheeses from different regions and families. The families include fresh cheeses, such as petit-suisse and fromage frais; soft cheeses with a coated rind, usually soft and white, such as Camembert; and soft cheeses with a washed rind, such as Munster. The rinds of these latter cheeses are typically orange-red from the frequent washings they receive as they age. Veined cheeses, those with blue veining or marbling, form another family. Hard uncooked cheeses, which are aged from three to six months, make up a group that includes morbier and Saint-Nectaire, and hard cooked cheeses constitute yet another family. From this latter cluster come Comté and Beaufort, which are aged for up to two years. Goat cheese can belong to any of the families, depending upon how it was made.

Another way to compose your cheese board is to choose three cheeses from the same region and accompany them with a wine, cider, or beer of that region. With goat cheese, of which I am especially fond, you can serve a "flight" from very fresh to aged. In every case, for the best flavor, remove your cheeses from the refrigerator at least an hour and a half before serving.

Pays de la Loire

Pain Perdu aux Cerises Tièdes

french toast with warm cherries

Although this dessert is humble farmhouse fare, the combination of tastes, textures, and colors makes it a splendid sweet.

¼ cup (2 oz/60 g) sugar

½ cup (4 fl oz/125 ml) water

1 star anise

1 tablespoon kirsch (optional)

1 cup (6 oz/185 g) stemmed yellow Rainier cherries or other large, sweet cherries

4 eggs

2 tablespoons milk or water

4 slices day-old brioche or other sweet bread, each ½ inch (12 mm) thick

3 tablespoons unsalted butter

confectioners' (icing) sugar

In a saucepan over medium heat, combine the sugar and water. Bring to a boil, stirring until the sugar dissolves. Add the star anise and the kirsch, if using. Cook, stirring occasionally, until a thin syrup forms, 4–5 minutes. Add the cherries and continue to cook, stirring often, until softened, 7–8 minutes. Remove from the heat and cover to keep warm.

In a shallow baking dish just large enough to hold the brioche slices in a single layer, whisk together the eggs and milk or water until blended. Add the brioche slices and let soak for 1–2 minutes. Turn them over and let soak on the second side until all the liquid has been absorbed.

In a frying pan over medium heat, melt the butter. Add the bread and cook, turning once, until golden, 6–8 minutes total.

Transfer a slice of the brioche to each of 4 warmed individual plates. Spoon an equal amount of the warm cherries and their sauce over each slice. Dust with confectioners' sugar and serve. Be sure to alert your guests about the unpitted cherries.

serves 4

Provence

Rissoles d'Abricots

jam-filled pastries

This is my version of a deep-fried pastry I had in Digne-les-Bains in the Basses-Alpes on market day. It was handed to me, wrapped in paper, piping hot from a huge deep-fat fryer.

The chalked board on the umbrella-covered table announced Rissoles. *Although the dough was not the sweetened pastry dough of the rézules, or rissoles, of Savoy, the principle is, I think, very much the same. In appearance, these* rissoles *rather resemble large ravioli that have been deep-fried and dusted with sugar. The vendor did have savory versions as well, and I sampled one made with a filling of spinach, and another with a filling of potato and cheese. The pastry was the same for the sweet and savory versions.*

DOUGH

2 cups (10 oz/315 g) all-purpose (plain) flour

2 egg yolks

1 tablespoon extra-virgin olive oil

2 tablespoons water

2 cups (1¼ lb/625 g) thick apricot jam with halves or chunks of fruit

canola or other light oil for deep-frying

confectioners' sugar (icing)

☗ To make the dough, put the flour, egg yolks, olive oil, and water, in that order, in a food processor. Process until a sticky ball forms. Transfer the dough to a floured work surface and knead until it is elastic and can be rolled out, about 7 minutes. Loosely wrap the dough in plastic wrap and let stand at room temperature for 30 minutes.

☗ Divide the dough into 2 equal pieces. On a large, well-floured work surface, roll out 1 ball of dough into a 16-by-20-inch (40-by-50-cm) rectangle about ⅛ inch (3 mm) thick. Visually divide the dough sheet into 4-inch (10-cm) squares. Place 3 tablespoons of the jam filling in the center of each square, smoothing and spreading it out to within ½ inch (12 mm) of the edges of the squares.

☗ Roll out the remaining ball of dough into the same-sized sheet. Lay the second sheet over the top of the first. With the edge of your hand, press the upper sheet to the lower one, making lines between the mounds of filling to seal the edges of the squares.

☗ With a pastry cutter or a sharp knife, cut along each sealing line, dividing the filled dough sheets into 4-inch (10-cm) squares. (At this point, you can cook the squares at once, or you can arrange them in a single layer, not touching, on a flour-dusted kitchen towel or piece of waxed paper, dust them well with flour, and cover them with another towel or piece of waxed paper. They will keep for several hours.)

☗ In a deep frying pan, pour in oil to a depth of 1 inch (2.5 cm) and heat over medium heat to 350°F (180°C) on a deep-frying thermometer, or until a drop of water flicked into the pan sizzles. Add the squares, a few at a time; do not allow them to touch. Cook on the first side until golden brown, about 2 minutes. Using tongs, turn them over and cook on the second side until golden brown, about 1½ minutes longer. Using tongs, transfer to paper towels to drain. Keep warm in a low oven until ready to serve, or serve as they are prepared, a few at a time.

☗ Just before serving, using a fine-mesh sieve, dust the pastries with confectioners' sugar. Serve hot.

makes about 20 pastries; serves 5 or 6

L'Affineur

Except for the very fresh cheeses, all cheeses are aged. Each type has its optimum point of ripeness, and it is at this point that it has fully matured. *Affineurs*, or master cheese maturers, buy cheeses of all kinds from producers and then age them in *caves*.

In Bordeaux, there is one such *affineur*, Jean d'Alos, whose shop and *cave* are near the river on the rue Montesquieu. His *cave* was hewn out of the rock hundreds of years ago and originally used by a wine merchant for storing casks. Looking at its cheese-laden shelves today, which are on three levels beneath the shop, is like taking a trip to all the regions of France. The subterranean walls are lined with hundreds of cylinders, pyramids, wheels, disks, and squares from Savoy, Auvergne, the north and Pas-de-Calais, Normandy, Lorraine and Alsace, Burgundy, the Alpes, and Provence, each cheese carefully tended by M. d'Alos and his white-smocked staff. Upstairs in the light-filled, intensely aromatic shop, his clients come to request a cheese for tonight's dinner or for a midday meal two days hence. M. d'Alos selects a cheese from the vast display in his shop or *cave* that will be perfectly ripe at that specified moment.

Crème au Caramel

Like chocolate mousse, crème au caramel *appears in many versions in restaurants of all persuasions, and it can even be purchased in individual four-pack servings at supermarkets. It is easy to make at home and rewarding, as it is an elegant dessert.*

> 1 cup (8 oz/250 g) sugar
> 2 cups (16 fl oz/500 ml) milk
> 2 cups (16 fl oz/500 ml) heavy (double) cream
> 8 eggs
> ¼ teaspoon salt
> 1 teaspoon vanilla extract (essence)
> boiling water, as needed

❦ Put ½ cup (4 oz/125 g) of the sugar in a 10-inch (25-cm) cake pan with 1½-inch (4-cm) sides and place it on the stove top over medium-low heat. Holding the edge of the pan with a hot pad, tilt the pan from side to side as the sugar melts and caramelizes. When all the sugar has melted and become a golden brown liquid, remove the pan from the stove. Tip the pan so that the sides and bottom are evenly coated with the syrup. Set aside.

❦ Preheat an oven to 325°F (165°C).

❦ In a saucepan over medium heat, combine the milk and cream and heat until small bubbles appear along the edges of the pan. Meanwhile, in a bowl, beat the eggs until blended. Add the remaining ½ cup (4 oz/125 g) sugar, the salt, and the vanilla and beat until blended. Slowly pour the hot milk mixture into the egg mixture while stirring continuously.

❦ Place the caramel-lined cake pan in a shallow baking pan. Pour the custard into the cake pan, filling it to the rim. Pour boiling water into the baking pan to reach halfway up the sides of the cake pan. Bake until a knife inserted into the center comes out clean, 35–45 minutes. Remove from the oven and let cool to room temperature.

❦ To unmold, slide a knife along the inside edge of the pan. Invert a shallow serving plate on top of the custard. Holding the cake pan and the plate firmly together, turn them over so the plate is on the bottom. Give the pan a shake and then lift it off. The custard should drop smoothly to the serving plate. Serve at room temperature or chilled.

serves 8

LE GLOSSAIRE

The following entries cover key French ingredients and basic recipes called for throughout this book. For information on items not found below, please refer to the index.

ANCHOVIES

Preserved with salt, which highlights their naturally sharp, briny taste, these tiny, silver-skinned fish are enjoyed in the south of France as a flavor element in savory dishes, sometimes evident in a recipe and sometimes only slightly present. Although the fish is also caught in the Atlantic Ocean, the finest anchovies are those found along France's Mediterranean coast. For the best-quality, freshest-tasting, and meatiest anchovies, look for those sold still layered whole in salt. They are available in 1-pound (500-g) tins or sold by weight from larger tins in specialty-food stores and many Italian delicatessens. If salted anchovies are unavailable, use a good brand of anchovy fillets packed in olive oil. Select those sold in glass jars rather than tins, which permit you to judge more easily their meatiness.

TO PREPARE SALTED ANCHOVIES FOR USE, rinse well under cold running water and scrape off their skins with a small, sharp knife. Split open along the backbone, cutting off the dorsal fins. Then pull out the spines and rinse the fillets well. Pat dry with paper towels, place in a glass or other nonreactive bowl, pour in enough olive oil to cover with a thin layer, cover tightly, and refrigerate. Use within 2 weeks.

ARMAGNAC

Named for the district surrounding Auch, the capital of Gascony in southwestern France, this fine brandy is distilled a single time (unlike twice-distilled Cognac) from local white wines, then aged in new casks (unlike the old casks used for Cognac) made from the tight-grained heartwood of local oak trees. The result is a more fragrant spirit, sometimes also described as earthier, than its better-known cousin. It is sipped after meals or used as an ingredient in both savory and sweet dishes of the region.

ARTICHOKES

These large, edible immature flower buds of a type of thistle were first brought to France from their native Italy by Catherine de' Medici in the sixteenth century. Today, distinctive varieties of the vegetable are grown in several different parts of the country. Brittany and Normandy are renowned for their enormous, globe-shaped variety, particularly the Camus artichoke, which is harvested from midspring to early winter. It requires trimming of its sharp-pointed leaves and prickly choke before the large, fleshy heart can be eaten. Although smaller globe-shaped varieties are also grown in the south, the most famous artichoke of Provence is the Violette, harvested in spring and autumn. A small, slender purple type about the size and shape of a large lemon, it may be eaten raw in its entirety when very young and is also cooked.

BEANS

In *potagers* (kitchen gardens) and on farms alike, the French raise a wide variety of beans, some to be eaten whole, pods and all, and some to be shelled and eaten fresh or dried and stored for future use. Fresh beans eaten pods and all are known as haricots verts, or green beans (although some varieties may be pale yellow). These are especially prized when small, slender, young, and very tender, with no seed development. Fava (broad) beans, known in France as *fèves*, resemble oversized lima beans and are enjoyed both fresh and dried. Unless very young and tender, shelled fresh favas are also generally peeled of their tough outer skins before cooking, although many Provençal cooks skip this step. Other beans that are eaten freshly shelled or dried for future use are typically referred to as *haricots*, a term that embraces a wide variety. These include flageolets, small, delicately flavored, pale green beans; creamy white beans such as the large *cocos* or the smaller *lingots*, for which dried Italian cannellini or American navy or white beans may be substituted; and speckled types such as Italian borlotti or cranberry beans.

TO SHELL ANY FRESH BEAN, hold the pod seam side up between your fingertips and press down and pull on the seam with your thumbs to split it open. Holding the open pod over a bowl, run a thumb or finger along the length of the pod's interior to pop out the beans.

BREAD CRUMBS

Used to make crisp toppings for oven-baked dishes or to lend body to fillings and stuffings, bread crumbs should be made from a country-style white loaf that is a day or two old, so that its crumb will be firmer.

TO MAKE FRESH BREAD CRUMBS, trim off and discard the crusts and process in a food processor with the metal blade until as coarsely or as finely textured as desired. To dry the crumbs, spread them on a baking sheet and bake in a preheated 325°F (165°C) oven for about 15 minutes. For toasted crumbs, continue baking the coarse or fine dried crumbs, stirring once or twice, until lightly golden, about 15 minutes longer.

CALVADOS

Distilled from the juice and pulp of apples, this potent specialty of Normandy in northwestern France is a dry, clear, amber-hued brandy fragrant with the perfume of the local fruit from which it is made. Although most commonly enjoyed after dinner or used as a flavoring for savory and sweet dishes, Calvados is also drunk locally as a midmeal *digestif*, referred to as *le trou normand*, "the Normandy hole." Traditionally sold in tall earthenware jugs crowned with a sprig of apple leaves, the brandy today is more often purchased in glass bottles.

CAPERS

Growing wild throughout southern France, the caper bush yields tiny gray-green buds that are preserved in salt or pickled in vinegar to produce a piquant seasoning or garnish used whole or finely minced.

CHEESES

"How can you be expected to govern a country that has 246 kinds of cheese?" complained French president Charles de Gaulle in 1962. How much more emphatic might his statement have been had he known that, in fact, almost 400 distinct varieties are recognized in the country, and that the preponderance of small-production farmhouse and monastery varieties may increase that level to as high as 750? Those highlighted in this book include:

BEAUFORT ~ Produced in the Savoy region of eastern France, this pale yellow cheese closely resembles the Gruyère of nearby Switzerland and is sometimes called Gruyère de Beaufort. It has a mellow, nutty flavor and a smooth, semifirm consistency with only a few small holes.

BLEU DE BRESSE ~ A popular cow's milk product made in alpine eastern France, this blue-veined cheese is enjoyed for its mild flavor and a creamy consistency soft enough for spreading with a knife.

CAMEMBERT ~ Rich, creamy, and slightly tangy, this specialty from the area surrounding the Normandy town of Camembert enjoys renown as one of France's greatest cheeses. It was acclaimed by no less a personage than Napoleon, who reputedly kissed the woman who served him the cheese when he visited its native village. Made of local cow's milk, the plump, disk-shaped cheese has a powdery white rind that develops yellow-orange flecks as ripeness approaches, at which time the buttery-yellow interior should be soft and smooth but not runny. Overripe Camemberts carry a strong scent of ammonia and should be avoided.

COMTE ~ Resembling the Swiss Gruyère produced nearby and sometimes called Gruyère de Comté, this nutty-tasting cow's milk cheese of the Jura region is considered to have a more mellow, less sweet flavor.

EMMENTALER ~ Noted for its mellow, slightly rich, nutlike flavor, this is the premier Swiss cheese, recognizable by its golden straw color and its holes as large as cherries. The name, modified to Emmental, also applies to a similar cow's milk cheese from France's Savoy and Franche-Comté regions.

FROMAGE FRAIS ~ This term applies to fresh *(frais)*, unripened curd cheeses made throughout France from skimmed or sometimes cream-enriched cow's milk, usually eaten at breakfast or for dessert with the addition of sugar, honey, jam, or fresh fruit.

GOAT CHEESES ~ Categorized by the French term *fromage de chèvre,* cheeses made from goat's milk range from day-old fresh cheeses mild and sweet enough to eat for dessert; to slightly older, mild, pleasantly tangy fresh cheeses; to more mature, creamy goat cheeses, often sold coated with herbs or wood ash, wrapped in chestnut or grape leaves, or marinated in olive oil; to well-aged, pungent cheeses hard enough to be grated.

GRUYERE ~ Named for the Swiss alpine village in which it originates, this cow's milk cheese has a more pronounced flavor than other Swiss varieties, the result of aging for 10 to 12 months. In France, the term also applies to the domestic Gruyère-type cheeses Beaufort, Comté, and Emmental.

MORBIER ~ A mild, smooth-textured cow's milk cheese that originated in monasteries in the Franche-Comté region. This variety is notable for the blue-black streak of edible ash running horizontally through its middle, which originated when monks produced the cheeses in two batches, spreading a thin layer of charcoal atop curds produced from the morning milking to protect them until those from the evening milking could be added.

MUNSTER ~ Soft and buttery in texture, but mildly to pungently aromatic in taste, this German-style cow's milk cheese, covered with a red rind, comes from Alsace and the Vosges in northeastern France.

PETIT-SUISSE ~ This term refers to several different brands of packaged, commercially manufactured, cream-enriched types of fromage frais, enjoyed for their rich flavor, mild taste, and smooth consistency.

RACLETTE ~ Resembling Gruyère, this cow's milk cheese, normally regarded as a Swiss product, is also produced in the Savoy region. Taking its name from *racler,* "to scrape," it is produced specifically for use in a special rustic dish popular in alpine regions.

REBLOCHON ~ A mild but flavorful cow's milk cheese produced in the Savoy region, firm but soft-textured when young and spreadable when slightly aged. The flattened cheese rounds are traditionally packaged between two thin wooden disks.

ROQUEFORT ~ The legendary blue-veined ewe's milk cheese produced only in the Aveyron commune of Roquefort-sur-Soulzon. Roquefort is savored for its rich, creamy to crumbly texture and tangy, salty flavor.

SAINT-NECTAIRE ~ Semihard and smooth with a mildly tangy flavor, this orange-rinded cow's milk cheese is made in the Auvergne region of France.

TOMME DE SAVOIE ~ This cow's milk cheese from the mountains of southeastern France (*tomme* means "cheese" in the local dialect) has a semihard texture, a fragrant aroma, and a mild, nutlike flavor. Also spelled tome de Savoie.

HERBS

French cooks grow many herbs in their *potagers* (kitchen gardens), gather them wild in the countryside, or buy them in their local markets. Among the many herbs used in France, those featured in this book include:

ARUGULA ~ Cooks have gathered this peppery-flavored salad herb in the wild since the days of the Roman Empire. It is included among the mixture of leaves known in Provence as *mesclun*.

BASIL ~ Thriving in the warmth of southern France, this sweet and spicy fresh herb is especially popular in the cooking of Provence. It pairs perfectly with sun-ripened tomatoes and goes well with other vegetables.

BAY LEAF ~ The long, pointed leaves of the evergreen Mediterranean laurel tree, *Lauris nobilis,* bay leaves may be added fresh or dried to any long-simmered dishes and are a classic element of the French herb bundle known as a bouquet garni.

CHERVIL ~ Resembling tiny Italian parsley leaves and carrying a hint of sweet anise flavor, this fresh springtime herb is especially popular in France's Basque region and in Touraine and Provence. It goes well with delicate foods, including salads, cooked vegetables, eggs, seafood, and chicken.

CHIVE ~ This thin green shoot of a member of the onion family is used fresh to add a hint of onion flavor to salads and mild-tasting ingredients such as eggs, cheeses, seafood, and poultry.

CILANTRO ~ Chinese or Arabic parsley is what the French call these fresh green leaves of the same plant that produces the spice known as coriander seeds. They give a spicy, astringent green taste to a wide variety of savory dishes. Also known as fresh coriander.

DILL ~ This sweet, mild, anise-scented herb is used in French kitchens to season vinegars and pickling brines, salads, and mild-tasting ingredients such as seafood, poultry, eggs, and cheeses.

LAVENDER ~ One of the definitive scents and sights of Provence, these fragrant purple blossoms cover entire fields and hillsides in the south of France and even flavor the meat of the animals, particularly lamb, who graze upon them.

MARJORAM ~ Milder in flavor than its cousin, oregano, this herb is used both fresh and dried throughout Mediterranean France. It goes well with grilled meats, poultry, and seafood and also frequently seasons vegetable and dried bean dishes.

MINT ~ More than 600 different types of mint exist. French cooks typically use the variety known as spearmint, which they call *menthe douce* (sweet) or *menthe verte* (green), adding its refreshing flavor to vegetables and roasts, particularly lamb. Fresh mint leaves are also infused in hot water to make an herbal tea.

PARSLEY, FLAT-LEAF ~ Southern European in origin, this widely versatile herb adds its bright, fresh flavor to many different kinds of savory foods. The flat-leaf variety, also known as Italian parsley, has a more pronounced flavor than the curly type, which is used predominantly as a garnish.

ROSEMARY ~ Taking its name from the Latin for "rose of the sea," this evergreen shrub thrives in the salt-spray air of Mediterranean France. Its highly aromatic flavor goes well with meats and poultry, as well as with tomatoes and other vegetables.

SAGE ~ Sharply fragrant, with traces of both bitterness and sweetness, this gray-green herb is particularly popular in Provence, where it often seasons pork, veal, game, and cured meats.

SORREL ~ This herb, with its long, narrow leaves, is noted for its highly acidic, tart, almost lemony flavor and is correspondingly very high in vitamin C. (The name derives from a Teutonic word for "sour.") Sometimes included raw in salads when very young, the delicate-textured leaves have the unusual property of melting to a purée when exposed to heat and are a popular source of color and flavor in sauces, soups, and stuffings featuring mild-flavored ingredients such as eggs, seafood, and veal.

TARRAGON ~ Native to Siberia, this heady, anise-flavored herb migrated across the kitchens of Asia and Europe, reaching French kitchens by the fifteenth century. Milder-tasting French tarragon is preferable to the more powerful Russian variety and is often used to perfume wine vinegar and Dijon mustards, flavor sauces and dressings, and season such ingredients as seafood, poultry, and eggs.

THYME ~ This aromatic herb grows wild throughout southern France and often flavors food without the cook's help, as game birds and wild rabbits like to feed upon it. A key element of the bouquet garni, it is considered a digestive aid and is often used to season rich meats such as mutton, pork, duck, and goose.

WINTER SAVORY ~ Strong and spicy in flavor, this evergreen Mediterranean herb goes well with robust ingredients such as dried beans, cured meats, pork, cheeses, and tomato sauces. In Provence, it is referred to as *poivre d'âne,* donkey's pepper.

CAUL FAT

Known in French as *crépine,* this thin membrane, which encases a pig's stomach, is interlaced with a delicate network of fat that resembles a lacy veil. Caul is traditionally used as an edible wrapper for homemade sausage mixtures formed into tiny bundles known as *crépinettes.* It is also used to wrap delicate veal roasts, to keep them moist in the oven, and to enclose pâtés, terrines, or even stuffed cabbage. Buy caul fresh or dry-salted from a full-service butcher. If it is too stiff to manipulate easily, soak it for about 5 minutes in warm water until pliable.

CHARCUTERIE

The French term *charcuterie* covers a wide variety of fresh and cured products derived from meats and variety meats (offal), all of which are traditionally sold in shops of the same name. Among the scores of products that fall under the heading, those referred to in this book include:

BOUDIN NOIR ~ "Black sausage," made from pork blood, *boudin noir* is a robust-tasting specialty produced throughout France.

JAMBON ~ The French term for ham, it can refer to a wide variety of different types, including *jambon cru,* raw salt-cured ham, popular all over France and used either thinly sliced as an hors d'oeuvre or as a seasoning or wrapper for cooked vegetables and other savory ingredients; and *jambon du pays,* literally "country-style ham," seasoned in the style of its particular region, such as the pepper-rubbed hams of Basque country.

PATE ~ Literally a "paste," this term refers to any number of hors d'oeuvre mixtures of seasoned ground meat and other ingredients, baked and served hot or cold in thick slices.

RILLETTES ~ Finely shredded meat, traditionally pork but sometimes goose, duck, or rabbit, that has been long cooked and then mixed with its melted fat and lightly seasoned before serving.

ROULADE ~ Salt-and-herb-cured pork belly similar to Italian pancetta.

SAUCISSE ~ The French term that covers a variety of different fresh sausages that require cooking before they are eaten. Noteworthy examples include the *poumoniers* of Savoy, which take their name from the French word for the lung meat they include along with robust greens such as spinach or chard; the small, delicate pork *diots* of the Savoy region, traditionally seasoned with nutmeg and cinnamon; *cervelas,* a sausage of Lyons, made of pork and flavored with truffles or pistachio nuts; and *boudin noir.*

SAUCISSON ~ Most often refers to a wide variety of large sausages preserved by smoking or drying and served in slices.

COGNAC

The Chevalier de la Croix-Marrons, who reputedly first developed Cognac some time around the seventeenth century, described the end result of distilling wine to make this world-renowned brandy as that of "capturing its soul." Produced in a strictly delineated region in western France surrounding the Charente town of the same name, Cognac is twice distilled from white wine made from grapes of the region, and is then aged for as few as 2 years or as many as 50 years in old oak casks that give it a distinctive amber hue and rich aroma and flavor. Many Cognacs are produced by blending older and younger vintages to make products of uniform quality.

CORNICHON

Prepared from a type of cucumber specifically grown to be picked when its fruits are still green and very small, cornichons are pickled in vinegar and served as a condiment with pâtés, terrines, and other charcuterie, as well as with the boiled beef dish known as pot-au-feu.

CREME FRAICHE

Thick enough to spread when chilled, but fluid enough to pour at room temperature, this tangy, slightly acidulated fresh cream is used as a topping for fruit and other sweets and is also a popular enrichment for sauces.

DIJON MUSTARD

The city of Dijon in Burgundy produces about half of the mustard in France, a distinctive product made by combining a fine flour ground from black and brown mustard seeds with verjuice, the juice from unripe grapes. A balanced blend of tangy, hot, and creamy flavors, it is used both as a condiment and as a seasoning for marinades, roasts, sauces, and dressings. Many dishes that include the words *à la dijonnaise* include a dose of the mustard.

FATBACK

The layer of fat that runs along the back of a pig. Used for making lard, for wrapping or covering roasting meats to keep them moist as they cook, and as an ingredient in sausages, pâtés, or terrines.

JUNIPER BERRY

This slightly resinous dried berry of a small evergreen shrub is a popular seasoning for game and pork dishes, particularly in the northeastern and alpine regions of France. Juniper berries are an indispensable ingredient in the charcuterie-and-sauerkraut dish known as *choucroute garnie* and are often included in marinades and stuffings, as well as in pâté and sausage mixtures. Before use, the berries are usually slightly crushed to release their aroma.

KIRSCH

A signature fruit brandy of Alsace, kirsch is twice distilled from highly acidic wild cherries along with their stones, which contribute a hint of almond flavor to the fruity but dry eau-de-vie. It is most often enjoyed after meals, sipped as a *digestif,* and is also included as a flavoring in fruit dishes, baked goods, and candies.

LARDONS

Strips of fat, commonly cut from salt pork or bacon, used with lean, dry meats or poultry. Sometimes lardons are inserted with a specialized needle; other times they are laid on top. The term is also used for diced and fried bacon.

LENTILS, PUY

Grown in and around the Puy-de-Dôme in the Auvergne, these tiny blue-green dried legumes have a finer flavor than other varieties of lentils and are prized because they hold their shape well during cooking.

MACHE

Known in English as lamb's lettuce or corn salad, this leaf vegetable, which resembles compact rosettes of slightly elongated watercress leaves, is harvested wild in France during autumn and is also cultivated from late summer to early spring. The flavorful, tender leaves are usually eaten raw in salads and may also be cooked.

NUTS

A wide variety of nuts are grown and harvested through-out France and used in many different ways, from roasted and salted and served with aperitifs to ground and used as ingredients in baked goods and desserts. Almonds thrive in Provence, where they are even eaten while still green and soft. Chestnuts, which grow well in the region south of Paris, complement game dishes and figure in many desserts. Spherical hazelnuts (filberts), grown in southwestern France and in Savoy, are favored in desserts, although they also go well with many savory dishes. Pine nuts, the seeds from the cones of a species of pine that thrives in Provence, are added to pâtés and terrines and used in baked goods. Pistachio nuts, also grown in southern France, go particularly well with poultry dishes and charcuterie and are popular in desserts. Walnuts are raised throughout the southern and eastern parts of the country, including the Dordogne, Gascony, Provence, and Savoy, with the most prolific source the area around Grenoble. They are popular in savory and sweet dishes.

TO TOAST NUTS, bake them in a single layer in a 325°F (165°C) oven until they just begin to darken, 5–10 minutes; remove from the oven and let cool to room temperature. Toasting also loosens the skins of hazelnuts and walnuts, which may then be removed by rubbing the still-warm nuts inside a kitchen towel.

OLIVES

Whether water-soaked and brine-cured or salt-cured and preserved in oil, a wide variety of olives are enjoyed in France's sunnier southern climes, nibbled on their own with aperitifs or included in hors d'oeuvres, salads, or other savory dishes. Among the best varieties are the small black Niçoise olives, for which similar varieties such as Nyons olives from the Drôme or sharper-tasting Greek Kalamata olives may be substituted.

PETITS POIS

Grown near Paris and in northern and western France, these green springtime peas are prized for their tiny size and exceptional sweetness. Peas freeze well, and when they are not fresh in season, frozen products labeled "petits pois" (little peas) can be used.

QUINCES

Grown in eastern France, these autumn fruits resemble large, lumpy, yellow-green pears. Unlike pears, they are inedible when raw, with an unpleasantly bitter taste and hard texture. Cooking, however, brings out a sweet, fragrant flavor and delicate consistency, which may be included in baked desserts or even some savory dishes, but most often is featured in jams, jellies, and confections.

SAFFRON THREADS

The highly aromatic dried stigmas of a variety of crocus, this costly spice is used in various parts of France, most notably in Provence, to add richly perfumed flavor and bright golden color to both savory and sweet dishes. Although saffron is grown near Orléans, west of Paris, the finest saffron is generally conceded to be that of Spain. For the best flavor, always buy the spice in the form of whole stigmas, or saffron threads, rather than in powdered form.

TOMATOES

Brought to Europe from the New World by Spanish explorers in the sixteenth century, tomatoes have become a definitive ingredient of southern French cooking, particularly when they are at their peak in summer.

TO PEEL A TOMATO, use a small, sharp knife to score a shallow X in its flower end. Dip the tomato into a saucepan of boiling water for about 20 seconds, then submerge it in a bowl of ice water. Starting at the X, peel off the loosened skin with your fingertips, using the knife if necessary to help. To remove the seeds, cut the tomato crosswise in half and squeeze gently.

VINEGARS

The word "vinegar" comes from the French *vin aigre,* meaning "sour wine," which describes what results when wine or some other alcoholic liquid or fruit juice undergoes a secondary fermentation caused by airborne bacteria, turning it acidic. Wine vinegars are prized throughout France for the power they have to sharpen the flavors of other foods. The best-quality wine vinegars start with good-quality wines and reflect the characteristics of the white or red wines from which they are made. Champagne vinegar, for example, has a particularly refined flavor. Raspberry vinegar has a distinctively fruity flavor, the result of steeping fresh berries in good-quality white wine vinegar. Cider vinegar reflects the taste of the apple cider from which it is made. French cooks also prize Italian balsamic vinegar. A similar French vinegar made from Banyuls, a sweet fortified red wine, is produced in the Pyrenees region of Roussillon.

STOCKS

For the recipes in this book, use good-quality canned or frozen broth, taking care not to purchase overly salted brands. Or prepare one of the following stocks when you have an afternoon to spare.

BEEF STOCK

6 lb (3 kg) meaty beef and veal shanks

2 yellow onions, coarsely chopped

1 leek, trimmed and coarsely chopped

2 carrots, peeled and coarsely chopped

1 celery stalk, coarsely chopped

1 cup (8 fl oz/250 ml) hot water

6 cloves garlic

4 fresh flat-leaf (Italian) parsley sprigs

10 peppercorns

3 fresh thyme sprigs

2 small dried bay leaves

❦ Preheat an oven to 450°F (220°C). Put the beef and veal shanks in a large roasting pan and roast, turning occasionally, until nicely browned, about 1½ hours. Transfer the shanks to a large stockpot, reserving the pan juices. Add cold water to cover generously, bring slowly to a boil, and skim off any scum and froth from the surface. Reduce the heat to low and simmer, uncovered, for 2 hours, adding water as needed to keep the bones generously immersed. Skim the scum from the surface occasionally.

❦ Meanwhile, place the roasting pan on the stove top and add the onions, leek, carrots, and celery to the fat remaining in the pan. Brown over high heat, stirring often, until the vegetables caramelize, 15–20 minutes; take care not to scorch them.

❦ When the shanks have simmered for 2 hours, add the browned vegetables to the stockpot. Pour the hot water into the roasting pan, bring to a simmer, and deglaze the pan, stirring to dislodge any browned bits; add this liquid to the pot. Place the garlic, parsley, peppercorns, thyme, and bay leaves on a square of cheesecloth (muslin), bring the corners together, tie securely with kitchen string, and add to the stockpot. Simmer over low heat, uncovered, for 6 hours longer (a total of 8 hours), or preferably the whole day.

❦ Remove the stockpot from the heat and remove the solids with a slotted spoon or skimmer. Pour the stock through a sieve. Line the sieve with cheesecloth and strain the stock again. Refrigerate, uncovered, until cool. Before using, lift off the fat solidified on the surface with a spoon. Store in a tightly covered container in the refrigerator for up to 5 days or in the freezer for up to 2 months.

Makes 4–5 qt (4–5 l)

CHICKEN STOCK

5 lb (2.5 kg) chicken parts, fat removed

3 qt (3 l) water

1 yellow onion, peeled and chopped

1 carrot, peeled and chopped

12 fresh flat-leaf (Italian) parsley sprigs

1 teaspoon minced fresh or ½ teaspoon crumbled dried thyme

1 dried bay leaf

❦ Place the chicken in a large stockpot and add all the remaining ingredients. Bring slowly to a boil, regularly skimming off any scum and froth from the surface. Reduce the heat to low and simmer, uncovered, until the meat has fallen off the bones and the stock is fragrant, 3–4 hours, periodically adding water to maintain the original level. Line a sieve or colander with cheesecloth (muslin) and strain the stock through it. Refrigerate, uncovered, until cool. Before using, lift off the fat solidified on the surface with a spoon. Store in a tightly covered container in the refrigerator for up to 5 days or in the freezer for up to 2 months.

Makes about 3 qt (3 l)

VEGETABLE STOCK

10 cups (2½ lb/1.25 kg) cut-up assorted fresh vegetables, such as leeks, celery, tomatoes, mushrooms, green beans, spinach, and Swiss chard

1 yellow onion, coarsely chopped

1 carrot, peeled and coarsely chopped

12 fresh flat-leaf (Italian) parsley sprigs

pinch of fresh thyme leaves

1 dried bay leaf

❦ Place the assorted vegetables, onion, and carrot in a stockpot. Place the parsley, thyme, and bay leaf on a square of cheesecloth (muslin), bring the corners together, tie securely with kitchen string, and add to the pot. Add cold water to cover the vegetables by 3 inches (7.5 cm), bring to a boil over high heat, and then immediately reduce the heat to low. Simmer, uncovered, until the stock is aromatic and flavorful, 1–1½ hours, adding water as needed to maintain the original level. Remove from the heat and pour through a fine-mesh sieve. Use immediately, or refrigerate, uncovered, until cool, then cover tightly and store in the refrigerator for up to 1 week or in the freezer for up to 2 months.

Makes 2–3 qt (2–3 l)

INDEX

ACKNOWLEDGMENTS

Georgeanne Brennan wishes to thank all the wonderful people who helped with this book: Robert Wallace, Jim Schrupp, Ethel Brennan, International Olive Oil Council, Diane Harris Brown, Warren Carroll, Linda Russo, Charlotte Kimball, Guy and Josselyene Quard, Huguette Front, Violette and Patrick Kapp, Paul Schrupp, Marie and Marcel Palazolli, Georgina and Denys Fine, Robert and Françoise Lamy, Susan and Michael Loomis, Denise and Jean-Pierre Moullé, Cameron and Gerald Hirigoyen, Anne Degrégnaucourt, Adele and Pascal Degrémont, Jean d'Alos, Pascal and Christine Arcé, Andre and Lillian Caplan, Wendely Harvey, Hannah Rahill, Sharon Silva, Lilia Gerberg, Kari Ontko, George Dolese, Noel Barnhurst, and Steven Rothfeld.

Noel Barnhurst wishes to thank his assistants, Noriko Akiyama and Jessica Martin. George Dolese wishes to thank his assistant Leslie Busch for her culinary abilities, patience, and good humor, and Waterborn Inc. for their fresh snails. Mary Ann Cleary would like to thank the following retailers for opening their cabinets and storerooms and generously making their collections available for this project: in San Francisco, The Butler & The Chef, Nest, Pierre Deux, Le Marché de Sion, and Sue Fisher King; in San Mateo, Draeger's; in Fairfax, Coquelicot; in Petaluma, Bluestone Main.

Steven Rothfeld would like to thank the following individuals for their generous assistance: Maryse Masse and Isabelle Durighello of Relais & Chateaux for finding him beautiful places to stay and photograph, André Chabert of the Château de Rochegude, Michèle Gombert of the Château de la Treyne, and M. & Mme. Lainé of the Château de Roumégouse. Thanks also to Hannah Rahill, whose mindful editorial and organizational skills, along with Kari Ontko's lovely sense of design, helped to create this beautiful book.

Weldon Owen wishes to thank the following for their help in creating this book: in San Francisco, Linda Bouchard, Ken DellaPenta, Sandra Eisert, Irene Elmer, Sharilyn Hovind, Beverly McGuire, Karen Richardson, and Kristen Wurz; and in France, Château de Roussan in Saint-Rémy-de-Provence.

OXMOOR HOUSE INC.

Oxmoor House®

Oxmoor House books are distributed by Sunset Books
80 Willow Road, Menlo Park, CA 94025
Telephone: 650-321-3600 Fax: 650-324-1532

Vice President/General Manager: Rich Smeby
New Accounts Manager/Special Sales: Brad Moses

Oxmoor House and Sunset Books are divisions of
Southern Progress Corporation

WILLIAMS-SONOMA INC.
Founder and Vice-Chairman: Chuck Williams
Book Buyer: Cecilia Michaelis

WELDON OWEN INC.
Chief Executive Officer: John Owen
President: Terry Newell
Chief Operating Officer: Larry Partington
Vice President International Sales: Stuart Laurence
Publisher: Wendely Harvey
Associate Publisher: Hannah Rahill
Copy Editor: Sharon Silva
Consulting Editor: Norman Kolpas
Design: Kari Ontko, India Ink
Production: Stephanie Sherman,
Christine DePedro, Chris Hemesath
Editorial Assistant: Lilia Gerberg
Food Stylist: George Dolese
Calligraphy: Jane Dill

THE SAVORING SERIES
conceived and produced by Weldon Owen Inc.
814 Montgomery Street, San Francisco, CA 94133
Telephone: 415-291-0100, Fax: 415-291-884

In collaboration with Williams-Sonoma Inc.
3250 Van Ness Avenue, San Francisco, CA 94109

Separations by Colourscan Overseas Co. Pte. Ltd.
Printed in Singapore by Tien Wah Press (Pte.) Ltd.

 Savoring® is a registered trademark of Weldon Owen Inc.

p 2: At the Château de Roussan in Saint-Rémy-de-Provence, a table set with a trio of crudités, guinea fowl with cabbage and chestnuts, and roasted potato halves with herb sprigs (see recipes on pages 42, 108, and 182, respectively).
pp 4–5: In Toulouse, the graceful arches of the Pont Neuf are reflected in the Garonne River. **pp 6–7:** Acres of vineyards and sunflowers carpet the fields outside Lacoste, one of the picturesque villages in the Lubéron mountains of western Provence. Most of this area has been designated national park land. **pp 8–9:** The trompe l'oeil ceiling of the fifteenth-century Cathedral of St. François de Sales in Chambéry, in Savoy, was painted in 1848. **pp 12–13:** The Mediterranean port of Collioure, in the Roussillon near the Spanish border, is renowned for its anchovies.